Political Economy

Recent Economic Thought Series

Warren J. Samuels, Series Editor
Michigan State University

Previously published:
*Feiwel, G. R.; Samuelson and
Neoclassical Economics*

This series is devoted to works that present divergent views on the development, prospects, and tensions within some important research areas of international economic thought. Among the fields covered are macro-monetary policy, public finance, labor, and political economy. The emphasis of the series is on providing a critical, constructive view of each of these fields, as well as a forum through which leading scholars of international reputation may voice their perspectives on important related issues. Each volume in the series will be self-contained; together, these volumes will provide dramatic evidence of the variety of economic thought within the scholarly community.

Political Economy
Recent Views

Larry L. Wade, Editor

Kluwer·Nijhoff Publishing
A member of the Kluwer Academic Publishers Group
Boston   The Hague   Dordrecht   Lancaster

Distributors for North America:
Kluwer Boston, Inc.
190 Old Derby Street
Hingham, MA 02043, U.S.A.

Distributors Outside North America:
Kluwer Academic Publishers Group
Distribution Centre
P.O. Box 322
3300AH Dordrecht, The Netherlands

Library of Congress Cataloging in Publication Data
Main entry under title:

Political economy, recent views.

  (Recent economic thought)
  Includes index.
  1. Economics — Addresses, essays, lectures.
2. Finance, Public — Addresses, essays, lectures.
3. Public choice — Addresses, essays, lectures.
4. Marxian economics — Addresses, essays, lectures.
5. State, The — Addresses, essays, lectures. I. Wade, Larry
L. II. Series
HB34.P64   1983   330   83-6090
ISBN 0-89838-083-9

Copyright © 1983 by Kluwer•Nijhoff Publishing. No part of this book may be reproduced in any form by print, photoprint, microfilm, or any other means without written permission of the publisher.

Printed in the United States of America

Contents

Preface vii

Acknowledgments xi

**1
Political Economy: Problems with Paradigms** 1
Larry L. Wade

**2
Modern Public Finance: The Neoclassical Approach** 27
L. Jay Helms
   Comment by Philip A. Klein 63

**3
Fiscal Behavior of the Modern Democratic State:
Public Choice Perspectives and Contributions** 69
William C. Mitchell
   Comment by Margaret Levi 114

**4
A Marxist Theory of the State** 122
Stephen Resnick and Richard D. Wolff
   Comment by Andrzej Brzeski 152

**5
Whither (Positive) Political Economy? One Reading** 157
Warren J. Samuels

Index 171

Contributing Authors 177

Preface

This volume contains original essays by outstanding scholars working within several of the dominant genres in contemporary political economy: neoclassical public finance, public choice, and Marxian analysis. Critical overviews of some of their major themes are offered in my introductory chapter and in Warren J. Samuels' concluding one, while more focused, if briefer, comments by other scholars follow each of the theoretical presentations in chapters 2 through 4. The book's aim is to alert, inform, and possibly provoke readers to a more careful examination of the important and manifold problems of theory and analysis raised by authors whose points of entry into the subject of political economy often differ substantially. At a time when problems of economic performance and political management frequently seem to have become not only severe but intractable, it is not unwise to consider again the ways in which greater sense might be made of these crucial matters.

The book's dialectical organization is intended to encourage readers to consider insights and objections that may not have been otherwise apparent and, hence, to reflect in a more critical fashion upon the limitations and advantages of various visions in this complicated and sometimes disorderly field. Since I am of the opinion that no fully satisfactory synthesis of the perspectives presented here is (probably ever) possible, no Procrustes has been summoned to make the attempt. Instead, several personalized versions or aspects of major models of political economy are offered and examined in the belief that all students of the subject will wish to explore both the logic of alternative approaches and of particular applications by scholars whose assumptions they share. It is desirable for students of economics and political science to be familiar with what surely are the central paradigms in the field, while many will concur that such a satisfying state is all too rarely witnessed. Thus this book.

The volume is organized as follows. Chapter 1 reiterates the ancient view — at least as old as Machiavelli — that all important and valid values and purposes cannot in principle be harmonized, that conflict is thus an enduring feature of all societies, and that political systems invariably show greater concern with this fact than any other. Eris lives! Economic conceptions, whether within or without the classical mold, concerning the proper or eventual role of the polity do not always take this fact sufficiently into account. It is argued that if some view the polity's appropriate social function to consist solely in providing public goods and adjusting externalities efficiently, or if others would assign it only a benign administrative function in a future just and reconciled community, they must face the prospect that much of politics, and thus economics, will remain forever inexplicable.

L. Jay Helms's lucid exposition of contemporary neoclassical public finance follows. It includes a most valuable discussion of important developments, not to say complications, made in that field in the 1970s having to do, most notably, with the *second-best* problems confronted by less than fully competent, which is to say real-world, governments.

Familiarity with the analytics involved is essential for all literate political economists, not excluding those of utterly different persuasion. Even Marx, one recalls, began with the classical framework. Philip A. Klein observes in his thoughtful comment that in many circumstances the conclusions of neoclassical public finance qualify greatly its relevance for public policy, even though such relevance is the raison d'etre of economic work. This is a sobering admonition and forces one to inquire whether genuinely attractive alternatives actually exist and, if so, whether they can equal the neoclassical system in generalizability and theoretical force or, instead, occupy a rather narrower ideological space. In any case, Professor Klein suggests, the most important theorizing remains to be done.

The public-choice approach to fiscal affairs in liberal society is taken up next in what is both a masterful survey of selected works in the field and, in some respects, an argument with, in William C. Mitchell's words, a "libertarian thrust." The individualistic premises underlying his discussion of the *new public finance* are ones conventional in orthodox economics but are being extended, in an increasingly familiar manner, by public choice theorists to explain and predict the behavior of individuals operating in political institutions. Professor Mitchell's essay is perhaps most interesting in its exploration of the distinctions between demand (citizen-based) and supply (government-based) models of public choice. Any notion that democratic states, given the interests of those who staff and manage them, make choices consistently, or even frequently, on the basis of social equity and efficiency becomes greatly strained in light of the inducements and compulsions identified. By drawing into question the efficacy of demand-based processes, the essay raises disquieting questions for those who have viewed the liberal democratic state as a beneficent or neutral instrument through which an overarching *public interest* might be realized, and forces us to consider the arrangements by which state power might reasonably be constrained. In her insightful comment, Margaret Levi voices similar dissatisfaction with the infirmities of demand-based public-choice models, and emphasizes the universal character of what is described as the predatory state. Its coercive potential, however, is said to be variously constrained (or amplified, presumably) by the mode of production in which it is embedded, and an historical dimension must necessarily be introduced if public-choice analysis is to enlarge its range of explanation and scientific power.

The last theoretical chapter, by Stephen Resnick and Richard Wolff, discusses the role of the state in perpetuating (reproducing) capitalism and the class structure with which it is identified. They question whether one popular Marxist view — that the state is a mere creature of economic forces in society — can explain the complex phenomena in which they are interested, and offer, as an alternative, an *overdeterminist* Marxist theory in which all social items are interdependent. The state's role in maintaining capitalism is thus contingent, a matter to be discovered rather than assumed. Thus, just as adherents to Marxian concerns cannot reject matters of state policy as irrelevant, neither can control of the state guarantee the changes in class composition which are thought to be desirable. It is apparently a matter for empirical investigation to determine *where* in society the processes necessary to maintain the capitalist mode of production are performed. That this has tactical significance is a point which the authors discuss. This problematic approach to the state is addressed by Andrzej Brzeski, who not only questions whether such a thesis is consistent with the core of Marxist thought but challenges the notion of overdetermination itself. Scientific hypotheses presume causal relationships (determinism?), while overdetermination, if accepted, means that "we can have little hope of understanding anything."

In the concluding chapter, Warren J. Samuels addresses some of the salient issues and problems dealt with by other contributors, suggests points of agreement and divergence, and cautions against the "stylistic perceptions" that can blind methodological partisans to important connections between politics and economics. In urging greater attention to positive political economy (and to the contributions that the other behavioral sciences can make in that regard), he is not unmindful of the relevance of normative theory to such an undertaking.

The reader is invited by these various exchanges to participate in his or her own way in an examination of the issues raised.

Acknowledgments

It is a pleasure to record my gratitude to Warren J. Samuels of Michigan State University, who, as editor of the series in which this volume appears, suggested, variously assisted with, and contributed to what I from the first regarded as a particularly useful enterprise. My departmental colleagues, Donald Rothchild, Alexander J. Groth, and John R. Owens were instructive consultants in the identification of themes to be addressed and helpful readers of draft manuscripts, for which I thank them.

The writers whose essays and comments are here contained showed themselves to be not only what was already known — talented and perceptive scholars — but sterling associates as well, unfailingly cooperative and responsive to my requests and suggestions. I thank them for that, as well as for the contributions each has made to my own education. It is my hope that readers will find themselves equally enlightened and thus similarly indebted.

1 POLITICAL ECONOMY: PROBLEMS WITH PARADIGMS

Larry L. Wade

Introduction

There is no entry for *political economy* in the last edition (1968) of the *International Encyclopedia of the Social Sciences* nor, less surprisingly, for a number of terms familiar to many readers: public choice, public goods, electoral-business cycle (or equivalent), among others. And, although many aspects of Marxism are discussed there at length, virtually no attention is given to Marx's, or his successors', views of government or the state and its relationship to economic systems and developments. Moreover, there is no discussion of the Keynesian view of politics, although Keynesian economics arguably dominates the thought of economic advisors to Western governments. These omissions do not reflect adversely on the generally impressive work of the encyclopedia's authors and editors, but indicate how substantial are the problems facing those intrepid scholars who would seek a higher synthesis of politics and economics. Entire seas have been left unfished.

This essay discusses several important and influential ways by which connections between economics and politics have been or might be addressed: (1) the Keynesian, which, it is argued, has misconceived democratic government as a plastic instrument that can be applied successfully to produce economic stability; (2) the Marxian, which, until recently at least, underestimated the problem of political as opposed to economic power; and (3) public choice, which extends the assumptions of classical economics to political and policy choices. No thorough treatment of such complex matters is possible here, but issues are posed that are fundamental to any full integration of politics and economics by these currently dominant academic paradigms.

Keynesian Economics and Politics

It was in orthodox academic circles that the synthetic tradition of political economy dissolved into the analytic sciences of economics and political science. The emergence of economics as a distinct profession with its own preoccupations can be observed in many ways, but emblematically in the title and content of Alfred Marshall's 1890 *Principles of Economics* when compared with John Stuart Mill's 1848 *Principles of Political Economy,* which although primarily economic, devoted five chapters to the description and purposes of government. To be sure, Marshall's great book is also replete with social and political commentary — and his moral concerns are no less obvious than Mill's — but it is a book in which modern economic analysis predominates and is strikingly more consistent, rigorous, and formal than Mill's. It was an analysis susceptible to extension and remarkable refinement, including mathematical treatments of the sort now familiar in economic texts and journals. While dominant, classical (or neoclassical, since Marshall) economics was never, however, entirely triumphant, even while it transcended the hyperfactualism and theoretical poverty characteristic of most alternative, mainly institutional, approaches. Contemporary Marxist and public-choice approaches have obviated these criticisms somewhat since each aims at a unified and systematic theory. Beyond doubt, the professionalization of economics produced a great theoretical edifice: one thinks of general equilibrium theory; economic optimization; capital and growth theory; the macrodynamic theories of income, employment, and prices; distribution theory; welfare economics; national income accounting; and modern public finance. It is not possible to believe that such achievements could have been made without the disengagement (at times rising to alienation) from political philosophy, political science, history, and sociology that accompanied their construction. For this reason, the sometimes tedious charges of formalism and ahistoricity leveled by Marxists, institutionalists, and other social scientists against modern economics are not altogether cogent: the mastery of one subject is preferable to dilettantism in several, a malady to which some critics of neoclassical economics are known to be prone.

Still, it is necessary to emphasize that modern economics developed into an intendedly positive subject without a corresponding positive theory of the rules and authorities (*governments* in Anglo-American, *states* in Marxist and European, parlance) that reflect, influence, or define economic circumstances.[1] Under conditions of the minimalist, that is, the prewelfare, preregulatory, or pregarrison state, perhaps inattention to political theory carried no great loss: a limited number of assumptions involving, mainly, utilitarianism, private property, the sanctity of contract, externalities, and public goods was judged sufficient to justify the building of an autonomous, market-oriented economic theory.

If neoclassical economics had little need for a rigorous theory of politics, government being a more easily comprehended and predictable matter until the early decades of the twentieth century, the same cannot be said for the revisionist Keynesian system of the 1930s, which suggested persistent state intervention in the economy in order to resolve the recurring business cycles (particularly their unemployment aspects) that afflict capitalist societies. Classical stalwarts saw nothing new in Keynes's economics — indeed many saw only an absurd repeal of Say's Law (that supply creates its own demand) and an irrational indulgence of the money cranks whose theories have ever appealed to opportunistic politicians — and some perceived in his political remedies the specter of Leviathan.[2] But the Keynesian heretics (now, according to Samuelson, having returned to the chapel as part of the "grand Neo-classical synthesis") failed to develop a theory of the means by which their policy recommendations were to be deployed, and the place of those recommendations among other political objectives. Nowhere in Keynes's own writings is a systematic view of the polity to be found, although, with diligence, one could perhaps be constructed from the casual and scattered asides, observations, and arguments to be found in his correspondence and essays. This would be a difficult task, however, for Keynes, lucid and scintillating as he often was, could also, by turns, be inconsistent and obscure.

On the philosophical plane, he was sure that the love of both money and power were prime motivations in human behavior (proof was found in his own conduct) and that pursuit of the former was preferable, socially speaking, to that of the latter. It is ironic to note, therefore, that the opportunities to pursue power were greatly and permanently enlarged by the Keynesian fascination with government's capacity to control aggregate demand and, hence, the economy generally — or so it was believed. For while the Keynesian remedies for rising unemployment and falling output (or for an overheated and inflationary economy) may imply little about the permanent scope of government (since taxing/spending/money could in principle expand or contract to any level required by the state of the economy), it has long since been clear that government intervention created new political alignments that make the possibility of contraction more an academic than a practical option. Keynes himself was generally blind to this prospect and to the political forces that an active democratic political system would set in motion. Writing in 1940, for example, he advanced the now remarkable proposition that: "It appears to be politically impossible for a capitalist democracy to organize expenditure on the scale necessary to make the grand experiment which would prove my case — except in war conditions."[3] The overloaded state — feared by conservatives, denied by some modern liberals, and welcomed by radicals as evidence for an approaching realization crisis — was not foreseen in Keynes's prepopulist democracy. Interestingly enough, Keynes had concluded his *General Theory* four years earlier with a most pertinent query; he wondered if his ideas were grounded "in the motives which govern the evolution of political society?"[4] No answer was given, and the observation was made that another book would be necessary to outline the problem. That much-needed book has yet to be written,[5] and the thought intrudes that the political treatise might have best preceded the economic one.

Most Keynesian specialists in public finance and macroeconomics have been content to suspend the political problem and to address the less arduous task of specifying the technical arrangements which, *if* adopted and followed, would, it was thought, maximize economic stability. They might have agreed that whether government will adopt a particular program, whether bureaucrats will apply it, and whether households, firms, and foreigners, as well as voters, interest groups, and social classes will accept it, cannot be known in the absence of a bureaucratic and political theory identifying the conditions under which acceptance is apt to occur. But no such theory existed in the 1930s, and perhaps the times could not await one.

The Keynesian model makes unselfconscious presumptions about political matters, which many, including erstwhile supporters, regard as increasingly suspect. In its most simplified form, the model identifies the manifold instruments by which modern governments are thought able to influence the economy, and assumes that government seeks to maximize a rationally established and stable utility function (involving tradeoffs among growth, employment, distribution, inflation). These goals require recurring intervention using particular instruments selected by rational and well-meaning statesmen on the basis of objective economic constraints and structure. The decision-makers whose behavior is to be influenced include firms (which establish demand for capital and imports), households (for consumption), and foreigners (for exports). In optimizing its utility function, government influences the demand of these decision-makers through, mainly, monetary and fiscal policies — through taxes, spending, interest rates, and credit. This model contains several implicit *political* and *administrative* requirements which are neither intuitively plausible nor consistent with known facts, particularly in democratic societies, but which are necessary if the model is to work.

1. A governmental elite must exercise hegemony over all other public actors and agencies (for example, in the United States, the president must dominate Congress, the courts, the Federal Reserve, the regulatory commissions, administrative agencies, and other levels of government).
2. The same elite must exercise hegemony over firms, households, and foreigners.
3. The same elite must persevere in its policies until its utility function is optimized.
4. Recognition periods and response lags are not significant in this process.

In a world characterized by a monolithic elite, an acquiescent public, and compliant foreigners, this *political* model might not lack interest. But in a pluralistic world and in open and contentious societies in which diverse interests can be made politically effective — either by replacing the controllers of policy or, no less effectively, by creative interpretation of the rules, legal delays, overt noncompliance, strikes, side-payments — the model has questionable practical force. Democratic institutions cannot be coordinated as smoothly as the model requires, and certainly not in the United States, where the separation of powers, an independent central bank, a bicameral and committee-dominated legislature, opposition and undisciplined parties, and federalism are institutions driven by multiple ambitions for political ascendancy, attracted to different economic forecasts, and influenced by the shifting pressures of diverse organized interests. Keynesian stability also requires an autonomy of national policy vis-a-vis other nation-states. If such autonomy was not apparent even in the postwar period of American preeminence, the fact of global interdependence had become universally recognized by the 1970s. The conflict between national and international stability was difficult, if not impossible, for the Keynesian system to resolve.

Full-employment objectives at home might require "begger your neighbor" trade, investment, and currency policies, which would not only disrupt other economies but, in rapid order, the domestic economy also, as inefficiencies accumulated, shortages developed, capital fled, inflation ensued, and trade stagnated as other governments retaliated. This is well known; what is less well recognized is that Keynesian stabilization techniques have no way of treating this issue beyond exhorting governments to somehow cooperate, even while their own constituencies demand other solutions. Thus, it may be appropriate for analytic, but not policy, purposes to ignore the facts of international and domestic pluralism and political responses as they bear on policy choices.[6] Politics, not economics, is the dismal science.

For Keynes, writing in the context of an economic crisis, a unitary state, a government formed from a disciplined parliamentary party, and what was in the 1930s a still relatively deferential society, the political assumptions underlying his model were more reasonable than in today's mobilized mass democracies. It seems not to have been well-understood that government interventions would create political and social commitments around which spending and taxing constituencies would form and make major retrenchments quite intractable. Expanded public involvement in labor markets, public enterprise, business regulation, and social welfare introduced new rigidities into the market, narrowed the scope of economic activity available for future manipulation, placed heavy tax burdens on both capital and labor, and by raising hopes and creating new entitlements in state dispensations, generated pressures for an ever-enlarged public sector.[7] Political organizations, by eroding the insulation of governments, led political elites to form inconsistent, unstable, and unobtainable *utility functions* — as in early 1980, when President Carter and a Democratic Congress promised a balanced 1981 budget to fight inflation, only to shift weeks later to budget deficits to combat unemployment (as the 1980 election approached). President Reagan's rejection of the Keynesian approach to 1970s stagflation (if indeed such an approach existed to that uncommon state) led to an initial policy stance of spending cuts (even as the 1981–1982 recession deepened), tax reductions, and deregulation leading to promised price stability and renewed growth through increased investment and market competition. Political calculations introduced numerous compromises (as with agricultural and export subsidies, protected programs such as social security, the perceived need for greater military spending), and investors appeared unconvinced as record deficits loomed and unemployment increased.

In spite of feigned shock, it was no revelation to experienced politicians when Mr. Reagan's budget director confessed in a moment of indiscreet candor that this particular utility function did not hang together and, further, that he had no confidence in the estimates emanating from the administration's short-term macroeconomic model.[8] The uncertainty of economic projections, caused partly by the unpredictability of political feedback, means that the range of possible outcomes generated by a forecasting model must be quite broad, thus providing decision-makers with the opportunity to choose those estimates that are most ideologically or politically congenial.

Given such knowledge, one is not surprised to learn that the Congress's bipartisan Joint Economic Committee concluded a 1981 report with this sobering assessment.[9]

> A review of the business cycles in the past 35 years shows that government attempts to shorten the duration or reduce the intensity of recessions through countercyclical programs initiated during specific downturns have been ineffective. In a number of instances, the effects of such efforts have been quite different from what was intended. Programs designed to reverse downward economic trends during recessions have frequently accelerated upward trends during the periods of recovery, sometimes with unfortunate results. The explanation for this phenomenon lies mostly in a series of delays that take place between economic performance, the perceptions of economists and policymakers, policy proposals, actions, and economic results.

The report noted that seven recessions had occurred in the period 1945–1980. Rarely had one been accurately anticipated (1981–1982 is a case in point), some predicted ones never occurred (as in 1980), and, once recognized, it had been impossible to know how long or deep a recession would be. Recognition lags are compounded by response lags. Automatic stabilizers may be triggered to desired effect, but most other antirecessionary fiscal policy requires decisions by both president and Congress, and even a short delay can come too late to alter the business cycle. But delays are often lengthy. In 1954, Eisenhower's public works and tax reductions were enacted several months after the economy had begun a strong recovery; a similar story was repeated in 1958. The 1960–1961 recession ended in February 1961, but the measures to counteract it (accelerated tax refunds, social security, housing and urban development spending) were passed after the recession had ended. Tax measures were delayed even longer: the Revenue Act of 1954 took fifteen months to pass;

the Revenue Act of 1964, thirteen months; the Revenue and Expenditure Act of 1968, eighteen months; the Tax Reduction Act of 1975 passed within one month, but not before the recession itself had passed. The public works program of 1972 was initiated to combat the 1969–1970 recession, and the 1973–1975 recession was dealt with by two public-works programs finally approved in 1976 and 1977. (The 1981 Economic Recovery Act's three-year tax cut was explicitly anti-Keynesian.) Moreover, there are serious implementation-lags even with timely policymaking: most obviously with public works (contracting, hiring, skilled-labor scarcity) but also with revenue sharing and public-service jobs. Even transfer payments, which in principle can enter the economy quickly, have been delayed so as to have had no effect in altering any postwar trade cycle.

Recognition lags are as great in the monetary as fiscal sphere, and while response times may be shorter (short-term interest rates and credit markets respond in a matter of weeks and long-term interest rates more slowly), there is little agreement on the time required before business and consumer demand responds as expected. If it is a lengthy period (six to nine months), or if, as some economists argue, it is both long and variable (that is, if it is impossible to predict how much time is required before policy impacts on the economy), rational countercyclical monetary decisions cannot be designed. Credit policy has a known capacity to dampen the economy, but it is questionable that it can be used as an economic stimulus.

Where do such realities leave the Keynesian revolution? Experience tempers the attractiveness of even the most elegant social theories (although elegance was never charged by Keynes' critics), and by the 1980s many economists and policymakers thought it a wiser course to focus government's attention on long-term structural forces in the economy and to concede that the wits of technicians and politicians were not capable of maintaining full employment, growth, and price stability by timely and, it was always thought, disinterested policy decisions. This is an unhappy conclusion when it is remembered that some business cycles approach the fabled *long-run* in duration, as in the 1930s.

By no means are all Keynesians convinced, however. In an address in late 1981, the distinguished economist James Tobin[10] rightly noted that, until the stagflation of the 1970s, productivity, living standards, employment, prices, and world trade had performed impressively for twenty-five years. Then, in the 1970s, a series of external shocks (Nixon's closing of the gold window in 1971, speculative booms in commodities, the 1973–1974 oil boycott, and a revitalized OPEC) contributed to the phenomenon of stagflation and compromised the Keynesian solutions. In point of fact, these shocks were external only to an apolitical Keynesian construct or model, not to the structure of the domestic and global political economy in which they were immanent: they were exogenous only to a mental picture that suppresses politics, aberrant only to a plan that sees economics as rational and political decisions as unnatural, akin to the work of leprechauns. Working from shaky premises, Tobin attributed the economic progress prior to the "abnormal" 1970s to the "apparent success" of Keynesian countercyclical policies (postwar structural circumstances were not mentioned), although, oddly enough, Tobin was well known for having earlier pronounced the 1960s (and the election of Kennedy) as the date from which academic Keynesianism had entered government and created a revolution in macroeconomic policy. This version would reduce the Keynesian laboratory from twenty-five to ten years (1960–1970), but even the *two* observations taken then, as the Joint Economic Committee observed, were not consistent with the theory — intervention was not effective in either 1960–1961 or 1969–1970. It is thus reasonable to conclude that countercyclical Keynesianism has in fact never been tried, or if tried, never well managed, or, if well managed, impossible to apply to an obstreperous world.

The counterrevolutions of Thatcher and Reagan, based on classical market solutions, will perhaps be judged with similar harshness: market solutions to income distribution, more market and less political determination of resource allocation, deregulation and desubsidization of firms and markets, supply rather than consumption incentives, must all accommodate a political test whatever their arguable economic merits. An economic program, in short, stands scant chance of success in the absence of a viable and complementary political theory, and conservative solutions are no more likely than Keynesian ones if the political variables involved are not understood and entered into policy choices.

Political Theory

If nascent and then triumphant nineteenth-century Western capitalism dominated politics, minimizing the need for political theory, late twentieth-century political systems — whether in the liberal industrial systems of the West, the self-identified Marxist-Leninist nation-states, or the mobilizational, traditional, or military oligarchies of the Third World — present a more equivocal picture. If gold traditionally bought the army, the odds are at least as strong today that the army will take the gold.

Certainly the problematics between politics and economics in the contemporary world seem to be broader than in simpler epochs.[11]

Unlike economics, the professionalization of political science, until recently an American near-monopoly, was not accompanied by and has not resulted in a unified theory or conceptual framework. This is not to say, however, that political science lacks theories, and an important task for political economists seeking to integrate their economic interests with a systematic understanding of political processes is to consider the implications for economic choices of contending political frameworks.

Samuel P. Huntington's 1974 essay neatly identifies these models (for the American context) in its title: "Paradigms of American Politics: Beyond the One, the Two and the Many."[12] The *One* refers to the ideological unity (or tyranny to some) emphasized in writings ranging from Tocqueville to the patriotic historians of the nineteenth-century to the carefully-argued schemes of Hofstadter, Potter, Boorstin and, above all, Hartz. The American consensus — a relatively constant but fluctuating agreement on liberty, equality, individualism, democracy and constitutionalism — is held to inhibit social conflict, enhance antigovernmental attitudes, extoll the individual, but at the same time, for some writers, to encourage injustice, rigidity, self-righteousness, Messianism, and impotent public authority. This political culture arose from unique circumstances (for example, the absence of feudalism, a country in which a majority of the population belonged to dissenting Protestant sects), but indispensably depends upon a large middle class whose economic interests have (or seemed to have) been served by the liberal ideology (if we may call it that, for it is an inconsistent amalgam of values) and the economic institutions and opportunities it legitimizes. If shared understandings prevail, conflict has not been altogether muted, for *this* liberal creed, unsystematic as it is, provides no rules for weighing and ranking its components; for example, liberty, implying achievement and hence hierarchy, has often been in conflict with equality, just as authority has been in conflict with individualism.

Indeed, it is precisely such contradictions in the One that have informed the Two as a model of American politics. The *Two* refers to class-based politics originating usually in economic relations, which divide society into few and many, rich and poor, the rulers and the ruled. The *Federalist Papers'* authors accepted class differences and conflicts and were concerned only to control them, it being no function of government to remove them. For the most part, however, partisans of the Two have sought to do just that: to unmask the reality of class cleavages and oppressions, to reveal thereby the depredations, injustices, and false consciousness encouraged by the One, all with the aim of reforming society along more just and egalitarian lines. The Progressive historians were notable contributors to this tendency — one thinks of V. L. Parrington and Charles Beard — as are a number of radical social scientists and Marxist scholars who have reinforced theories of the Two more recently.[13]

For those who see a more complex political world, theories of the *Many* provide an alternative. These would include Madison's "factions," Bentley's and Truman's "group theory," Dahl's "polyarchies" and "dispersed inequalities," Lowi's "interest-group liberalism," and Wilson's "organizational politics."[14] On some occasions, views of the Many shade into class and quasi-Marxist views, with most emphasizing the economic basis of political behavior — Truman's dominant model shows such an emphasis, for example. Other formulations point to the autonomy of cultural/moral communities, ethnicity, race and other factors in interest-group politics, but *economic* or not, none is guilty of the Panglossian *pluralistic* innocence ascribed to writers in the field by some critics. Lindblom, for example, has claimed that "many works" on interest groups " . . . treat labor, business and farm groups as though operating at some parity with each other,"[15] although the fact is that no major writer has so contended. Huntington has asserted that supporters of the "pluralist paradigm" are "favorably disposed toward that process, seeing a rough approximation of the public interest emerge out of open, competitive struggle in the political free market, where *it can be assumed* [italics added] that constitutional and governmental structures do not significantly discriminate among groups in terms of their access to the political process."[16] Actually, no significant scholar has ever made such an *assumption,* and virtually all explicitly reject it. It is unfortunate that caricatures of interest groups cum pluralistic models have become so widely accepted, because the implications for political economy of the more sophisticated versions are profound. In Lowi's view, for example, interest-group liberalism has overwhelmed an uncritically indulgent and irresponsible state and created a *crisis of authority* in the process. Intergroup and marketplace competition has been minimized by a *receivership state* which subsidizes, insures, and protects immunity-seeking *interests* from the insecurities of a competitive world, while, ironically, eroding its legitimacy by so doing, since constitutionalism declines as responsibility and accountability are evaded. Lowi's scheme has points in tandem with O'Connor's innovative Marxian explanation of the rise of the modern *welfare* state: one is required to provide the infrastructure and social *harmony* essential to continued accumulation in late capitalist societies.

Both Lowi and O'Connor perceive great difficulties with the evolved arrangements, which draw the future of the liberal state into question.

So, for that matter, does Wilson's analysis, which points to the lost ideological or philosophical struggle waged by large business interests over free enterprise and the limited state, and to the resulting pragmatic holding actions fought over whether government should now do more or less, not whether it should exit from the enormous undertakings it has assumed over the last half-century. The expanded state is beyond significant shrinkage, its management sensitive to the gratification of a *middle-classified* and more ideological society, while the sustained political organization of the poor remains exceedingly difficult. In Wilson's model, socioeconomic and political factors interact in complex but perceptible ways to allocate perceived costs and benefits (illusions, fiscal and otherwise, are common) in concentrated or diffused patterns, thus giving structure to contemporary political conflicts.

The implications of Wilson's analysis are many, but for the political economy the most significant involves the inherently uncertain balance between contingency and necessity. Unrelieved by political knowledge, plans to manage economies on Keynesian or other principles, to pose rational criteria demarcating public and private sectors, to improve the delivery of public services, to enhance equity, or to reorder society fundamentally, in short, to realize *any* pure value, are, to Wilson, recipes for certain failure. Politics involves the perpetual balance of shifting values, good or bad, depending on one's social and ideological position. The dominance of one condition requires the suppression of equally valid other states, and opportunity-costs obtain in the sphere of values as with all other choices. That scholars, politicians, and activists speak as if tradeoffs of cherished values are not necessary — that efficiency and equity can be made synonymous, as can individual egoism and social order, that all will be for the best in that best of all possible worlds yet to be born — is simply demogoguery or self-deception. It is perhaps this aspect of pluralism that is so distasteful to its critics, for it is, within limits, a relativistic perspective that locates social welfare not in the substance of policy (where values must be sacrificed) but in the procedures for political participation and responsible decision-making: for example, in Truman's "access" or Lowi's "juridical democracy," or in Calhoun's "concurrent majority" for that matter. A procedural, unlike a substantive, view of the public interest has the virtues of modesty and tentativeness, and differs as much from the grand equilibrium that is to reconcile individual utilities in neoclassical economics as from the value-harmonized community that is to populate socialism's elysian meadows.

Marxism: An Integration

If conventional economics lacked political theory, and if political theory had separated from economics, there remained one tradition, the Marxian, in which this was, at least intendedly, not the case. Classical Marxism insisted upon a holistic approach to thinking and action. If the driving force of social change was rooted in economic facts which in turn gave rise to certain social and political institutions and conflicts, it was apparent that no (or few) significant historical events could be understood by sciences which focused only on the polity (or its subsystems), or society (with its diverse status-orderings). Social stratification and power were linked indissolvably to the organization of the means of production, a fact which so-called bourgeois social science is said to often obfuscate in the form of various apologetics and legitimations. The charge of reductionism (monocausality) often leveled at the Marxist approach loses some of its force if one believes that an equally insidious reductionism of a very different type is encouraged by a social science that pays more attention to the subsystems of polity and economy than to their interrelationships.[17] The demand that societies be seen as wholes is an emphatic and persistent challenge to non-Marxist scholars. Ironically, however, it has become a challenge to Marxist writers as well, for there is a serious question whether Marxian political economy, given the nature of contemporary polities, is capable of further broad development without devoting greater attention than it has to the polities of liberal, or late capitalist, states as well as to those in other places, including the self-proclaimed Eastern European and Asian socialist (vocabulary deserts us) states and the multiple political orders of the Third World.

To be sure, it is by no means clear what is now unique or distinctive in Marxian social science, there being no final arbiter in these matters: teleological elements are found to be emphasized, attenuated, or ignored altogether, depending on the author in question.[18] In different writings, social classes are understood as organized along an obvious and grand economic cleavage or as so complex that simple proletarian and bourgeois divisions can on important occasions be discerned only dimly, if at all.[19] Marxian historicism in one form denies the possibility of a *generalized* sociocultural theory, the aim being to understand and transform *particular* socioeconomic systems, while in another variation historicism is viewed as consistent with the enduring importance of some liberal political values, such as civil rights and liberties.[20] Nor is there a distinctly Marxian stance toward specific policy issues, the evaluation of political regimes, the proper balance between theory and praxis, or even what *capitalism* and *socialism* are.²¹ As with non-Marxist scholarship, common themes may consist less in the lyrics than the music — but even on that score the harmony is often imperceptible, with dogmatism from some quarters disrupting scientific discourse from others. Moreover, if Marxism comes to consist simply in the awareness that economic relations create antagonistic social classes and that class conflict is a great engine of historical change, there can be little disagreement from any quarter. Perhaps the uniqueness of Marxism is based on positive acceptance of the need to produce radical change of a particular type — socialism — in capitalist societies and the militant conviction that theory and struggle are reciprocal activities to be tested and proved in the arena of actual conditions.

While there is an academic dimension, theory-building for most practitioners is a practical task by which bourgeois legitimations are unveiled, proletarian objectives clarified, and tactical possibilities assessed, selected, and engaged. As in non-Marxist realms, efforts in these directions range from the pedantic to the insightful and profound. For all these reasons, one must necessarily speak of Marxian *approaches* to political economy, for Marxism provides, except in well-known dogmatized circles, an evolving, rather than settled, perspective on theory and action. If Marxian *political* theory is underdeveloped, it is not because all Marxists think it unimportant, although some may, but because of identifiable circumstances. Marx's own view of the state is nowhere elaborated, consisting only of random and unsystematic observations, but there seems little reason to conclude that he thought the matter without significance. Engels' famous reference in *Anti-Duhring* (1878) to socialism's replacement of the state by the administration of things also identified the state as a *special* repressive force, a view entirely consistent with Marx's much earlier contention in the *Poverty of Philosophy* (1840) that "political power is precisely the expression of antagonism in civil society" and that "there will be no political power, properly so-called," when civil (meaning bourgeois) society is replaced by the workers' association. It is a necessary burden of Marxist political analysis to demonstrate (or amend or refute) these *special* and *precise* themes, not, as sometimes attempted, by axioms and definitions, but by the scientific and inductive reasoning upon which Marx insisted. That states/governments possess repressive instruments is their defining characteristic, but it is an empirical matter as to how and under what conditions they are used, in whose interest and to what extent, and the degree to which state activity involves repression, for much of it does not except in the most resourceful interpretations.

Even in otherwise sophisticated Marxist analyses of states, there is sometimes found an unsettling ad hoc quality: whatever the state does or does not do, whether something is done on one occasion but not on another, is equally explained by its role as the great coordinator of bourgeois interests. This may or may not be true, but is in any case scientifically uninteresting if there is no way in principle by which the hypothesis might be rejected. A related and more subtle issue involves the rather frequent resort in Marxist studies of politics to the *functional-purposive* fallacy, avoidance of which is also best achieved through carefully designed and refutable empirical studies. If, for example, the function (objective consequence) of the welfare state was to stave off the collapse of capitalism, or if the function of nominal as opposed to real tax rates is to obscure how limited tax progressivity actually is, one cannot, given that knowledge alone, deduce that it was the conscious purpose (intention) of the framers of policy to save capitalism or to create a fiscal illusion. Function and purpose may or may not be synonymous, but cannot be assumed to be so. Miliband argues persuasively, as have non-Marxists such as Schumpeter, that neither Marx nor Engels were devotees of economic determinism (a "meaningless, abstract, senseless phrase" according to Engels). They accepted that, depending on circumstances, politics and economics are reciprocally involved in social change, although certainly the economic base is *primary* and hence the necessary starting point for understanding.[22] But the primary base can be influenced by political factors, as Marx recognized when he applauded the prospects of universal suffrage in Britain as a great contribution to socialism (even though he was later skeptical of its saliency).

Marx's notion of democracy resembled Rousseau's: "an association in which the free development of each is the condition for the free development of all," as it was defined in the *Communist Manifesto*. Operationally, the foundations of democracy were found to consist in the practices of the Paris commune (*The Civil War in France,* 1871): the instruments of repression (police, army, bureaucracy) were to be abolished, voting rights made universal, judges elected and subject to recall, administrative appointments to be for short terms. Two of these — voting rights and bureaucratic/police euthanasia — raise serious issues for political theory, the rest being less substantial (although no doubt important in nineteenth-century Europe). These democratic practices, of course, are to operate in a greatly changed economic context, specified (in at least initial form) in the *Communist Manifesto,* and range from the vital (the abolishment of private ownership of the means of production) to the now commonplace (free public education), but, in toto, are rather mild compared to some contemporary socialist agendas assembled by the Leninist tradition. Income and inheritance taxes will equalize incomes, everyone will work, credit, communications and transportation will be *centralized,* public enterprise will be extended, agricultural lands improved, et cetera. Since such undertakings will obviously require an administrative apparatus (but not a *bureaucracy,* that being the old ruling class' administrative system), as well as decisions on allocative priorities (to be made, apparently, by representatives selected on the basis of universal suffrage), the stage would still seem to be set for something resembling a political process, with all that such a process implies in the Marxian vocabulary.

The demystification of the liberal capitalist state, a topic on which much contemporary Marxist analysis centers, is a task still lacking its Voltaire[23] — certainly it is a more difficult one than was Marx's demystifying of the German monarchy's surrounding fog of feudalism and Hegelian idealism[24] — and raises the most profound questions involving the Marxian and liberal conceptions of power.

Consider, for example, one of the great *rationalizations* of the American political system, James Madison's *Federalist 10,* in which the main source of social conflict is defined in lucid terms (which Marx would later echo):

> . . . the most common and durable source of factions has been the various and unequal distribution of property. Those who hold and those who are without property have ever formed distinct interests in society.

Particular economic interests — agricultural, manufacturing, mercantile, financial, creditors, debtors — form subsidiary cleavages. To Madison, the regulation of these interests is the "principal task" of modern legislation, but "it is vain to say that enlightened statesmen will be able to adjust their clashing interests and render them subservient to the public good." Harmony on larger ends is not to be expected: people's different circumstances give them a "zeal" for different opinions on every subject, including government, have "inflamed them with mutual animosity and rendered them much more disposed to vex and oppress each other than to co-operate for the common good." Property is the usual and chief source of conflict but, continues Madison (anticipating Freud):

> So strong is the propensity of mankind to fall into mutual animosities that where no substantial occasion presents itself the most frivolous and fanciful distinctions have been sufficient to kindle their unfriendly passions and excite their most violent conflicts.

For Madison it was an illusion to contemplate the eradication of conflict; the problem therefore was to control its potentially tyrannical effects. His proposed political institutions (and the facts of geography) might do so, and might also inhibit other "improper and wicked projects," including an "equal division of property." Madison, it is apparent, was neither an equalitarian, nor an advocate of popular democracy, unless "auxiliary precautions" were taken to discipline it. He was, rather, a republican constitutionalist, and thus, in the classic sense, a liberal, that is, a partisan of liberty. He confronted what history had revealed to his time, and since as well: the twin problems of permanent social conflict and the need for political institutions that could simultaneously divide, limit, and control both social and political power so that oppression or its threat might be minimized. The famous dictum of *Federalist 51* is an unambiguous presentation of the first problem of politics: "In framing a government which is to be administered by men over men, the great difficulty lies in this; you must first enable the government to control the governed; and in the next place oblige it to control itself." Economics is a decidedly *secondary* question. Populists and majoritarian democrats of the present often deplore Madison's political engineering and have adopted or been assigned the liberal label, but have often neglected to confront rigorously the problem Madison posed.[25]

Madison's is the quintessential statement of (American) political liberalism, suggesting that those arguments are decidedly wrong which hold, as do those of one influential Marxist, Ralph Miliband, that the liberal view of politics contains the "hidden assumption" that "conflict does not, or need not, run very deep; that it can be managed by the exercise of reason or good will, and a readiness to compromise and agree." In contrast, the Marxist approach to conflict is said to be "very different." In that scheme, the "antagonists are irreconcilable and the notion of genuine harmony is a deception or a delusion, at least in relation to class societies."[26] Miliband is apparently referring to certain (unidentified) slack-baked varieties of contemporary liberalism which are indeed blushingly idealistic. But serious political liberalism is built on more formidable terrain.

Madison and Marx differ not in being, respectively, sentimental and realistic, but in Marx's view that conflict is not, or need not be, a permanent feature of human nature. To Marx, as he is usually understood, profound conflicts are rooted in an economic system in which surplus value is extracted from labor in the interest of a dominant class. If exploitation should cease, so necessarily would the most menacing source of human conflict. Clearly, Madison would have regarded this view as hopelessly credulous: to him, as to Hamilton, Adams, and their associates, social conflict is an ineradicable fact of all history, past and future. They agreed with David Hume, whose influence on Madison is apparent, that all important and valid human ends cannot *in principle* be reconciled and, hence, that power and political institutions are and must be enduring historical facts.[27] Political antagonisms are inevitable, and while the interests will change, the conflicts, not to say the bloodshed, will surely continue. The terrible fact of power is, of course, met directly in many Marxist treatments of prior or existing states/governments, but a more robust confrontation of the liberal view of the permanence of political power would be a welcome and potentially enlightening undertaking. Would Madison or Marx have been more surprised by this century's mass crimes? The Marxist emphasis on dynamics and dialectics — on change — is important and, to some disputed degree, correct. Certainly there is little reason to doubt that capitalist societies, like all others, are transitory systems, and comprehending and effecting the course of change is a necessary activity. And it would be an eccentric approach indeed that did not give concerted attention to the role of economic developments and interests in shaping politics.[28] But nowhere has primal power been eliminated, although, very importantly, its exercise has been made more legitimate and restrained in some places than in others, and pronounced skepticism is a reasonable response to beliefs that a more benign or withered polity will follow any particular economic transformation.

In registering the claim that the control of political power is the most fundamental of social problems, political liberals are to be distinguished from economic liberals as well as Marxists. If economic liberalism has become distorted by some libertarians to justify freedom for an exploiting class (or unrestricted accumulation) they promote an idea that is not broadly attractive. Liberalism as restraint on state power is far more enticing.

It is important to realize that it is not historically sound to hold (although it is widely believed) that political and economic liberalism developed simultaneously. The former existed long before the latter, and, logically, an attack on economic liberalism need not include one on political liberalism. Unfortunately, there is great confusion on this issue, leading to the result that liberal democracy is often so excoriated in radical political economy that the impression grows, implausibly, that some critics would prefer (to use Sartori's term) "illiberal democracy."[29] Both terms in liberal democracy might be evaluated highly in either capitalist or socialist economic systems. Political liberalism may, however, not be *practically* possible in both economic types: that remains to be seen, but the data thus far are not encouraging. The great insight of the Marxian tradition reminds us forcefully that key cultural practices are not freestanding and unrelated to the material organization of society. If capitalism has indeed lost its vitality, as many ideologically diverse scholars assert, one hopes to be decisively wrong on this crucial issue. The speculation that, class domination having ended, rights/liberties will take on universal vitality and be extended to the entire society for the first time, rests on estimates convincing only to those who understand "the economic law of motion of modern society," while the historical record gives no reason for benighted others to expect such a convenient outcome. Political economists are admonished by Madison to examine the proposition: governments exist primarily not to manage economies (in whoever's interest) but to prevent societies from disintegrating into chronic and unrestrained civil strife. Political reform can hope only to civilize power, never eliminate it. From this point of view, economic functions are of secondary importance in polities, a by-product of primary ones. Government is not merely a mechanism by which questions of distribution (or appropriation of the product), allocation, stabilization, growth are decided authoritatively. Governments, in this view, manage economies only incidentally.

Public Choice: An Integration

The demystification of politics and government is not a uniquely Marxist undertaking. The development over the last quarter-century of the economics of politics or public choice has, albeit for very different reasons, served often to undermine many conventional myths that surround the operation of liberal democratic politics.[30] In retrospect, it was no doubt inevitable that orthodox economists would come to apply their perspectives to political decisions, confronted as they were with growth in governments that could not readily be explained, as in the presumptively efficient minimalist state, by market imperfections and the existence of pure or mixed public goods. The great twentieth-century expansions in Western governments undermined profoundly the normative elegance — produced "leakages," in Bartlett's deft description — of the efficient distributions made by the stylized market of economic theory.[31] It was apparent that a general solution to the problem of optimality would require analysis of the nature of collective or public choices, that is, governmental decisions. The disconcerting fact that rules and institutions do not exist by which public decisions can be made (even conceptually) efficient was an early discovery,[32] and one that has led many theorists to a pronounced suspicion of public activity.[33]

Public-choice analysis is based upon the characteristics of *economic man:* Individualistic, rationalistic, maximizing. Its positive expression considers the resources commanded by individuals, the objectives they seek, the political rules and institutions through which they interact, and the consequences which interaction produces. Normative public choice evaluates these consequences for social or individual welfare and advances various schemes (usually alternative decision-rules) by which inefficient or absurd outcomes might, in the opinion of the advocate, be reduced or eliminated. Most interestingly, the normative concerns so generated have led public choice increasingly in the direction of classical political theory as the perennial questions of justice and the avoidance of tyranny augment the now-recognized limits of efficiency as a basis for evaluating political as opposed to market allocations.[34] Political theorists will rejoice at this, for it had been their criticism that early (and, in retrograde quarters, current) public choice had not appreciated the uniqueness of politics as a social process: political systems can never, in all of their aspects, be efficient in the economic sense, even though inefficient polities are far more durable than efficient economies.

A straightforward definition of public choice is given by Buchanan: it "... may be summarized as the 'discovery' or 're-discovery' that people should be treated as rational utility-maximizers in *all* of their behavioral capacities" — that is, in politics no less than economics.[35] The thrust of analysis has been to apply the conventions of micro-economic theory to political processes. Just as in imperfect industrial organization, analysis has emphasized the extent to which monopolistic public policymakers, by maximizing their own interests, are led rationally to reduce social welfare. Attention is directed at the means by which changes in decision-rules might produce happier, non-zero-sum outcomes.[36] A good deal of work in public choice seeks to penetrate the public interest rhetoric that surrounds political activity and the related and misguided myth that, since policymakers are not profit-seekers in the ordinary sense, their allocations are somehow more regardful of the public interest than market allocations. Politicians and bureaucrats, however, can be viewed as less than public-interest-maximizers: as power, vote, fame, applause, budget, or ideology maximizers. The problem for political reform is not to eliminate these entirely normal motivations, but to align them with institutional checks in such a way as to produce more responsive outcomes in the classical manner of free markets.

Paralleling public choice is recent work concerning property rights. Both tendencies use common methods and theory and arrive frequently at similar conclusions: traditional arguments on behalf of public actions derived from notions of market failure (public goods, externalities) are inappropriate if failure is due to an inadequate specification of property rights. The conventional assumption, stated systematically by Pigou and adopted in the standard texts, was that, since external effects of private action were not reflected in prices and thus misallocated resources, governmental intervention was justified.[37] The range of appropriate public action has often been seen as extremely broad, indeed, could justify virtually any intervention since externalities are very widespread: education, welfare, communications, transportation, environment, land-use, and so on all generate externalities, some beneficial, some costly. R. H. Coase's 1960 demonstration challenged this wisdom: if the producer and consumer of an effect were free to trade, if transaction costs were zero, and if their property rights were well defined, they would be led, in the conventional market manner, to remove the externality.[38] Resources would not be misallocated. The Coase conclusion has immense significance by delegitimizing the intellectual case for much public activity. It also has more practical applications. For example, Burton has argued cogently that specifying property rights in sub-Saharan Africa would alter the vast, centuries-long rape of the commons that has produced a desert and untold human suffering across an entire continent. No nomadic group has had incentives to plant, husband, and conserve grazing land given the sure knowledge that the benefits of such effort would accrue to those who prefer to reap without sowing. Bureaucratic solutions — education, agricultural assistance, et cetera — will not suffice in the absence of property entitlements that would restrict access to sown lands to the sowers.[39]

Public choice has also reintroduced a healthy institutional focus into economic analysis. Assumptions drawn from the theory of the firm are reasserted in light of the incentives that are said to motivate members of nonmarket institutions, such as interest groups, political parties, legislative committees, bureaucracies, judicial office (but also universities, trade unions, charitable foundations). A legitimate criticism, however, has been that public-choice analysts have often failed to appreciate the actual workings and rules of these institutions.[40] Public-choice models continue to be poorly specified, are rarely subjected to rigorous testing, often identify congenial facts while ignoring contrary ones, and withal, have failed to operationalize key political variables such as power and influence.

From a radical perspective, public choice will be said to suffer from the infirmities attributed to orthodox market analysis. In the economic approach to decision making, individualism, subjectivism, and the primacy of exchange combine, in the view of one Marxist critic of "vulgar economics," to yield a limited and distorted methodology.[41] According to this critique, to understand society in terms of individuals is to obscure the extent to which individuals are best understood in terms of society. The capitalist need not be viewed as a profit-maximizer nor the politician as a vote-maximizer, since their behavior is not dependent upon their subjective characteristics but upon the laws of historical development. Similarly, exchange among individuals (money for commodities, votes for policy, political contributions for favors) obscures the particular social setting in which individuals are embedded. Many cultural historians, sociologists, and political scientists will find merit in such criticisms. Nonetheless, public-choice analysis, when conducted by those who are historically and politically sensitive as well as methodologically adept (and not those merely so adept), shows substantial promise as a source of sharpened insights, intelligent political criticisms, and suggestive policy proposals.

Conclusion

Academic political economy today is in a state of agitation and intense activity, reflecting, no doubt, an even more tumultuous world scene. Deep economic and political crises afflict every region and type of political system, from the affluent polyarchies of the West, and the military, traditional oligarchies, and transformational political systems of the Third World, to the self-proclaimed Marxist-Leninist states. Armed ideologies, social instability, chronic deprivation, failed economic plans, and perplexed governments alarm and dismay those who seek a more just, productive, stable, and peaceful globe. The certitudes of many schools of political economy have been shown, time and again, to be perverse or limited in application, but the hope persists that, with different rules, or different policies, or different politico-economic structures, the worst of these traumata would be remedied.

Is it conceivable that, somehow, an acceptable combination of rules, policies, and social organization will emerge eventually from academic and practical work to reconcile the ancient antinomies of equity, efficiency, power, participation, liberty, and legitimacy? If this essay answers skeptically, if it suggests that values relating to these matters are in principle often antagonistic, that all major paradigms of political economy have serious delinquencies and face intractable dilemmas, there is no reason to conclude that schemes of political economy are equally deficient or equally unhelpful in addressing practical problems. This is patently not the case, for selective applications of political and economic theory have contributed greatly to improvements in material welfare, the practice of democracy, and the growth, in places, of liberty. Further improvements will require similar selectivity.

Notes

1. Many foreign observers — Baron von Hubner, H. G. Wells, G. K. Chesterton, Giovanni Sartori — have shared Lord Bryce's observations that "America has no theory of the State and felt no need of one — The nation is nothing but so many individuals. The government is nothing but certain representatives and officials." See Samuel P. Huntington, *American Politics: The Promise of Disharmony* (Cambridge: Harvard University Press, 1981). As Huntington notes, the idea of the State matured in the age of absolutism and "implied the concentration of sovereignty in a single, centralized, governmental authority" (p. 35). The growing use of the term in American social science serves to simplify analysis but also mystifies the political process by suggesting the existence of a supreme *essence* with, presumably, discernible purposes and functions. Operationally, the State seems normally to be the divided and fractious Federal government, although half the public sector consists of state and local activity.

Recent and informative views on state-society relations are available in Stephen R. Graubard, ed., *The State* (New York: Norton, 1981).

2. See, for example, the essays in Henry Hazlitt, (ed.), *The Critics of Keynesian Economics* (New York: Van Nostrand, 1960). For more recent assessments, see Harry G. Johnson, *The Shadow of Keynes* (Chicago: University of Chicago Press, 1978); John Hicks, *The Crisis in Keynesian Economics* (New York: Basic Books, 1974). An excellent balanced treatment is Alex Leijonhufvud, *On Keynesian Economics and the Economics of Keynes* (London: Oxford University Press, 1968).

3. John Maynard Keynes, *The New Republic*, July 29, 1940.

4. John Maynard Keynes, *The General Theory of Employment, Interest and Money* (London: MacMillan, 1936).

5. William Beveridge's *Full Employment in a Free Society* (New York: Norton, 1945) was an effort to specify the policies and institutions by which the state might achieve Keynesian objectives. Perhaps extrapolating from his own large and generous personality, Lord Beveridge endowed his state planners with both benevolence and wisdom. I am not certain that he had ever visited Las Vegas.

6. See Allan Peacock, *The Economic Analysis of Government* (New York: St. Martin's Press, 1979) for a more extended discussion.

7. See Robert Skidelsky, ed., *The End of the Keynesian Era: Essays on the Disintegration of the Keynesian Political Economy* (New York: Holmes and Meier, 1977); Fred Hirsch and John H. Goldthorpe, eds., *The Political Economy of Inflation* (Cambridge: Harvard University Press, 1978); and the excellent essay by Norman J. Vig, "Post–Keynesian Economics and Politics: Toward an Expectationist Theory of Democracy?" *World Politics*, 34 (October 1981): 62–73.

8. William Greider, "The Education of David Stockman," *The Atlantic Monthly* (December 1981): 27–54.

9. "The 1980 Midyear Review of the Economy: The Recession and the Recovery," Joint Economic Committee, 96th U.S. Congress, 2nd session (August 1980).

10. James Tobin, "Reagan's Counterrevolution," *New York Review of Books*, 28 (December 3, 1981): 11–14.

11. An influential statement of this position is Max Weber's 1921 article, "Class, Status, Party," in Hans H. Gerth and C. Wright Mills, trans. and eds., *From Max Weber: Essays in Sociology* (New York: Oxford University Press, 1946).

12. *Political Science Quarterly,* 89 (March 1974): 1–26.

13. See, among many others, Manuel Castells, *The Economic Crisis and American Society* (Princeton: Princeton University Press, 1980); James O'Connor, *The Fiscal Crisis of Capitalism* (New York: St. Martin's Press, 1973); Alan Wolf, *The Limits of Legitimacy: Political Contradictions of Contemporary Capitalism* (New York: Free Press, 1977); Edward S. Herman, *Corporate Control, Corporate Power* (Cambridge: Harvard University Press, 1981); Albert Szymanski, *The Capitalist State and the Politics of Class* (Cambridge: Winthrop, 1978; Edward S. Greenberg, *Serving the Few* (New York: Wiley, 1974); G. William Domhoff, *The Powers that Be: Processes of Ruling Class Domination in America* (New York: Random House, 1978); C. Wright Mills, *The Power Elite* (New York: Oxford University Press, 1956).

14. James Madison, *Federalist Ten;* Arthur Bentley, *The Process of Government* (San Antonio: Principia, 1949) first published in 1908; David B. Truman, *The Governmental Process,* 2nd ed. (New York: Knopf, 1971); Robert Dahl, *Pluralist Democracy in the United States* (Chicago: Rand McNally, 1967); Theodore J. Lowi, *The End of Liberalism: The Second Republic of the United States,* 2nd ed. (New York: Norton, 1979); James Q. Wilson, *Political Organizations* (New York: Basic Books, 1973).

15. Charles E. Lindblom, *Politics and Markets: The World's Political Economic Systems* (New York: Basic Books, 1977), p. 193.

16. Huntington, *American Politics,* p. 8.

17. Often by Marxists themselves. See Ernest Mandel, *Late Capitalism* (Atlantic Highlands, N.J.: Humanities Press, 1975), ch. 2, for a criticism of single-factor analysis, for example, of surplus value, anarchy of production, et cetera. In Mandel's view, any of the many variables in the capitalist mode of production can be more or less autonomous, depending on circumstances. To many non-Marxists, of course, Marxist monocausality consists in an excessive emphasis upon the mode of production as such, yielding a world that is less contingent than they believe it to be.

18. For example, Ralph Miliband, *The State in Capitalist Society* (New York: Basic Books, 1969) writes of Britain that "sooner or later" the "working class and its allies in other classes will rule the nation, and the socialist society they will create will not require the establishment of an all-powerful state on the ruins of the old" (pp. 276–77). O'Connor, in *The Fiscal Crisis of the State,* is less certain of the American outcome, concluding only that socialism has a "fighting chance" if the political struggle is correctly managed (pp. 252, 253–56). It is interesting to contrast Miliband's assurance that British socialism will not require an all-powerful state with Bob Rowthorn's analysis of what would be required to extricate Britain from world capitalism. See his *Capitalism, Conflict and Inflation* (London: Lawrence and Wishart, 1980), ch. 3. For those who wish to understand some strategic thinking of the Labor Party's radical wing, this is an excellent source.

19. As with Afrikaner nationalism and racism in John S. Saul and Stephen Gelb, *The Crisis in South Africa: Class Defense, Class Revolution* (New York: Monthly Review Press, 1981).

20. Wolf, *The Limits of Legitimacy,* cautions radicals to regard civil liberties as more than mere capitalistic legitimations, although why they are not precisely that is not clear. A transhistorical commitment to civil liberties is a feature of many contemporary Marxist studies.

21. Albert Szymanski, *Is the Red Flag Still Flying?* (London: Zed Press, 1978) answers

his question with an emphatic yes: socialism is alive and well in the Soviet Union. Miliband, *Marxism and Politics* (Oxford: Oxford University Press, 1977), is completely without illusions on this score, and Edward S. Malecki, "The Capitalist State: Structural Variations and Its Implications for Radical Change," *Western Political Quarterly*, 34 (June 1981): 246–69 includes the Soviet Union among the capitalist states, albeit a totalitarian one. Since Malecki regards capitalism as ranging from classical laissez-faire to Soviet practice, one wonders if the term conveys very much useful information. Wage-labor seems to be at the heart of it, but, if so, expectations for the demise of capitalism may be in need of revision.

22. Miliband, *Marxism and Politics*, ch. 1.

23. For a telling rejection of Marxist claims of capitalist mystification, see Guenter Lewy, *False Consciousness: An Essay on Mystification* (New Brunswick, N.J.: Transaction Books, 1982).

24. See Gustav A. Wetter, *Dialectical Materialism* (New York: Praeger, 1958), pp. 17–29.

25. James MacGregor Burns, *Deadlock of Democracy* (Englewood Cliffs, N.J.: Prentice-Hall, 1963) is such an attack on the Madisonian Model.

26. Miliband, *Marxism and Politics*, p. 17.

27. Douglas Adair, " 'That Politics May Be Reduced to a Science': David Hume, James Madison, and the *Tenth Federalist*," *Huntington Library Quarterly*, 20(1957): 343–60.

28. Although there are very different understandings of the *transformation rules* involved. For example, contrast those of Marx with those of Joseph Schumpeter, *Capitalism, Socialism and Democracy* (New York: Harper and Bros., 1942), and Daniel Bell, *The Cultural Contradictions of Capitalism* (New York: Basic Books, 1976).

29. Giovanni Sartori, *Democratic Theory*, ch. 15. We are also reminded that the great liberal writers Locke, Montesquieu, and Constant focused on the rule of law and constitutionalism, not capitalism. These matters approach the status of universals; that is, a good opinion of them is shared by ideologists of very different outlook. The insistence that the liberal (and other) political writers be seen as ideologists, not philosophers, seems an unnecessarily severe position. For an example of the general approach at desanctifying political theory, see E. M. Wood and N. Wood, *Class, Ideology and Ancient Political Theory* (Oxford: Basil Blackwell, 1978). Also see Richard Ashcraft, "Political Theory and the Problem of Ideology," *The Journal of Politics*, 42 (August 1980): 687–705, who argues for the dubious proposition that claims of "universal values" would "evaporate into obscurity" if the actual historical context of political commentary were exposed. It is hard to see why constitutionalism, for example, is in any way compromised by understanding that its emphasis first served aristocratic, now bourgeois, and (later?) proletarian interests.

30. The assumptions, problems, and development of public choice are treated at length in Dennis C. Mueller, *Public Choice* (New York: Cambridge University Press, 1979). A short *history* by one of the founders is James M. Buchanan, *The Economics of Politics* (London: The Institute of Economic Affairs, 1978). William C. Mitchell's essay in the present volume should be consulted for other works in the public choice genre.

31. Randall Bartlett, *Economic Foundation of Political Power* (New York: The Free Press, 1973), p. 10.

32. Kenneth Arrow's *Social Choice and Individual Values*, 2nd ed. (New York: Wiley, 1963) advanced the proof that, under minimal assumptions of voter sovereignty, individual voting can lead to arbitrary ("imposed or dictatorial") outcomes (p. 59). Duncan Black, *The Theory of Committees and Elections* (Cambridge, Cambridge University Press, 1958) traces historically a neglected older form of the argument.

33. But not all. Damaging to political efficiency as Arrow's "possibility theorem" might

have seemed, it has often been recognized and then inexplicably ignored by scholars committed to the view that the decisions of liberal governments bear a close correspondence to the preferences of the electorate. For a discussion of this tendency in the work of Richard Musgrave, see L. L. Wade, "Political Theory and Public Finance," in W. Samuels and L. L. Wade, eds. *Taxing and Spending Policy* (Lexington, Mass.: Lexington Books, 1980).

34. See, for example, James M. Buchanan, *The Limits of Liberty* (Chicago: University of Chicago Press, 1975), and, if he may be included as an economic reasoner in politics, John Rawls, *A Theory of Justice* (Cambridge: Harvard University Press, 1971).

35. Buchanan, *The Economics of Politics,* p. 17.

36. Constitutional rules, for example, are examined in James M. Buchanan and Gordon Tullock, *The Calculus of Consent* (Ann Arbor: University of Michigan Press, 1962). Also see James M. Buchanan and Richard E. Wagner, *Democracy in Deficit* (New York: Academic Press, 1977), and Geoffrey Breton and James M. Buchanan, *The Power to Tax* (Cambridge: Cambridge University Press, 1980). On bureaucratic and legislative rules, see William A. Niskanen, *Bureaucracy and Representative Government* (Chicago: Aldine, 1971).

37. A. C. Pigou, *Wealth and Welfare* (London: Macmillan, 1912). John Burton, "Externalities, Property Rights and Public Policy," in *The Myth of Social Cost* (London: Institute of Economic Affairs, 1978), pp. 71–91, quotes Paul A. Samuelson's *Economics,* 9th ed. (New York: McGraw-Hill, 1973), p. 475, as a typical example: "Whenever there are externalities, a strong case can be made for supplanting complete individualism by some kind of group action."

38. R. H. Coase, "The Problem of Social Cost," *Journal of Law and Economics,* 3 (October 1960): 1–44.

39. John Burton, "Externalities, Property Rights and Public Policy," pp. 84–7.

40. For example, George Stigler's assumption that regulatory agencies serve the interests of the regulated is based on his understanding of the political dynamics involved. It is very much a partial truth, however, as the studies published in James Q. Wilson, *The Politics of Regulation* (New York: Basic Books, 1980) make clear. Similarly, William A. Niskanen's, *Bureaucracy and Representative Government* misstates bureaucratic dynamics in important respects. See L. L. Wade, "Public Administration, Public Choice, and the Pathos of Reform," *Review of Politics,* 41 (July 1979): 344–74.

41. Rowthorn, "Neo-classicism, Neo-Ricardianism and Marxism," in *Capitalism, Conflict and Inflation,* ch. 1.

2 MODERN PUBLIC FINANCE: THE NEOCLASSICAL APPROACH

L. Jay Helms

Public finance is a notably broad field of study. It explores issues ranging from the philosophical to the technical; it employs methodologies extending from the mathematical to the metaphysical. A substantial component of mainstream public finance, however, is characterized by two features: (1) it addresses normative questions of public policy — it is prescriptive, rather than descriptive; and (2) it utilizes the neoclassical microeconomic theory of how consumers, producers, and the government interact through markets and prices.

This approach to public finance, which can be termed normative public microeconomics, is closely tied to the development of economic science over the last two centuries; at the same time, however, it has undergone substantial revisions in the last decade, as different policy questions have been asked and new answers provided. Accordingly, we seek to present a unified framework within which the problems and prospects of the approach can be understood and developed.

The author wishes to thank Professor James D. Rodgers for helpful comments on an earlier draft.

We begin by setting the scene with a brief description of the strands of economic thought which have over time led to the development of neoclassical public finance and welfare economics. Only by reference to this historical context can we meaningfully, if imprecisely, define the term *neoclassical*.

Second, we present a model of neoclassical welfare economics, finding a formal characterization of the problem and of its solution: the production plan and the allocation of outputs among consumers which is Pareto optimal (making any given person as well off as possible given the utility of every other person). This provides the normative framework for the analysis. We then describe the outcome of the laissez-faire process and show that this outcome (the competitive equilibrium) will itself be Pareto optimal under certain assumptions.

Third, we discuss the limitations of this optimistic conclusion about free markets, showing how markets may fail to generate desirable outcomes as a result of externalities, large fixed costs in production, or a maldistribution of income. In each case we show how the government might intervene in the marketplace to insure that (modified) competitive forces would still yield outcomes which the normative theory finds to be optimal.

Finally, we consider the important case where the government may not be able to intervene so effectively in the economic system and explore the more difficult questions of optimal public policy for a government with restricted powers. Looking again at externalities, fixed costs in production, and maldistribution, we find that government responses in these more realistic settings may be guided by quite different decision rules and that recognizing the limitations to government power raises entirely different questions for theory, analysis, and policy.

The Historical Setting for Neoclassical Public Finance

To understand the nature of neoclassical public finance, it is useful to trace the development of the neoclassical paradigm from its origins in classical economics and to compare it with its major alternative, the Marxian approach.

Classical Economics

Although one could argue persuasively that 1776 was but a point on the continuum of the development of economic thought, the publication that year of Adam Smith's (1723-1790) *The Wealth of Nations* has traditionally been regarded as signaling the birth of modern political economy and the beginning of *classical* economics. The classical approach is particularly interesting and important because it provided the shared ancestry for both the Marxian and the neoclassical traditions which would emerge a century later.

Smith is most often remembered as an apostle of laissez-faire, articulating the notion of the efficiency of free domestic markets and free international trade:

> [For] every individual . . . it is his own advantage, indeed, and not that of the society which he has in view. But the study of his own advantage naturally, or rather necessarily leads him to prefer that employment which is most advantageous to society. . . . He generally, indeed, neither intends to promote the public interest, nor knows how much he is promoting it. . . . [but] he is in this, as in many other cases, led by an invisible hand to promote an end which was no part of his intention. By pursuing his own interest he frequently promotes that of the society more effectively than when he really intends to promote it.[1]

This notion would emerge nearly two centuries later as the Fundamental Theorems of Welfare Economics — the linchpin of neoclassical economics and the point of departure for neoclassical public finance. In the meantime, however, the classicists devoted little attention to the allocative efficiency of markets in the sense conceived of today; for a hundred years economists would largely ignore consumer welfare and demand and so would not be led to explore the essential issues of market equilibrium and normative public finance.

Because of this lack of focus on the demand side of the market, classical economics became a cost-oriented study. *Natural prices* of commodities were determined solely by the cost of production. Although it was realized that market prices could in fact be greater or less than natural prices (during the blockade of a town or an unusually good harvest),

> The natural price, therefore, is, as it were, the central price, to which the prices of all commodities are continually gravitating. Different accidents may sometimes keep them suspended a good deal above it, and sometimes force them down even somewhat below it. But whatever may be the obstacles which hinder them from settling in this center of repose and continuance, they are constantly tending towards it.[2]

Thus the classical approach to prices largely ignored the forces of market price formation and the role of prices as a tool of public policy.

The Physiocrats in France had emphasized the primacy of land as a factor of production: only in agriculture could one produce more (corn, say) than one started with. Manufacturing was the mere *rearrangement* of inputs and was therefore *sterile*. The classicists, in contrast, devoted more attention to the role of labor. David Ricardo (1772–1823) is credited with the development of much of the labor theory of value and the idea that labor was only *productive* when devoted to the creation of physical commodities. The notion that different commodities embodied (were produced, directly or indirectly, by) different amounts of labor facilitated the definition of the natural prices of goods.

Costs, and therefore natural prices, were not always conceived of as being immutable. The discovery of the principle of diminishing returns (increasing costs) in production (given land's limitations in quantity and unevenness in quality) led Thomas Malthus (1766–1834) to pessimistic conclusions regarding the economy's ability to provide for long-term growth: the geometric increase in population would ultimately overwhelm the arithmetic increase in output. This view, which attained prominence despite the simultaneous progression of the Industrial Revolution, led to an intense study of the distribution of (inevitably limited) income. For the classicists, income distribution was a zero-sum game the outcome of which would be determined by the relative bargaining power of landowners, capitalists, and laborers constrained by the biological requirement that wages not fall below a subsistence level.

To summarize, the classical economists (1) focused on cost as the determinant of natural prices, downplaying market forces and the role of demand; (2) viewed labor as an essential factor of production, with the generation of physical commodities being the only productive use of resources; and (3) believed that economic growth was inherently incapable of keeping pace with population growth, resulting in a continuing struggle over distribution between landowners, capitalists, and laborers. With this as background, we can now better see how, in the mid and late nineteenth century, Marxian and neoclassical thought emerged from this common origin.

Marxian and Neoclassical Economics

Karl Marx (1818–1883) built upon and developed the Ricardian concept of the labor theory of value; indeed, labor would play the crucial role in the Marxian analysis of the workings of the market. Moreover, the special nature of labor would be the essential ingredient in the theory of growth and distribution. Two major themes in this theory are: (1) that technological displacement would cause the demand for labor to lag farther and farther behind supply as the labor force increased; and (2) that the distribution of income would be determined by the struggle between labor and the owners of the means of production. Both factors would lead to capitalists *exploiting* labor in the sense of paying subsistence wages while requiring hours of work in excess of that necessary to make that payment possible. The resulting class conflict, combined with the historically inevitable downturn in the rate of profit, would lead to crises and eventual collapse.

The neoclassical economists took a much different tack. The central role and special nature of labor was rejected: land and capital achieved coequal status as factors of production and, since rents and profits were considered as *legitimate* a payment to a factor of production as were wages, the emerging theory had no room for a characterization of profits as exploitative. The classical and Marxian distinction between productive and nonproductive uses of resources, already being questioned by classicists such as John Stuart Mill (1806–1873), was eliminated altogether. Instead, the new approach was to attach importance to any good — or service — which provided utility.

The concept of utility led Alfred Marshall (1842–1924) to develop a new approach to prices and the market mechanism. Whereas the classicists had thought of demand primarily as the quantity of a good which was required for some specified purpose, Marshall posited that demand would depend on price: the downward sloping demand curve, derived from the diminishing marginal utility a good provides as its quantity rises, was born as a formal construct. Similarly, increasing marginal costs of production would lead to upward sloping supply curves. Demand and supply, interacting through the market mechanism, would determine price; gone was the cost-determined *natural* price.

> We might as reasonably dispute whether it is the upper or the under blade of a pair of scissors that cuts a piece of paper, as whether value is governed by utility or cost of production.[3]

Moreover, the issues of growth and distribution received diminished attention: the former would wait for John Maynard Keynes (1883–1946) to propose alternative theories to the neoclassical assumptions of full employment, while the latter was (until much later) regarded merely as a consequence of the pricing of goods and services.

General Equilibrium and Neoclassical Public Finance

The primary emphasis of the neoclassical approach, then, is on the market mechanism: prices, rather than being any sort of reflection of inherent or technological characteristics of goods and services, are simply the signals that determine the quantities which consumers will demand and firms will supply and which thereby channel resources to their preferred uses. Accordingly, in public finance we may seek to alter the uses to which goods are put by using taxes to change these signals. Alternatively, we may seek to use these signals to assist in the evaluation of the desirability of public investment projects, as through cost-benefit analysis.

Modern public finance, however, awaited two further developments: first, the introduction by Leon Walras (1834–1910) of the analysis of general equilibrium; and second, the completion of the mathematical formalization of the analysis in the mid twentieth century by a number of economists including Gerard Debreu, Kenneth Arrow, Tjalling Koopmans, and Paul Samuelson. With these innovations, the framework for neoclassical public finance was complete.

Neoclassical Welfare Economics

Because normative public finance largely concerns itself with *breakdowns* in the market mechanism and the appropriate governmental response to such breakdowns, it is appropriate to develop a simple model of the market within which we can demonstrate the welfare properties of the competitive market. Then, in subsequent sections, we will use the model to illustrate the types of policy recommendations neoclassical public finance would propose when markets fail to produce desired results.

Central Planning

We will consider a simple economy which consists of one producer or firm (a farmer/rancher), two consumers (A and B), and two goods (let good one be corn and good two be cattle). The producer can divide his acreage between corn production and cattle grazing. With his fixed amount of land, the less corn he produces, the more cattle he can raise:

$$y_2 = f(y_1) \qquad (1)$$

where y_1 is the amount of corn and y_2 is the amount of beef he can supply in the marketplace. The function f is graphed in figure 2–1, where it represents the production possibilities frontier. We assume the production possibilities set is convex (as drawn), reflecting diminishing returns.[4]

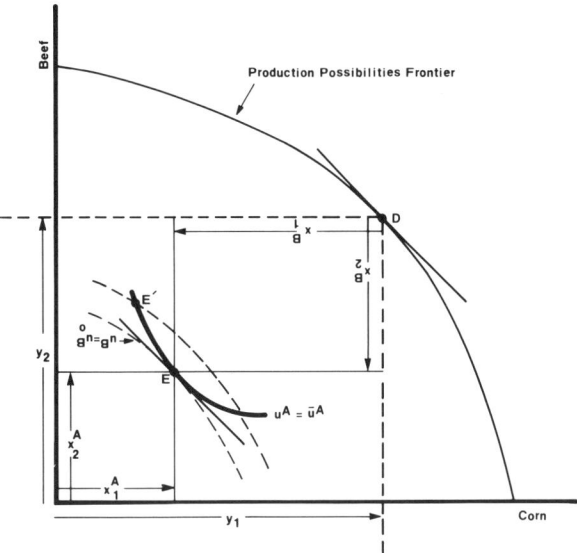

Figure 2-1
Description of the Pareto Optimum in the Standard Case

Each consumer has a utility function which depends on the amount of each good he consumes:

$$u^A = u^A(x_1^A, x_2^A)$$
$$u^B = u^B(x_1^B, x_2^B) \tag{2}$$

where x_1^A and x_2^A are the amounts of corn and beef A consumes and x_1^B and x_2^B are the amounts of corn and beef B consumes. We will assume that each consumer's indifference curves are convex, as illustrated for A by the heavy solid line in figure 2-1.

Of course, a production plan (y_1, y_2) and an allocation of the output $(x_1^A, x_2^A, x_1^B, x_2^B)$ proposed by an efficient central planner are *feasible* only if 1 holds and the amount produced by the firm is equal to the total amount allocated to consumers for each good:

$$y_1 = x_1^A + x_1^B$$
$$y_2 = x_2^A + x_2^B. \tag{3}$$

A feasible plan, satisfying 1 and 3, will provide utility to A and B as given by 2. A feasible plan may *favor* either A or B (in the sense of producing more of the commodity that one of them prefers or distributing more of the goods to one of them). A feasible plan is said to be *Pareto optimal* (or *Pareto efficient*) if it is not possible to find another feasible plan which makes B better off without making A worse off (or vice versa). In other words, the plan must be maximizing B's utility given the level of A's utility ($\bar{u}^A$), and so must be the choice of $(y_1, y_2, x_1^A, x_2^A, x_1^B, x_2^B)$ which solves

$$\max u^B(x_1^B, x_2^B) \tag{4a}$$

$$\text{subject to } u^A(x_1^A, x_2^A) = \bar{u}^A \tag{4b}$$

$$y_2 = f(y_1) \tag{4c}$$

$$y_1 = x_1^A + x_1^B \tag{4d}$$

$$y_2 = x_2^A + x_2^B. \tag{4e}$$

Note that 4b ensures that the plan maintains A's utility at $\bar{u}^A$, 4c is the production constraint 1, and 4de are the allocational constraints 3.[5] Although we do not know what level of $\bar{u}^A$ a central planner would choose, surely the desired plan solves 4abcde for *some* $\bar{u}^A$.

The solution to this problem is illustrated in figure 2–1. The firm produces y_1 units of corn and y_2 units of beef and so operates at point D on the production possibilities frontier. We then draw an Edgeworth-Bowley box with the northeast corner at point D. A's consumption of the two goods is measured relative to the origin and the solid axes, increasing in quantity as we move up and to the right; B's consumption is measured relative to point D and the dashed axes, increasing in quantity as we move down or to the left. Thus, any point in the box corresponds to a division of the total available output between A and B.

Constraint 4b requires that the output be divided between the two consumers so as to keep A on the indifference curve corresponding to $u^A = \bar{u}^A$, as shown. The division which makes B as well off as possible (subject to that constraint) is at point E, where his utility is u_0^B. Any other point which gives A the required utility, such as point E', is on a lower indifference curve for B. (B's indifference curves are shown as dashed lines. Note that since B's consumption is measured from point D downwards and to the left, curves to the northeast represent lower utility levels.) Thus at the Pareto optimum we will have the indifference curve for B tangent to the indifference curve for A. Since the negative of the slope of an indifference curve is the marginal rate of substitution, we find that A and B must have equal marginal rates of substitution (MRS) between corn and beef ($MRS^A = MRS^B$).

The discussion in the preceding paragraph found the optimal allocation between A and B *given* A's utility $\bar{u}^A$ and the production plan (point D). We must ask, however, how D is determined. Recall that the negative of the slope of the production possibilities frontier is the marginal rate of transformation (MRT) between corn and beef. At a Pareto optimum we must have equality between the consumers' MRS and the MRT, as shown in figure 2–1 by the tangents through points D and E being parallel. To see why this is so, suppose that it were not — say MRT = 3 > 2 = MRS. When we say that the marginal rate of transformation is equal to three, we mean that the farmer could produce one less unit of corn and instead produce three more units of beef. When we say that the marginal rate of substitution (for both consumers) is equal to two, we mean that they would be indifferent to giving up one unit of corn and receiving in return two units of beef. Then MRT = 3 > 2 = MRS could not occur at a Pareto optimum, since it would be possible to make B better off by producing one less unit of corn and three more units of beef, taking the one unit of corn away from A while giving him two of the extra units of beef (thus leaving A as well off as before) with B receiving the surplus unit of beef (thus making him better off).

To summarize, in order for a central planner's production and allocation decisions to be Pareto optimal, they must (1) leave all consumers with the same MRS, and (2) equate this common MRS with the MRT in production: $MRS^A = MRS^B = MRT$.[6]

When maintaining A's utility at $\bar{u}^A$, the best feasible production and allocation decisions by the planner would provide B with utility u_0^B. Point J in figure 2–2 represents this possibility. The decision to set A's utility at $\bar{u}^A$ was, of course, arbitrary. Had the planner decided at the outset to maintain A's utility at a higher level, say u_1^A, it would have only been possible to raise B's utility to, say, u_1^B, as shown by point N. In general, the higher the utility level decided on for A, the less utility a production/allocation plan could provide for B. This set of tradeoffs between A's and B's welfare is shown in the utility possibilities frontier — the solid curve in figure 2–2. The choice between points on the frontier is essentially a question in income distribution, an issue to which we will return later.

Competitive Equilibrium

The analysis above has made the heroic assumption that an omniscient planner can fully control both production and the allocation of output in the economy. The concept of a Pareto optimum in the central-planning problem is useful, nonetheless, because it provides an upper limit on how

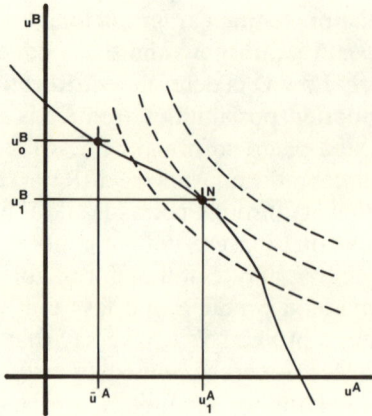

Figure 2–2
The Utility Possibilities Frontier

well any social mechanism could perform. In this section we will describe an alternative social mechanism: laissez-faire competition. In the next section we will compare the outcome of free markets with the Pareto optimum.

We begin our description of a competitive economy with five assumptions:

A1. When producers maximize profits (subject to the production constraint) and consumers maximize utility (subject to a budget constraint) they have no control over prices — they take them as given parametrically.
A2. Each consumer's utility depends on his own consumption choices only.
A3. Each firm's production possibilities do not depend on the actions of any other firm or any consumer.
A4. All consumers have continuous, convex preferences (indifference curves).
A5. Each firm's production possibilities set is convex.

Assumption A1 says that neither producers nor consumers have any monopoly or monopsony power; in other words, we are considering a *competitive* economy — one in which all agents are price takers. Assumption A2 says that no consumer is the victim (or beneficiary) of any externality, while assumption A3 indicates that there are no externalities in the production sector either. Assumptions A4 and A5 are the standard convexity assumptions which were invoked in figure 2–1.

A price system is said to be a *competitive equilibrium* (or general equilibrium or Walrasian equilibrium) if supply equals demand for each good at those prices, that is, if all markets clear.

Formally, we may describe a competitive equilibrium in the simple two consumer, one producer economy as follows: Each consumer makes consumption choices to maximize utility subject to his budget constraint; thus for A the consumer's problem is to choose (x_1^A, x_2^A) to solve

$$\max u^A (x_1^A, x_2^A)$$
$$\text{subject to } px_1^A + x_2^A = M^A \tag{5}$$

where M^A is A's income. Note that we have selected beef as the numeraire with price one, while the price of corn, expressed in terms of beef, is p. The solution to 5 generates demand functions $x_1^A = x_1^A(p, M^A)$ and $x_2^A = x_2^A(p, M^A)$ which result from the consumer selecting goods to equate his marginal rate of substitution to the price ratio: $MU_1^A/MU_2^A = MRS^A = p/1 = p$ where MU_1^A and MU_2^A are A's marginal utilities of goods one and two. Analogously for consumer B (who faces the same price), we have $MU_1^B/MU_2^B = MRS^B = p/1 = p$.

The firm will choose its output mix (y_1, y_2) to maximize profits subject to the production constraint:

$$\max py_1 + y_2$$
$$\text{subject to } y_2 = f(y_1). \tag{6}$$

The solution to 6 generates supply functions $y_1(p)$ and $y_2(p)$ which result from the producer selecting an output mix such that the marginal rate of transformation is equal to the price ratio: $MRT = p/1 = p$. Note that the MRT is the amount by which beef production must be decreased in order to produce one more unit of corn. The MRT is thus the marginal cost of corn (in terms of beef, the numeraire) and so the condition $MRT = p$ can be interpreted as marginal cost pricing.

In order for p to be a competitive equilibrium price, we must have market clearance:

$$y_1(p) = x_1^A(p, M^A) + x_1^B(p, M^B)$$
$$y_2(p) = x_2^A(p, M^A) + x_2^B(p, M^B). \tag{7}$$

There are two important differences between 7 and condition 3 required for the feasibility of the central planner's production/allocation plan: first, a pattern of production and allocation can only arise as a competitive equilibrium if a single price (and consumer incomes) can be found which will induce consumers and producers to supply and demand the given quantities; this is reflected in the use of supply and demand *functions* in 7 but not in 3. Second, 7 guarantees that the given levels of y_1 and y_2 can in fact be produced, since 1 is built into the problem 6 which provides the supply functions. Thus 7 is a complete verification of the viability of a competitive equilibrium.

Although it is not obvious that supply and demand can be made equal as in 7 at any price, the existence of a competitive equilibrium under very general conditions was proven by Abraham Wald[7] and by Arrow and Debreu.[8]

The Fundamental Theorems of Welfare Economics

We have presented above the solutions to two completely different problems. First, we asked what production/allocation plan an omniscient central planner would dictate to achieve a Pareto optimum constrained only by the technical feasibility and market clearance conditions 1 and 3. Note that in this problem the producer is told what to produce and the consumers are told what they may consume — there are no prices, no markets, and no free choices by economic agents. Second, we asked what result would arise in the marketplace if consumers and producers were left on their own to do as well as they could for themselves by maximizing utility and profits respectively given a price at which supply and demand would be equal. There is no central planner seeking to ensure that the outcome is Pareto optimal. The Fundamental Theorems of Welfare Economics show that these fundamentally distinct problems can generate identical results.

First Fundamental Theorem of Welfare Economics: Given assumptions A1-A3, every competitive equilibrium is a Pareto optimum.

Although we will not formally prove this result here, it is easy to see why it is true.[9] In a competitive equilibrium consumers are maximizing utility subject to a budget constraint at price p, so $MRS^A = MRS^B = p$. Diagrammatically, on figure 2-1 the straight line through point E is A's budget line, with a slope of -p. His demands will place him at point E, where an indifference curve is tangent to the budget line, so $MRS^A = p$. Similarly, B's consumption choices are viewed looking downward and to the left from point D. The same straight line serves as B's budget line, with slope equal to -p. He demands point E, where the indifference curve is tangent to the budget line, since any point above the line gives lower utility (since consumption levels for B are decreasing as we move to the northeast) and any point below it is unaffordable. Thus MRS^B = p also. Producers are maximizing profits given the same price at point D, where the production possibilities frontier (with slope equal to -MRT) is tangent to the isoprofit line (with slope equal to -p), so MRT = p. These conditions will then guarantee that $MRS^A = MRS^B$ = MRT, which are exactly the conditions required for a Pareto optimum, thus guaranteeing that the market outcome will be Pareto optimal.

The converse statement is also true if we add the convexity assumptions:

Second Fundamental Theorem of Welfare Economics: Given assumptions A1-A5, any Pareto optimum can be achieved as a competitive equilibrium if the distribution of income is correct.

This says that any Pareto optimal production/allocation plan which a central planner might propose could as well be achieved via the unregulated laissez-faire economy, if only the distribution of income were appropriate.

Two comments on these results are in order. First, they are rather remarkable — they say that a completely directed economy can do no better than can an undirected economy in which each agent acts solely to further his own interest. Adam Smith's work clearly foreshadowed these results; however it took economic science some two centuries to progress to the point where Smith's conjectures could be stated and proved as formal propositions.

Second, however, these results are limited in their applicability in two fundamental ways: (1) if any of assumptions A1–A5 are violated it may not be possible for the market to duplicate the Pareto optimum a central planner might propose; and (2) the First Theorem merely says that a competitive equilibrium will be Pareto optimal — not that it will be desirable in any larger sense. This concern is underlined by a careful reading of the Second Theorem, which assures that a *particular* Pareto optimum can be achieved through the market *if* income is appropriately redistributed.

Let us recapitulate briefly. We began by describing the historical development of neoclassical analysis, showing the emerging emphasis on price signals and markets. Then we proceeded to describe a particular model of an economic system, deriving conditions for a Pareto optimum under central planning and for the competitive equilibrium. The assumptions, focus, and methods reflected in this model epitomize the neoclassical approach. Finally, we discussed the Fundamental Theorems of Welfare Economics and stressed their limitations. These limitations have traditionally provided the rationale for government intervention in the market; moreover, it is the failure of one or more of the five assumptions to hold, or a concern with distributional equity (which transcends the Pareto concept), that poses the policy questions which public finance addresses.

First-Best Taxation and Expenditure Policies

If any of the assumptions of the Fundamental Theorems of Welfare Economics are violated, the free market's competitive equilibrium will not in general be Pareto optimal. It is important to distinguish carefully what this means: it means that while some production plan which is technologically feasible and some allocation scheme which is satisfying 3 could make some consumers better off while leaving the rest as well off, the unaided competitive market is unable to achieve that outcome. It is this possibility which has historically been the rationale for government intervention.

A crucial question, however, is how much more effective the government can be than the market in achieving a Pareto optimum. Until the 1970s, the focus in public finance was on what are now termed *first-best problems:* those in which the government has the necessary tools at its disposal to restore the economy to a desired point on the utility possibilities frontier. Thus, if the suboptimality arose because of an externality in production (for example, the factory pollutes the air in the process of turning raw materials into a finished product), a first-best solution might be to tax the factory so as to force it to take account not only of the direct costs of its inputs but also the indirect costs imposed in the form of environmental degradation. If the government is able to levy such a tax, and assumptions A1–A5 are met elsewhere in the economy, the government can simply intervene in the sector which gives rise to the problem and still rely on the competitive economy to function elsewhere.

In *second-best problems* the government does not have available sufficiently powerful policy tools fully to restore Pareto optimality, or it may choose not to use all available tools due to legal constraints, high administrative costs, or for other reasons. The problem of the *next best thing* to do is much more complex analytically, and will typically have ramifications for the rest of the economy as well.

Even if all five assumptions are met, the economy may be characterized by such a skewed distribution of income that society may decide to undertake a program of income redistribution. In this case, despite the (Pareto) efficiency of the system, government intervention is justified on the grounds of distributional equity. In the first-best setting, such equity is easily obtained by lump-sum income transfers (positive or negative for each person as required). This allows a different point on the utilities possibilities frontier to be reached, so that both Pareto efficiency and distributional equity are achieved. In the more realistic second-best setting, lump-sum transfers are usually not available. If the government must rely on taxes (such as a progressive income tax) which distort economic decisions (reduce work incentives) in addition to redistributing income, it will be necessary to sacrifice Pareto efficiency in order to improve distributional equity.

We shall begin by considering first-best policy responses when the competitive economy is prevented from being Pareto efficient (1) due to the presence of consumption externalities and (2) because of large fixed costs in the production process (a form of nonconvexity). Then we will consider redistributive policies in the first-best setting. Later we shall examine the much more complicated second-best responses in each of these cases.

Consumption Externalities

A key assumption of the competitive model is that agents, consumers as well as producers, interact with one another only via the market mechanism. Direct interactions, referred to as externalities, violate assumptions A2 or A3 and can occur either within or between sectors: when one consumer's behavior affects another consumer (for example, A's smoking in the elevator causes B's eyes to water) we refer to the phenomenon as a consumption externality; when one producer affects another (the upstream factory's pollution reduces the downstream fishery's catch) we have a production externality; and when the effects spill over from one sector to the other (as when the airport's noise harms nearby homeowners) we have a mixed externality.

Note that we did not define externalities simply as instances in which one agent's actions have an effect on another agent. That definition is rather broader and includes not only the occurrences described above, but also instances where, for example, people's propensity to drive cars on summer weekends increases the demand for gasoline and, by causing its price to rise, makes others worse off. Such *pecuniary externalities* are transmitted via the price system alone and, accordingly, pose no problem for the validity of the Fundamental Theorems. Indeed, the increased price is providing exactly the correct information: gasoline, now in greater demand, is a dearer commodity and should be valued more highly — optimality still obtains. *Technological externalities*, as those in the preceding paragraph are sometimes called, are more troublesome, since the agent who is creating the externality receives no market signals indicating the gravity of the harm (or benefit) that others receive.

We will use the earlier model to illustrate a consumption externality. Our producer has decided to give up growing corn altogether. Instead, he devotes the resources not used in cattle production to constructing radios. Both consumers enjoy owning one or more radios, but unfortunately, while B always plays his radios softly or uses earphones, A is less considerate and plays them loudly, disturbing and irritating B, who cannot tolerate A's choice of music. With good one representing radios (rather than corn) and good two still representing beef, the utility functions are

$$u^A = u^A(x_1^A, x_2^A) \tag{8a}$$

$$u^B = u^B(x_1^B, x_2^B; x_1^A). \tag{8b}$$

Note that x_1^A enters B's utility function because of the externality.

Now let us find a Pareto optimum in this economy. If we hold A's utility constant at $\bar{u}_A$ and make B as well off as possible subject to that constraint, we are solving the following problem:

$$\max u^B(x_1^B, x_2^B; x_1^A) \tag{9a}$$

$$\text{subject to } u^A(x_1^A, x_2^A) = \bar{u}_A \tag{9b}$$

$$y_2 = f(y_1) \tag{9c}$$

$$y_1 = x_1^A + x_1^B \tag{9d}$$

$$y_2 = x_2^A + x_2^B. \tag{9e}$$

Note that this problem differs from 4abcde only in that x_1^A enters B's utility function, reflecting the externality.

Figure 2–3 describes the economy much as figure 2–1 did for the standard case. The predetermined level of utility for A is maintained along the solid indifference curve, so our solution will be somewhere on that curve. Two of B's indifference curves are shown as dashed lines. Note, however, that 8b tells us that the concept of indifference to combinations of x_1^B and x_2^B must be understood here as holding the level of the externality, x_1^A, constant. Without externalities, the optimum was at point E where A's indifference curves are tangent to B's curves. That result does not carry

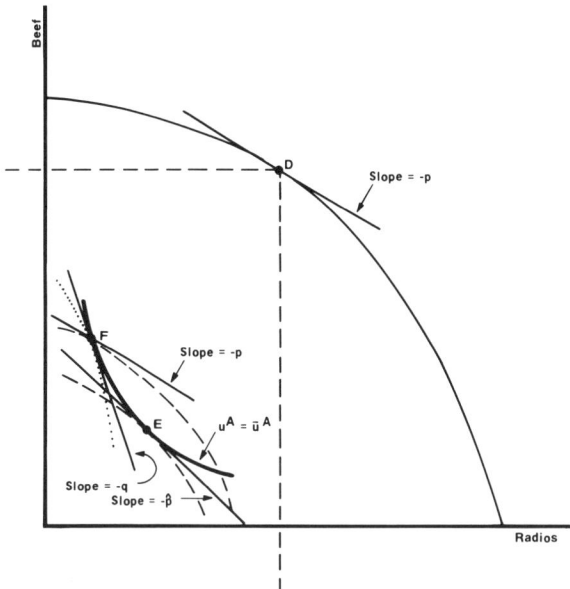

Figure 2-3
Description of the Pareto Optimum with
Consumption Externalities

over once assumption A2 is violated, however. To see this, let us suppose that E *were* Pareto efficient, say with $\text{MRS}^A = \text{MRS}^B = 2$. This means that A is indifferent to giving up one radio and getting two units of beef instead. But B would *increase* his utility by trading two units of his beef to A in return for a radio because, although such a trade would move him along an indifference curve for fixed x_1^A, it would in fact reduce x_1^A, making B better off than before owing to the reduced radio noise.

As an omniscient planner would realize, the trade described above would have two effects on B: first, it would alter his consumption of the two goods in such a way as to leave him indifferent to the change; this is the direct effect. Second, the trade has an indirect effect of reducing the externality, increasing his utility. This can be seen more clearly by collapsing the formal problem by substituting 9c into 9e to eliminate y_2:

$$\max u^B(x_1^B, x_2^B; x_1^A) \qquad (10a)$$

$$\text{subject to } u^A(x_1^A, x_2^A) = \bar{u}_A \qquad (10b)$$

$$y_1 = x_1^A + x_1^B \tag{10d}$$

$$f(y_1) = x_2^A + x_2^B. \tag{10e}$$

Then let us eliminate x_1^A and x_2^A from 10a and 10b by substituting from 10d and 10e:

$$\max u^B(x_1^B, x_2^B; y_1 - x_1^B) \tag{11a}$$

$$\text{subject to } u^A(y_1 - x_1^B, f(y_1) - x_2^B). \tag{11b}$$

For a fixed production plan (point D), 11a shows the direct and indirect effects of giving B one more radio. If indifference curves for B were drawn to include both effects, they would be steeper than before, as shown by the dotted line in figure 2-3. This is because it takes more beef to compensate for taking one radio away from B when one recognizes that radio will instead be used by A and create an externality.

From the planner's perspective, this *augmented* indifference curve is the relevant one, and the true Pareto optimum is at point F, where this new curve is tangent to A's indifference curve. At that point we can refer to B's *augmented* marginal rate of substitution:

$$AMRS^B = MRS^B - MRS^B_{ext}$$

$$= \frac{MU_1^B}{MU_2^B} - \frac{MU_{ext}^B}{MU_2^B} \tag{12}$$

where MRS^B_{ext} is the (negative) amount of beef that B would give up if receiving one more unit of the externality (that is, A's consumption of radios) in order to leave his utility unchanged, and MU^B_{ext} is the (negative) marginal utility that B receives from A's consumption of radios. Then at the optimum $AMRS^B = MRS^A$.

With respect to production, the relationship between the MRT and MRS^B is the same in the standard case, since neither B's consumption nor the production process creates any externalities; at an optimum we will have $MRS^B = MRT$ in addition to $AMRS^B = MRS^A$, as previously noted. Since MRS^B_{ext} is negative, these relationships and equation 12 imply that, at the optimum,

$$MRS^A = AMRS^B > MRS^B = MRT. \tag{13}$$

It will not be possible, however, to achieve this Pareto optimum as a competitive equilibrium. The reason for this is that, if both consumers and the producer face price $\hat{p}$ for radios, utility maximization will yield $MRS^A = \hat{p}$ for consumer A, $MRS^B = \hat{p}$ for consumer B (since B takes the level of the externality, which is out of his control, as given), and $MRT = \hat{p}$ for the producer. Thus $MRS^A = MRS^B = MRT = \hat{p}$, which is the same marginal condition that would obtain if there were no externality: the market fails to take the externality into account.

Within the confines of the market system, what corrective policy might be recommended? The problem here is that A is buying too many radios, driving down MRS^A to too low a level. If an excise tax were imposed on A's purchase of radios, then his consumption, and hence the externality, could be reduced to the optimal level.[10] The amount of the appropriate tax is simply $t = -MRS^B_{ext}$. With such a tax, A would face a gross-of-tax price of $q = p + t$ while B and the producer face the untaxed price p — in effect, A is facing a price for radios which not only reflects the costs of production, but also the costs he imposes on B when using the radios: $-MRS^B_{ext}$. Then, with the tax in place, the Pareto optimal conditions 13 can be met with $q = p + t = MRS^A = AMRS^B > MRS^B = MRT = p$. In figure 2-3 we see that, at the optimal point F, A's indifference curve is tangent to the price line with slope -q, while B's (non-augmented) indifference curve is tangent to the price line with slope -p, as is the production possibilities frontier at point D.

If the government has complete freedom to impose whatever taxes it chooses, the optimality of competitive equilibrium can be fully restored by a policy of corrective taxation where the taxes are made to reflect costs not priced in the marketplace.

Production with Large Fixed Costs

Thus far we have focused on corrective policies when there are problems in the consumption sector. To consider what might go wrong on the production side, let us consider an economy with only one consumer. In such an economy there is no question about how the firm's output will be distributed (and, of course, there can be no consumption externalities); we need only be concerned with the selection of the optimal configuration of outputs.

Going back to the example used above where the firm produces radios and beef, figure 2-4 shows the Pareto optimum at point D, where the production possibilities frontier is tangent to the single consumer's indifference curve. (Any other point which is feasible, such as D', is on a lower indifference curve.) At point D we have MRT = MRS, and the same point will be achieved as a competitive equilibrium with price p = MRT = MRS. This is to be expected, since the assumptions required for the Second Fundamental Theorem are met in this case.

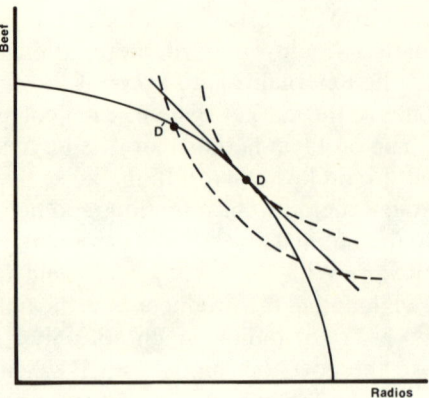

Figure 2-4
The Pareto Optimum with Only One Consumer

We now consider an important category of cases in which assumption A5 — convexity of the production set — is likely to be violated. Many production processes require certain large fixed costs to be incurred before any output will be forthcoming.[11] Thus, in the case of automobile manufacturing it is necessary to set up an assembly plant; when providing telephone service the utility must install expensive central office equipment, telephone lines, and the like; and a railroad company must install tracks and purchase trains before any transportation can be provided.

In our example of radio and beef production, we would like to think of a situation in which radios can be produced on the land only after incurring fixed costs C for setting up production; these costs are avoidable only by deciding to produce no radios at all.[12] The production function might then be written as

$$y_2 = \begin{cases} f(y_1) & \text{for } y_1 > 0 \\ f(0) + C & \text{for } y_1 = 0 \end{cases} \quad (14)$$

as illustrated in figure 2-5. The production possibilities frontier consists of point G and the solid curve except for point G'. The distance between G' and G is C, the fixed costs. Is it preferable for the firm to produce at point D or to avoid the fixed costs of radio manufacturing by specializing in raising cattle at point G? If the indifference curve through D cuts above point G, as does I_1I_1, then the consumer is better off at point D; however, if the indifference curve cuts below point G, as does I_2I_2, it would be

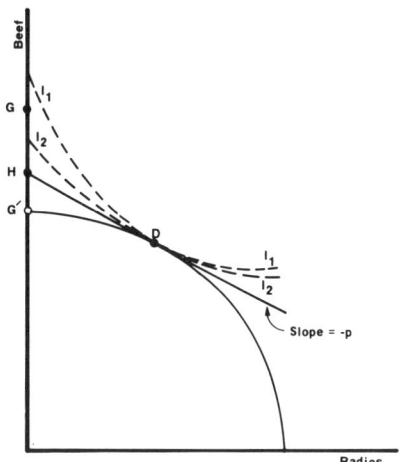

Figure 2–5
Production Choices with Large Fixed Costs

preferable for no radios to be produced and the fixed costs to be saved at point G.

Even in the former case, where the optimum is at point D, the market will not be effective in achieving that outcome. The consumer, facing a budget set given by the line with slope -p (as shown in figure 2–5), will choose point D; however, the firm, facing those prices, will choose point G. The reason for this is that since the line with slope -p is also an isoprofit line for the firm, production at any point along the line, such as point H, would generate the same level of profits (if it were feasible). But G is even more profitable for the firm than H, since no radios are produced at either point, but point G yields more beef. Since G is better than H, and H represents the same profit potential as D, G must be better than D, and no radios will be produced, despite the Pareto optimality of point D. The market fails to achieve the Pareto optimum due to the violation of assumption A5.

In cases such as these, two questions arise: (1) Is this a situation (like I_1I_1) where the firm should operate or a case (like I_2I_2) where it should not? (2) If the firm should (from a social perspective) operate (at point D) and yet in the free market it will choose not to do so, how can we ensure efficient production? We have seen that the market itself may well not provide an answer to the first question; the result has been the evolution of the subdiscipline of cost-benefit analysis.[13] Once it is determined that production at point D is optimal, the government must either motivate the private concern to produce at that point (perhaps by providing a subsidy if and only if radios are produced), impose regulatory constraints, or run the industry under direct government control and/or ownership. In fact, we often see precisely these policies adopted, especially for utilities, mass transit, and certain recreational facilities.

Distributional Equity

In a first-best setting the government has at its disposal all necessary policy tools, including lump-sum taxes or subsidies which may vary from individual to individual. Accordingly, any desired distribution of income is attainable; as a result, we have to this point largely finessed the issue of the consumers' incomes. (That is, we have worried more about the slope of their budget lines than about their distance from the origin.) In general, first-best issues of income distribution are not of interest in modern public finance, precisely because they are so easily solved (using a totally unworkable tool).

Although the *attainment* of the *best* income distribution presents a trivial and uninteresting question in this setting, the more difficult question involves deciding how the *best* distribution is to be determined. Clearly it is not sufficient simply to look at the market value of each consumer's endowments (including endowments of human capital) and attribute any ethical properties to the resulting distribution. This is the approach which Samuelson decried when stating:

> Perhaps the bourgeois penchant for laissez-faire is the only case on record where a substantial number of individuals have made idols of partial derivatives, i.e., imputed marginal productivities.[14]

Many of the classical and early neoclassical economists approached the problem of the optimal distribution of income by asserting that societal well-being — or social welfare — could simply be measured as a sum of individual utilities. Thus, in our two-person economy we would have W = $u^A + u^B$. This approach of *utilitarianism* or *hedonism,* which Samuelson terms "old welfare economics," is often associated with Jeremy Bentham and retained some respectability until the 1930's. Public finance economists of that era pointed out certain of its implications, the most important of which is an argument for a perfectly egalitarian income distribution. Suppose A and B initially have incomes of $\bar{M}^A$ and $\bar{M}^B$, respectively, with $\bar{M}^A < \bar{M}^B$ (as shown in figure 2–6) and that they have the same

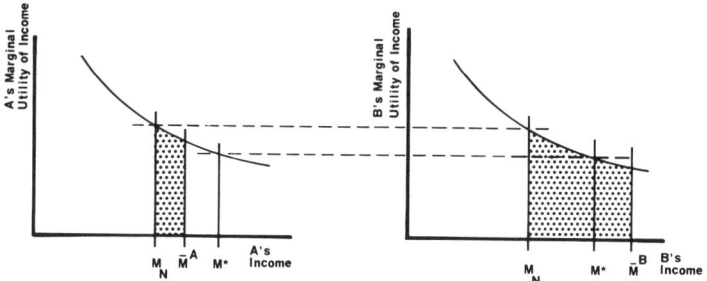

Figure 2-6
Utilitarian Maximization of Total Utility (Minimum Total Sacrifice)

utility function. Since the marginal utility of income declines as income increases, A has a higher marginal utility of income than B. Then taking a dollar from B hurts him less (in terms of utils) than giving the same dollar to A would help A. The principle of *maximum total utility* would require taxing B and subsidizing A until they had identical after-tax incomes M*. (At this point they have equal marginal utilities, and taking further income away from B would no longer reduce B's utility by less than giving the income to A would increase his.) If the tax must raise revenue (say to finance a project with large fixed costs), both A and B would have their after-tax incomes reduced by the same number of dollars below M* (say to M_N). This result is also consistent with the principles of *minimum total sacrifice* and *equal marginal sacrifice* (each consumer's utility sacrifice is indicated as a shaded area in figure 2–6).

Other (presumably wealthier) economists argued for a principle with less radical implications: the *equal absolute sacrifice* criterion. Since B is wealthier than A and has a smaller marginal utility of income, more income can be taxed away from him than from A if each is to have his utility reduced by the same amount (the shaded areas in figure 2–7). The implication here is that taxes increase with income, but the degree of progressivity (or regressivity) depends on the actual shape of the marginal utility curves.

Understandably, these results, together with the entire notion that social welfare can be ascertained simply by adding individual utilities, came under severe attack:

> Today such arguments are not very fashionable since it is as easy to assume one's conclusions with respect to appropriate policy as to assume the premises of these arguments. Not only is the former more direct, it is more honest.[15]

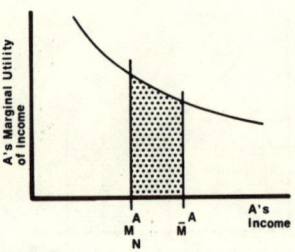 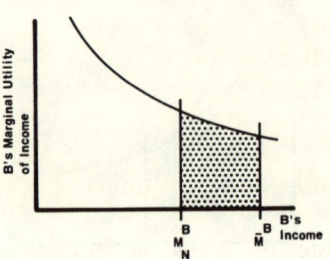

Figure 2–7
Equal Absolute Sacrifice

In reaction to such criticisms, one of two tacks can be taken. First, one can simply deny the validity of social-welfare evaluations at all except, perhaps, for conceding that a policy which makes *everyone* better off is desirable. While this approach saves the economist from making normative statements, it also leaves the question of optimal income distribution — and indeed most policy questions — unresolvable. Second, one can note that society does indeed make choices which make some better off at the expense of others, in effect deciding that the gains to some outweigh the losses to others. This implies that some points on the utility possibilities frontier of figure 2–2 are indeed considered preferable to others. As a result, one can construct a Bergson-Samuelson social-welfare function reflecting these social preferences; in the two-person economy this function would be written as $W = W(u^A, u^B)$. On figure 2–2 the dashed lines are *social indifference curves,* which connect points of equal social desirability (equal values of W). The best attainable point, N, is the welfare optimum or *bliss point*.[16] Positive economics can provide no guidance in the construction of W (except perhaps that it be an increasing function of individual utilities); at best it is a description of the perceived social decision rule.

In practice, the Bergson-Samuelson social-welfare function has been a useful construct for use in public finance. It does not, however, reflect such notions as the *benefit principle,* which asserts that those who receive the benefits of government services should be the ones to pay for them, or any concept of deservedness, which presumes that those whose work or risk-taking generates extraordinary income (or utility) are entitled to receive those rewards.

More importantly, all of the previous discussion presupposes the first-best assumption that lump-sum transfers can be freely made. Where they

MODERN PUBLIC FINANCE 51

cannot, and devices such as the income tax must be used instead, the difficult questions of how these taxes affect incentives must be clearly addressed.

Second-Best Taxation and Expenditure Policies

Consider the policy recommendations detailed above: (1) in the case of externalities, it was necessary to levy an excise tax on certain purchasers of radios but not on others; (2) in the case of large fixed costs in production, it was necessary for the government to nationalize the firm and run it less profitably than it would be run in the private sector or to devote tax revenue to providing a subsidy to the firm; (3) to address equity concerns, it was necessary for the government to establish a system of lump-sum subsidies and taxes in amounts which vary from person to person.

All of these recommendations involve the use of extremely powerful tools — tools which administrative costs or political considerations may preclude the government from even considering. If the government is limited in the tools it may employ, what is the *second-best* thing it can do? Surprisingly, it is only since 1970 that such issues have been extensively explored. The reason for the late development of second-best analysis is that it typically involves conceptual and mathematical complexities far beyond those previously encountered. The reward for pursuing such analysis, however, is that it takes a step toward reality in its description of available government policy choices.

In the seminal article in the area, Archibald Lipsey and Kelvin Lancaster showed that when some markets or sectors of the economy are subject to distortions or imperfections which the government cannot fully restore to a first-best condition, it is in general *not* optimal to use first-best policy prescriptions in the unaffected sectors.[17] This result, often referred to as the Lipsey-Lancaster Theorem or The Theorem of the Second Best, implies that if any facet of the economy is not first-best in nature, then policy recommendations for the *entire* economy are affected. One might expect that this would complicate analysis enormously, and in fact it does just that. It is important to note that there is no single second-best set of tools; constraints on government may take any of a number of forms. We shall therefore take up our two examples of market inefficiency, in each case focusing on what could make the problem a second-best one, and how the solutions might be expected to differ from those proposed in the first-best context. Finally, we shall return to the question of distributional equity, also in a second-best setting.

Consumption Externalities

It would be almost impossible for the government to impose excise taxes which were individually tailored to reflect the relative offensiveness of one's consumption patterns. In a second-best world, we might recognize that the government is limited to imposing excise taxes which are the same for all purchasers. In that case the uniform tax might be quite different from the tax we would like to have imposed on the generator of the externality alone.[18]

Moreover, we find that if the government cannot impose a lump-sum tax/subsidy program, the question of, say, an optimal pollution tax becomes intertwined with two further issues.[19] (1) If the revenue raised by the corrective pollution taxes is inadequate (or excessive) to meet the government's revenue requirements, what is the best pattern of other (distorting) taxes to employ, and how should the pollution tax itself be adjusted? (2) Suppose the pollution tax itself has undesired distributional consequences. For example, the optimal registration-fee structure for automobiles might charge more for older cars, since they are typically equipped with fewer emission-control devices and are in inferior condition, therefore causing more pollution. However, the desire for such a differential tax structure would doubtless be tempered by the recognition that older cars tend to be driven by poorer people for whom the tax would be particularly burdensome.

Production with Large Fixed Costs

Let us now return to our model with a single consumer and a producer who must bear certain fixed costs in the production of radios. Suppose the profit-maximizing competitive producer would, in the absence of government intervention, choose to raise cattle and to produce no radios. The government, however, has undertaken a cost-benefit analysis and has determined that it would be socially desirable to induce the producer to produce at point D in figure 2–5 (which is reproduced as figure 2–8), since the indifference curve through that point cuts the vertical axis above point G. Political and budgetary considerations prevent the government from either nationalizing the firm or providing a direct subsidy. Instead, a public regulatory body decides to set the price of radios at the level which maximizes the consumer's welfare; this level may not be the same as the competitive price. However, in order to provide the producer with a fair rate of return, without allowing price gouging, the commission is bound to

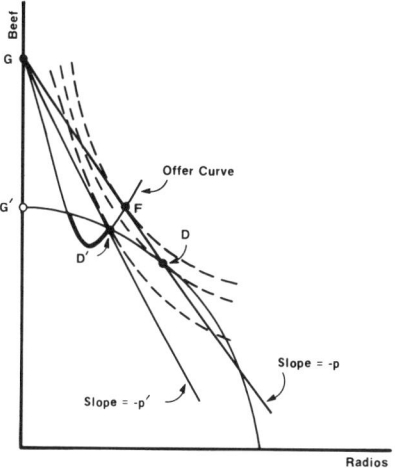

Figure 2–8
Second-best Production Policy

set a price which will keep profits from the producer's land at the same level as they would have been without the regulation (that is, as if the firm produced at point G). Say this profit level is M, the vertical distance from the origin to point G. The consumer (who also owns all of the firm's stock) then is assured that, whatever the commission decides about pricing, his dividend income will be equal to M.

The government's welfare maximization problem is to choose the price, p, of radios to solve

$$\max u(y_1, y_2) \tag{15a}$$

$$\text{subject to } y_2 = f(y_1) \tag{15b}$$

$$y_1 = x_1(p, M) \tag{15c}$$

$$y_2 = x_2(p, M) \tag{15d}$$

Note that if constraints 15cd were eliminated this would be the first-best problem of the unconstrained central planner: we would merely be seeking to maximize utility subject to the production constraint, which is done at point D. However, this first-best optimum is not attainable here because of these additional constraints.[20] The reason for this is because if the commission set the price at p (on figure 2–8), so that point D would be on the budget line as shown, the consumer would instead demand point F where his indifference curve is tangent to the budget line. Point F, however, is infeasible (it is above the production possibilities frontier). Thus, the price which would *enable* the consumer to choose point D is not one at which he would *willingly* choose that point.

The nature of constraints 15cd can be best seen by looking at the offer curve, shown in figure 2–8. This is the locus of points which the consumer would demand at some price given income M; that is, it is the locus of tangencies of indifference curves with rays emanating downward and to the right from point G. (Point F is one such point.) Since the consumer spends his entire income M, the firm will make the requisite profit anywhere along the offer curve. The offer curve, then, is the set of (y_1,y_2) pairs which meet the constraints 15cd. Of these points, only those on the production possibilities frontier also meet the feasibility constraint 15b; these points (and those below the frontier) are in the thickened part of the offer curve. Then, of those points satisfying all constraints, the best is D', which will be chosen by the consumer at price p'. (Other points on the thickened part of the offer curve are on lower indifference curves with a higher price of radios.) Point D', then, is the second-best optimum: although point D is also on the production possibilities frontier and is on a higher indifference curve, the consumer cannot be made to voluntarily choose it. Moreover, we observe that at point D' we have MRS $\neq$ MRT, in contradiction to the first-best allocational rule. Moreover, p' $\neq$ MRT, so we do not have marginal cost pricing.

Note the ironic nature of the second-best solution: in trying to maximize the consumer's utility, the commission is thwarted in its attempt to reach the first-best point D precisely because the consumer is himself maximizing utility given the price seen in the marketplace. And whereas in the first-best world self-interest is the *invisible hand* leading the consumer to an optimum, in this second-best world self-interest leads the consumer away from the feasible point D to an infeasible point F. The next best thing the government can do is to set the price higher so that the consumer chooses point D'.

Distributional Equity

Many taxes which might be imposed to restore market efficiency will have equity implications, as in the previous example of a corrective pollution tax falling more heavily on the poor than on the rich. Suppose, though, that all assumptions required by the Fundamental Theorems are met. There will still be a need for government tax policies if revenue must be raised for the provision of services which are traditionally or necessarily provided in the public sector (such as police and fire departments, court systems, national defense and the like) or if perceived distributional inequities remain.

We have seen how in a first-best setting it is simply necessary to have a lump-sum tax-subsidy structure to move the economy to the point of greatest social welfare along the utility possibilities frontier (point N in figure 2–2). If we assume, more realistically, that the government can only use a tool, such as the progressive income tax, which will distort work incentives, the government will be faced with a tradeoff between distributional equity and production efficiency.

We can best model this phenomenon by modifying our two-good example such that the producer must employ labor in beef production, rather than foregoing the production of corn or radios to produce beef. The two goods, then, will be leisure time and beef: for consumer A, x_2^A is the amount of beef consumed and x_1^A is the amount of leisure time. Thus, if there are a total of T hours per period (say 24 hours per day or 8760 hours per year), the amount of labor supplied by A is $\ell^A = T - x_1^A$.

Suppose A's marginal product of labor is w^A. While A is a greenhorn, B is a veteran rancher and has a much higher marginal product, w^B. The production technology exhibits constant returns to scale with no fixed costs, so the production function, which we have been writing as $y_2 = f(y_1)$, can be written explicitly as

$$y_2 = w^A \ell^A + w^B \ell^B. \tag{16}$$

Under perfect competition, both A and B will be paid wages equal to their marginal products (note that beef is still the numeraire). Then A's utility maximization problem is

$$\max u^A(x_1^A, x_2^A)$$
$$\text{subject to } x_2^A = w^A \ell^A \tag{17}$$
$$x_1^A = T - \ell^A,$$

where we have put leisure, rather than labor, in the utility function so that both marginal utilities will be positive. Note that the firm will have zero profits (because of the constant returns to scale) and so consumers' incomes consist only of their wages. For convenience, we can eliminate x_1^A from 17 by substituting for it from the last constraint, leaving

$$\max u^A(T - \ell^A, x_2^A)$$
$$\text{subject to } x_2^A = w^A \ell^A. \tag{18}$$

This maximization problem will generate demand functions for leisure and, by implication, labor supply functions $\ell^A = \ell^A(w^A)$ and indirect utility functions $u^A = v^A(w^A)$ which depend on the wage rate. Of course, analogous expressions are available to describe B's maximization problem, labor supply function, and indirect utility function.

Suppose, now, that the government is concerned that A's inexperience results in his having such a low wage rate that he is left in poverty. If lump-sum redistribution is not possible, a decision may be made to impose an income tax at rate t (a *flat tax* or *linear tax*) to finance a demogrant, s, to be paid to all citizens. For those with high incomes, the income tax paid will be larger than the demogrant received; those with low incomes will receive net subsidies.[21] Take-home pay will then be $(1 - t)w^A\ell^A + s$ for A and $(1 - t)w^B\ell^B + s$ for B. When faced with this tax-subsidy system, A's maximization problem becomes

$$\max u^A(T - \ell^A, x_2^A)$$
$$\text{subject to } x_2^A = (1 - t)w^A\ell^A + s. \tag{19}$$

which generates labor supply and indirect utility functions which depend on the net wage and the level of the demogrant:

$$\ell^A = \ell^A((1 - t)w^A, s)$$
$$u^A = v^A((1-t)w^A, s). \tag{20}$$

Using a Bergson-Samuelson social-welfare function, $W = W(u^A, u^B)$, the government welfare-maximization problem can be written as a choice of t and s to solve

$$\max W(v^A((1-t)w^A, s), v^B((1-t)w^B, s)) \tag{21a}$$
$$\text{subject to } t[w^A\ell^A((1 - t)w^A, s) + w^B\ell^B((1 - t)w^B, s)] = 2s + R. \tag{21b}$$

where R is the amount of government revenue required for purposes other than providing the demogrant. The constraint 21b is the government's balanced budget requirement (although R could incorporate desired or allowed increases or decreases in the national debt). The term in brackets is the total of A's and B's gross wages, so the left-hand side of 21b is total government revenue, which is spent to provide the demogrant (s for each consumer) and other government services (R).

Each worker's labor supply, and thus the bracketed amount in 21b, is a decreasing function of both t and s, as higher taxes and subsidies reduce work efforts. Let us consider a purely redistributive tax when no other revenue need be raised (R = 0). Then for any tax rate t there will be a demogrant s = s(t) which satisfies 21b and balances the budget; figure 2–9

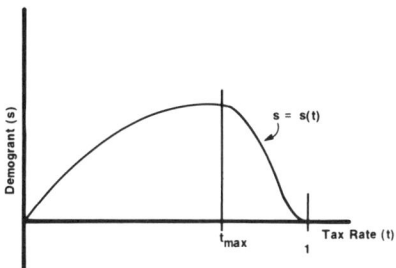

Figure 2–9
Feasible Demogrant (s) as the
Tax Rate (t) Varies

shows this relationship. When $t = 0$ no demogrant can be financed; necessarily, $s = 0$. Typically the demogrant which can be financed from the tax revenues will continue increasing as t increases until it reaches a maximum at $t = t_{max}$. Thereafter, the disincentive effects of taxation are so great that revenue actually declines as t is increased further. Thus we can regard the demogrant which can be provided as a function of t and R. This reduces the government's problem to a simple choice of t (s then being determined by $s = s(t)$) as shown in figure 2–9 to solve:

$$\max W(v^A((1-t)w^A, s(t)), v^B((1-t)w^B, s(t))). \tag{22}$$

The solution to this problem is illustrated in figure 2–10. For A, increased tax rates are less important (given his low income) than the ac-

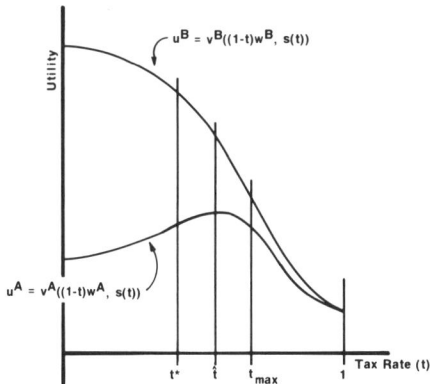

Figure 2–10
Consumer Utilities at Different
Tax Rates (with $s = s(t)$)

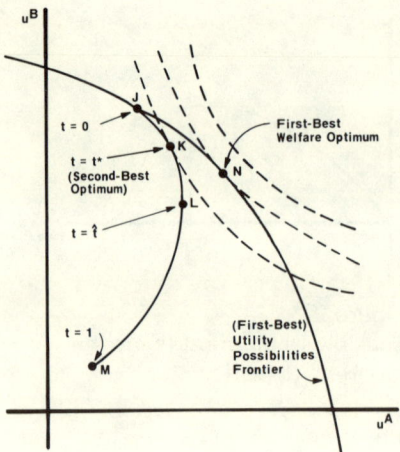

Figure 2–11
The Equity-Efficiency Tradeoff
(*Second-best Utility Possibilities Frontier*) with a Linear Income Tax

companying increases in the demogrant which make him better off until $t = \hat{t}$. After that point the combination of the burden of the tax and the eventual falloff in the rate of increase in s as t approaches t_{max} causes utility to decline. On the other hand, because B's wages are higher than A's, his tax payments rise faster than the demogrant can rise as t increases; the tax-grant program is a device for transferring wealth from B to A, so B is made worse off as that program is enlarged. The optimal tax, t*, is the one which maximizes the social welfare function, balancing A's increased utility as t increases against B's decreased utility. The precise level of t* will depend on the form of the social-welfare and utility functions.

The nature of this equity-efficiency tradeoff is best seen by reference to the utility possibilities frontier in figure 2–11. Without government intervention (t = 0) the consumers are at the Pareto efficient point J on the frontier. Note that, although social welfare is maximized at point N on the frontier (the point of tangency with the social indifference curve), that point is not attainable without lump-sum taxation. If only the income tax-demogrant system we have described above is available, increasing the income tax raises A's utility and lowers B's, improving distributional equity but drawing the economy below its (first-best) utility possibilities frontier due to the reduction in work effort and therefore in output. The second-best optimum occurs at point K ($t = t^*$); further increases in taxes make A better off but so reduce B's utility that social welfare falls. If taxes are raised beyond point L ($t = \hat{t}$), both A and B are made worse off, so the second-best utility possibilities frontier connecting points J, K, L and M bends backward. Societies which are more concerned with distributional equity will be willing to tolerate being further below the first-best utility possibilities frontier in the interest of equalizing the distribution; the size of the pie is shrinking, but it is being cut more evenly as the tax rate is increased.

Actually solving for optimal income-tax rates is quite difficult. In general, the pathbreaking work by James Mirrlees,[22] Anthony Atkinson,[23] Nicholas Stern,[24] Eytan Sheshinski,[25] and others[26] has revealed that optimal taxes tend to be higher when there is a greater dispersion of wage rates (and so more pretax inequality to be concerned with); when labor supply functions are more inelastic (minimizing the work disincentives from taxation); and when R is higher (increasing the need for net tax revenues).

Conclusion

We have distinguished between first-best policy analysis and second-best policy analysis presenting examples of each in a unified framework. First-best analysis, the traditional approach, provides useful and familiar decision rules: absent market imperfections, marginal rates of substitution and marginal rates of transformation (marginal costs) will be equated to the market price, and therefore to each other. In the presence of externalities, the price facing those responsible for the pollution must be modified (by taxes) to reflect the external costs imposed; when there are large fixed costs in production, marginal cost pricing is still appropriate, but subsidies may still be necessary to induce the firm to produce. Distributional concerns are effortlessly swept away with lump-sum taxes and subsidies.

Second-best analysis, in which the limitations on government power are recognized, began to flower in the 1970s. Economists challenged the relevance of first-best questions and the applicability of the resulting policy prescriptions. Marginal cost pricing may no longer be called for if there are large fixed costs in production and direct government subsidies cannot be provided. Polluters may not be presented with prices fully reflecting the effects of their pollution, and marginal rates of substitution may be forced away from marginal rates of transformation by taxes if distributional concerns cannot be addressed with lump-sum taxation.

In the idealized first-best setting the utility and profit-maximizing behavior of consumers and producers serves to further the public interest, or can be made to do so by appropriate government intervention in the marketplace. In a second-best world consumer and producer behavior tends to defeat, rather than facilitate, the attainment of optimality.

The prospects of second-best analysis are formidable. Any time a sector of the economy is subject to imperfections which the government cannot remedy — monopoly, public goods, or distorting taxes by other government agencies, for example — the Theorem of the Second Best tells us that traditional first-best policy rules are no longer applicable, even in unaffected sectors, and second-best modeling must be undertaken. Unfortunately, the problems confronting second-best analysis are equally formidable. Mathematical and conceptual complexity increases enormously as the price of modeling these situations. Moreover, the very theorem which justifies this approach presents the further warning that even second-best rules will be inapplicable if the economy has imperfections beyond those modeled. To some extent, then, the results have been negative ones, advising us of the limits of the generalizability of our policy recommendations.

Normative public microeconomics does not stand in splendid isolation; it relies crucially on positive results: labor supply and demand studies tell us the nature of the equity-efficiency tradeoff in redistributive taxation; studies of tax incidence will influence our estimation of the desirability of alternative taxes; studies of the public-choice mechanism can be drawn upon in deciding how to model the scope and limitations of government authority and objectives. It is the normative analysis, however, that provides the final link between positive economics and public policy.

Notes

1. Adam Smith, *An Inquiry into the Nature and Causes of the Wealth of Nations*, Edwin Cannan, ed. (London: Methuen, 1961), Book IV, chapter II, pp. 475–477.
2. Ibid, Book I, chapter VII, p. 65.
3. Alfred Marshall, *Principles of Economics*, Ninth (Variorum) edition, C. W. Guillebaud, ed. (London: MacMillan, 1961), Vol. I, p. 348.
4. The production possibilities set is the set of points with $y_2 \leq f(y_1)$; it includes the area underneath the production possibilities frontier 1 as well as the frontier itself. However, because it is always desirable to be on, rather than under, the frontier in the models we consider, we shall write the technical feasibility constraints as an equality, rather than as an inequality.

5. See the previous footnote. This constraint will hold as an equality (that is, the planner will choose to be on the frontier of the production possibilities set) as long as the consumers are not satiated.

6. For a more complete treatment of the optimization problem see Francis M. Bator, "The Simple Analytics of Welfare Maximization," *American Economic Review*, 47 (March 1957): 22–59.

7. Abraham Wald, "On Some System of Equations in Mathematical Economics," *Econometrica*, 19 (October 1951): 368–403.

8. Kenneth Arrow and Gerard Debreu, "Existence of Equilibrium for a Competitive Economy," *Econometrica* 22 (July 1954): 265–90; Debreu, *Theory of Value* (New York: Wiley, 1959).

9. See Paul A. Samuelson, *Foundations of Economic Analysis* (Cambridge, Massachusetts: Harvard University Press, 1947), chapter 8 and Tjalling Koopmans, *Three Essays on the State of Economic Science* (New Haven: Yale University Press, 1957), essay I.

10. This type of corrective tax is sometimes referred to as a *Pigovian* tax, after A. C. Pigou. See Pigou, *The Economics of Welfare* (London: Macmillan & Co., 1932), part II, chapter XI.

11. By this we mean *large* relative to marginal costs, so that average costs exceed marginal costs over some relevant output range.

12. Note that we are considering avoidable *fixed costs* rather than unavoidable *sunk costs* which are incurred even at zero production levels and are thus economically irrelevant.

13. See, for example, Richard Layard, ed., *Cost Benefit Analysis: Selected Readings* (New York: Penguin Books, 1972) and Ezra J. Mishan, *Cost-Benefit Analysis* (New York: Praeger Publishers, 1976).

14. Samuelson, *Foundations of Economic Analysis*, p. 225. Chapter 8 of this book provides an important discussion of welfare economics.

15. Ibid., p. 227.

16. Bator, "Welfare Maximization," pp. 22–59.

17. Archibald Lipsey and Kelvin Lancaster, "The General Theory of Second-Best," *Review of Economic Studies* 24 (December 1956): 11–32.

18. Peter A. Diamond, "Consumption Externalities and Imperfect Corrective Pricing," *Bell Journal of Economics and Management Science* 4 (Autumn 1973): 526–38.

19. Agnar Sandmo, "Optimal Taxation in the Presence of Externalities," *Swedish Journal of Economics* 77 (1975): 86–98.

20. A second-best maximization problem can always be expressed as a first-best problem subject to additional constraints. See Diamond and James A. Mirrlees, "Optimal Taxation and Public Production I: Production Efficiency," *American Economic Review* 61 (March 1971): 8–13 for a discussion of a problem similar to the one discussed here; this paper is the seminal work in optimal commodity taxation when public production is also allowed.

21. This is essentially the proposal made by George McGovern in 1972. Although this stand clearly hurt McGovern's election prospects, a quite similar proposal, the Family Assistance Plan, was made in 1969 by the man who defeated him for the presidency.

22. James Mirrlees, "An Exploration in the Theory of Optimum Income Taxation," *Review of Economic Studies* 38 (April 1971): 179–208.

23. Anthony Atkinson, "How Progressive Should the Income Tax Be?" in M. Parkin, ed., *Essays in Modern Economics* (London: Longman Group Ltd., 1973).

24. Nicholas Stern, "On the Specification of Models of Optimum Income Taxation," *Journal of Public Economics* 6 (July 1976): 123–62.

25. Eytan Sheshinski, "The Optimal Linear Income Tax," *Review of Economic Studies* 39 (July 1972): 297–302.
26. See references cited in David F. Bradford and Harvey S. Rosen, "The Optimal Taxation of Commodities and Income," *American Economic Review Papers and Proceedings* 66 (May 1976): 94–101 and Richard W. Tresch, *Public Finance: A Normative Theory* (Plano, Texas: Business Publications, Inc., 1981), chapters 15 and 16.

Selected Bibliography

Arrow, Kenneth J., "The Organization of Economic Activity: Issues Pertinent to the Choice of Market vs. Non-Market Allocation," in Robert Haveman and Julius Margolis, eds., *Public Expenditures*, 2nd edition (Chicago: Rand McNally, 1977) pp. 67–81.

Barber, William J., *A History of Economic Thought* (New York: Penguin Books, 1977).

Bator, Francis M., "The Simple Analytics of Welfare Maximization," *American Economic Review* 47 (March 1957): 22–59.

Baumol, William J., "On Taxation and the Control of Externalities," *American Economic Review* 62 (June 1972): 307–22.

Baumol, William J. and Bradford, David, "Optimal Departures from Marginal Cost Pricing," *American Economic Review* 60 (June 1970): 265–83.

Bradford, David F. and Rosen, Harvey S., "The Optimal Taxation of Commodities and Income," *American Economic Review Papers and Proceedings* 66 (May 1976): 94–101.

Coase, Ronald H., "The Problem of Social Cost," *Journal of Law and Economics* 3 (October 1960): 1–44.

Diamond, Peter A. and Mirrlees, James A., "Optimal Taxation and Public Production, I: Production Efficiency," *American Economic Review* 61 (March 1971): 8–13.

Koopmans, Tjalling, *Three Essays on the State of Economic Science* (New Haven: Yale University Press, 1957), essay I.

Layard, Richard, ed., *Cost-Benefit Analysis: Selected Readings* (New York: Penguin Books, 1972), especially the introductory chapter.

Mishan, Ezra J., *Cost-Benefit Analysis* (New York: Praeger Publishers, 1976).

Roll, Eric, *A History of Economic Thought* (Englewood Cliffs, New Jersey: Prentice Hall, 1972).

Ruff, Larry E., "The Economic Common Sense of Pollution," *The Public Interest* 19 (Spring 1970): 69–85.

Samuelson, Paul A., *Foundations of Economic Analysis* (New York: Atheneum, 1974), chapter 8.

Tresch, Richard W., *Public Finance: A Normative Theory* (Plano, Texas, Business Publications, Inc., 1981).

Comment by Philip A. Klein

Professor Helms has offered an interesting paper based on spelling out the consequences of relaxing some of the more stringent assumptions made in traditional welfare economics and its applied counterpart, public finance. As he notes, second-best analysis — popularized after 1970 — allows for the possibility that the government may not have powerful enough tools to restore Pareto optimality or may not choose to attempt such a restoration. He correctly notes that in cases where there are imperfections which the government cannot or will not remedy — monopoly and public goods are two he specifically mentions — welfare economics must resort to second-best modelling.

The problem with this whole approach would seem to be that, while the type of analysis Professor Helms dwells on is interesting up to a point, it is precisely the cases beyond the scope of his models which are most interesting and which indeed produce the major challenges for modern economics. One can engage in technical analysis as to which of several highways is *the best*, but the debate is relatively sterile if *the best* road does not go where you have decided to go. Much the same charge can be levelled at modern economic modelling of the sort described in this paper. The relaxed assumptions produce slightly more realistic approximations of the real economy with which we must contend, but they leave untouched the primary challenges which that economy thrusts upon us. That those challenges involve questions which, assuming they can be handled by models at all, can be handled only by models of enormous complexity may be unfortunate, but as a profession dedicated to confronting problems in the world as it is, economists have no choice but to tackle the task head on.

"A feasible plan is said to be Pareto optimal (or Pareto efficient)," Professor Helms tells us in time-honored fashion, "if it is not possible to find another feasible plan which makes B better off without making A worse off (or vice versa)." Let us apply this logic to our criminal-justice system and assume that B represents all the individuals in the community save A, a homicidal maniac. Obviously executing A, or even jailing him, will make him worse off, even though everyone else may be better off (that is, safer). There is no price system in the world that can be applied to this situation that will enable us to assess how much better off the Bs will be relative to how much worse off A will feel. The point need not be belabored. This is simply a very incomplete framework within which to develop sound public policy. It is as true of economics as it is for a criminal-justice system, yet economists continue in one way or another to regard it as a useful perspective from which to begin analyzing the welfare implications of various public-policy alternatives.

The problem is partly that while it is possible to move some small way toward greater realism by relaxing some of the assumptions, one cannot move far enough to get to the critical policy challenges of the day. Thus Professor Helms begins with a consideration of Pareto optimality in a world where a central planner can control totally the production of output and its allocation in the economy and then moves on to laissez-faire competition when production and its allocation are accomplished, under certain highly restrictive assumptions, by market prices. In that world he assumes, as is the custom, that the consumers maximize utility and the producers maximize profits. He shows that Pareto optimality can be achieved in the second situation just as in the first, adding in his second welfare assumption the caveat " . . . if the distribution of income is correct." He distinguishes between Pareto optimality and what might be "desirable in a larger sense" without telling us anything about what desirability in a larger sense might be. But it is surely that *larger sense* in which policymakers must operate in devising public policy — and among the things they have to consider are criteria by which to alter income distribution from the way it emerges from the operation of prices in the economy as conditioned by all the factors which impinge on it. Professor Helms, of course, knows all this. But the question must nonetheless be asked, how far does his analysis go in helping us develop sound public policy in the world as it is?

He goes on, for example, to consider "first best tax and expenditure policies," posing the problem as "how much more effective the government can be than the market in achieving a Pareto optimum?" quite ignoring the caveat of the immediately preceding section — that solutions of Pareto optimality might not be optimal in some "larger sense." Then he considers the assumption of first best — that the government has the tools to achieve some point on "the utility possibilities frontier" — in the face of certain types of externalities, suggesting that an omniscient planner can restore optimality by a "policy of corrective taxation" to offset the costs to the community and notes that "society does indeed make decisions which make some better off at the expense of others." That is, society does indeed require more than Pareto optimality, for precisely the kind of reasons the criminal-justice example introduced earlier suggests. Where does this leave economic analysis as a guide to public policy?

The limits to which the model under consideration is pushed is the world of the second best in which the options open to the government are limited. Here, Professor Helms concludes, his analysis leads to essentially negative results because, aside from enormous mathematical, conceptual, and modelling difficulties, "even second-best rules will be inapplicable if the economy has imperfections beyond those modeled." The real economy is, of course, riddled with imperfections.

The problem with this approach, however, begins with the first-best case where Pareto optimality emerges from the magical equating of marginal rates of substitution to marginal rates of transformation via market-clearing prices. Here Professor Helms argues the analysis is useful because it suggests how externalities should be paid for via the imposition of taxes. But all of this can work only if one abstracts from market imperfections.

Economists in general, and welfare economists in particular, have spent far too much time and energy on plowing the relatively arid pasture called Pareto optimality. Notions of Pareto optimality enable economists to nibble at the edges of significant problems, but never to attack the major challenges. Professor Helms hints at some of this by suggesting that one may have to sacrifice Pareto efficiency to obtain "distributional equity" although, interestingly, he says not a word about where these notions of distributional equity might come from. A major limitation of Pareto optimality has always been that income (and wealth) distribution must be consigned to the limbo of ceteris paribus assumptions if the notion is to operate at all.

Nowhere does Professor Helms ask about the welfare consequences of concentrated economic power. Nowhere does he consider the optimality implications of the conflict between the size (scale) requirements of modern technology and the necessary diminished automaticity (that is, decline in competition) which the resultant market domination will bring. Nowhere does he consider the critical question of what consumers' "utility" may be and where it comes from, nor the interactive process involving both individuals *and* the economy which in fact creates "wants."

The argument being made is not that Professor Helms' presentation is illogical or even uninteresting. Rather the argument is that it is largely irrelevant to the policy problems which policy makers must face. The ongoing determination of what we mean at any time by *welfare* is the preeminent challenge to the field of economics. Recognition that our notion of welfare is indeed another name for the emergent value system — a system which transcends the price system — is the beginning of economic policy making. We use all prices to express some values, but we do not express all values with prices. Pareto optimality, even when it is used with full recognition of its assumptions, can nonetheless be introduced only if it is granted that individuals are related to the economy in a way which enables each individual's utility to contribute to the total utility in the economy, rather than having his notions of utility even *partially shaped* by the economy. But people interact with each other, both as consumers and producers; they influence the economy and the economy influences them. Both are influenced as well by exogenous sources. The emergent values require resource allocation partly via market prices, and partly by administrative fiat (for example, we need a strong national defense, "regardless of cost").

The analytical apparatus Professor Helms restricts himself to can make a modest contribution to problems such as externalities but only if the critical value questions are finessed. What, for example, is meant by "perceived distributional inequities"? Where do they come from, and how are they recognized?

The difficulty with the neoclassical approach is that it must necessarily assume that market pricing and the process of evaluation are coterminous. But they are not. The neoclassical approach, therefore, permits the intrusion of the government only by letting it alter market prices (via taxes, transfers, et cetera). The *criteria* governing public allocation (via Congress, the executive or judicial processes, et cetera) come from somewhere — they are, indeed, part of the economy just as they influence it and are influenced by it. This interaction is essentially the process of creating values, and that in turn is the true role of the economy, of which markets and mere allocation are but a part.

Professor Helms has performed a valuable service because his "essentially negative" conclusions suggest what must be dropped if economics is to confront realistically the task of developing public policy for the only economy we have — the economy operating in the real world with all its imperfections, contradictions, dangers, and potentials.

While we recognize that simplification, abstraction, and formalism are necessary to the process of theorizing, theory is perforce good only if it leads to sound public policy. But cost-benefit analysis, to use a term dear to the hearts of welfare economists, suggests that the costs of abstraction derived from notions of Pareto optimality are too high when the theory produced is too abstract to apply to the most pressing challenges of the real world.

Professor Helms is probably correct in his implicit assumption that modern welfare economics is in large part based on a neoclassical approach to public finance. The latter is sometimes referred to as *normative microeconomics*. But applying *positive economic analysis* to problems in the real world cannot get very far without asking questions which this approach is never very comfortable asking. How do participants in the economic process develop their notions of self-interest? What is the process by which consumers perceive *wants;* and what are the welfare implications for an economy in which unequal power and distorted information-flows lead producers to shape wants — for their own purposes — in which the notion of consumer sovereignty is, therefore, ambiguous, at best? What are the welfare implications of allocating resources by dollar votes when both income and its origin — wealth — are distributed not only unequally, but in a way which one cannot argue has any particular relationship to welfare by any conceivable definition? How shall we develop a theory of welfare for an economy, in short, in which many of the participants are *manipulated by* the system rather than manipulating the system? No one believes that Adam Smith's *invisible hand* actually works. But welfare economics has great difficulty in finding an alternative mechanism for transmogrifying individual objectives — however determined and of whatever characteristics (complementary, competing, et cetera) — into a collective result that can by any comprehensible standard be *defined* as collective welfare, let alone pushed to any maximum or optimum by forces either endogenous or exogenous to *the economy*.

In short, the modest headway toward greater realism made by neoclassical public finance leaves public policy issues in very much the same predicament as they have always been. It is vital, of course, that students of political economy be entirely familiar with the analytics and current state of conventional public finance, and Professor Helms has presented that field in lucid and highly competent terms. If it is only a beginning for inquiry, it is not least valuable because its deficiencies illuminate the immense challenge confronting those who would suggest that the most interesting questions begin with Professor Helms's conclusions.

3 FISCAL BEHAVIOR OF THE MODERN DEMOCRATIC STATE: PUBLIC CHOICE PERSPECTIVES AND CONTRIBUTIONS
William C. Mitchell

> *The fundamental business of our representatives is taxing and spending.*
>
> — E. S. Phelps
> "Rational Taxation"
> *Social Research*
> 44 (Winter, 1977): 657

My concerns center on political processes and, more particularly, American governmental decisions pertaining to the raising and spending of public monies. Fiscal choices are at the heart of politics. As Aaron Wildavsky has often noted, budgets are key political documents for they register the allocative and distributive choices that have been made or are being proposed. In this chapter I attempt to describe, integrate, and assess certain contributions of modern pubic choice to these questions of fiscal policy. The work of Bartlett, Borcherding, Breton, Browning, Buchanan and Tullock, Niskanen, and Tollison, to mention some of the more prominent, loom large. My survey is highly selective, but it is hoped not unreasonable or unfair. Nontechnical contributions as well as work with a certain libertarian thrust are emphasized. Highly specialized empirical investigations are occasionally cited but not extensively discussed. Although important in a science of public choice, they are here deemed of lesser import to general students of public choice and finance. While cognizant of the value of surveys of the literature, I seek here a synthesis or a consistent point of view. The synthesis draws unequally upon two divergent perspectives: demand and supply models. In the former, citizen-consumers reign supreme; in the latter, politicians, bureaucrats, and governments play roles not unlike those ascribed to monopolistic businesses by, say, J. K. Galbraith. With important qualifications, I view the consumer as powerful in the economy and the citizen as relatively powerless in the polity.

Elements of Public Choice

The political institutions of a society provide the framework within which the preferences and resource commitments of its citizens are transformed into collective actions that are expected to yield utility. Just as the distribution of income and wealth, the availability of markets, et cetera, determine price-quantity-quality outputs in the market, so wealth, votes, and the presence of certain democratic institutions determine the distribution of political power and the responsiveness of policies in achieving the preferences of voters.

Modern public-choice views representative government not as a separate, sentient entity capable of acting in the public interest; rather government is treated as a political activity carried on by rational, self-interested individuals. Public policies are the product of many individuals with different values, preferences, beliefs, and knowledge. Some are office holders and employees of the state, but most are simply citizens with extraordinarily limited roles in collective decision processes. The vast majority of citizens do not get an opportunity to vote directly on most issues, even at local levels of government. Because of the large number of issues, their complexity, and the high cost of adequate information (among other reasons), actual decision-making is delegated to representatives. The important decisions for the ordinary citizen are made by representatives selected in an at-large voting process where the principle of majority rule usually is in force (even if plurality rules formally apply, as in congressional elections).

The individual citizen-voter uses political institutions to shop, as it were, for publicly supplied services in a manner somewhat analogous to shopping behavior in the market. In both systems the citizen seeks to obtain the best or optimal bargain obtainable. Public choice maintains that political institutions and activities can be understood by use of economic analysis quite comparable to that traditionally applied to market institutions and activity.

The politician or elective public official, including aspirants, plays a role analogous to that of an entrepreneur in the economy. Like businessmen, politicians seek to maximize their own utility, an aim accomplished by maximizing either votes or their probability of being returned to office.

Elected officials realize that any given policy stance will please some voters, displease others, and escape the attention of many. The same action can change their power or influence with colleagues, bureaucrats, and organized interests. Reconciling these differences requires bargains, compromises, logrolling, and, in general, strategic choices. Successful politicians are those who can adopt policies which keep them in office, maintain or improve influence with other politicians, and enlist the aid of bureaucrats. Presumably, much of this interaction restrains irresponsible behavior. The extent to which this occurs is a subject of some difference among public-choice theorists. A few, including Anthony Downs and Mancur Olson, have an apparent faith in the efficacy of politics, while others, notably James M. Buchanan and Gordon Tullock, are skeptical about the efficacy of the *unseen hand* of political bargaining. The latter contend that political institutions are highly imperfect reflectors of preferences, that information costs are immense, that the probability of successful action is remote, that cost-benefit calculations are more difficult than in the market, and, that efficiency goes unrewarded. Institutional arrangements, then, serve to increase irresponsible behavior and inefficient policies. Most likely, political processes encourage everyone to distort, dissemble, and exaggerate their demands. The ever-present prospect of receiving substantial gains, at little or no cost to oneself, is a major motivating force in the polity, since costs and benefits are rarely internalized as they must be in most market activity.

It is within this general setting that the fiscal choices of a society are made or enacted. The obvious questions confronting analysts include: (1) the supply of government output or, more precisely, the size of the public budget; (2) composition of the output or expenditures; (3) choice of revenue sources, instruments, and rates; and (4) variations of these magnitudes through time. While public-choice analysts approach these questions within the well-defined paradigm of economics, the theories that have evolved over the past thirty years are by no means fully consistent. In fact, I shall contend that two major schools of thought vie in supplying answers to these questions.

Unlike economic theory, which began with production or supply-oriented models, public choice began with demand-inspired models. But, whereas economics took a century to discover demand and appropriate means for integrating supply and demand analyses, public choice began to emphasize the other side of the market only a decade after the demand-oriented work of Black and of Downs.[1] Indeed, libertarian economists from Virginia Polytechnic Institute have viewed theories of imperfect competition and monopoly as more appropriate and useful in the study of politics than the markets for which they were originally designed.

Demand-Based Models: Votes and Optimal Budgets

At least two major and conflicting public-choice explanations are used to account for the fiscal choices of individuals and governments. One reflects or emphasizes the demands of citizens, while another emphasizes government and supply-side considerations. We begin with the demand-based framework.

Early statements of demand-based theory by Lindahl, Hotelling, Bowen, and Black tended to view policy as emerging from the direct and active demands of citizens disappointed with the inefficiencies of markets.[2] Governmental intervention was felt to promise, if not guarantee, greater efficiency by providing desired public goods, reducing welfare losses stemming from monopoly, correcting market externalities, generating more equitable income distributions, and moderating business fluctuations. In brief, the failures and imperfections of markets so sharply delineated by welfare economists provided a compelling rationale for expansion of the state. It was assumed that political processes, although unexamined, would provide right policies that would be implemented effectively by government. The question of just how officials could achieve these ideals was never raised, let alone explored. Apparently, some combination of benevolence, political competition, and constitutional constraints were to work in tandem to produce desired results.[3] This ideal, which is to say nonexistent, political world so prevalent in welfare economics continues to hold sway in the standard economics textbook exposition of market failure. Although more recent discussions are accompanied by policy evaluations of alternatives, little if anything is said about their political feasibility. How and why typical political processes select among policies is rarely broached. Such analyses would seem to be logical extensions of demand models, since one wishes to know how individual policy preferences are mobilized and acted upon.

Unitary Governments

Because demand models assume that governments are relatively passive and do not actively seek to control their environments, one should hardly be surprised to learn that most demand models treat governments as single, hierarchical entities seeking a single goal. Downs made these assumptions explicit. His analysis was facilitated by ignoring bureaucracies, constitutional separation of powers, and federalism. With its roots in the heuristic conceptualization of the firm, the political model possesses considerable appeal. Nevertheless, researchers have shown the limitations of that view even in economics. If such a theory is at odds with reality in the market, consider the discrepancy in political systems. Governments, including nondemocratic ones, can hardly be considered as unitary agents of ruling parties. Indeed, analysts usually find it difficult in practice to say who rules or makes what decisions under what conditions and why. Governments are usually far greater in size than business firms and much more loosely organized. One must assume (in fact one knows) that different interests and goals exist among governmental participants. Far from having a unitary interest, governments harbor many conflicting departmental and individual interests.

Different decision-makers are selected by different means, decide under quite different circumstances, are rewarded and penalized in different ways and at different levels and rates, and ultimately are responsible to different agents in different ways. For example, politicians are elected for fixed terms while bureaucrats are typically chosen through some civil service procedure and accorded considerable security of tenure. Ordinary employees are hired for a wage and are often represented by a powerful union. Local governments are often managed by appointees hired by politicians and have no security of tenure. Under these restricted conditions alone, one should expect that different decision-makers will react to the fiscal situation of government in radically different ways. Just how they respond will be considered when we review supply-based models, for those models are most sensitive to the complexities and inefficiencies of collective choice.

Competitive Vote-Maximizing Parties and Budgets

Downs, the preeminent theorist during the late 1950s and early 1960s, viewed the political problem in a much more sophisticated manner: monolithic but *competing* parties vie for the support of voters by offering policies and/or promises that accurately reflect the wishes of *consumer-voters*. The basic decision rule followed by Downsian governments is simple: ... expenditures grow until votes gained at the margin equal votes lost from additional taxes.[4] Downs based his model on the competitive marketplace, with vote-maximizing serving as the analogue to profit-maximizing among competitive firms. While governments are treated as electoral strategists, their strategies are really the passive responses of voter-representatives in the same sense that competitive firms are price-takers resolving quantity-quality dilemmas under the rigorous discipline of market competition. Downsian governments are self-interested, but those interests are readily reconciled with those of the utility-maximizing citizenry. Although the monopoly power of government was recognized, its implications were hardly as fully developed as they were to become in the supply-size models. In fact, Downs's view encourages the belief that governments are responsive, responsible and can not only tax/spend effectively and efficiently but can also compensate for the alleged imperfections and failures of markets. Downs recognized that polities and markets differ in fundamental ways, but these differences were not developed in his first book.

Downs's failure to distinguish simultaneous spending and taxing choices in market decisions from nonsimultaneous choices that dominate in politics is also noteworthy. Governments can avoid market discipline whenever they are permitted to separate taxing and spending choices. In short, democratic governments compare spending policies in terms of their marginal vote-getting potential *independently* of revenue decisions and only rarely reconcile spending and revenue proposals simultaneously, as suggested by Downs's original decision rule. The absence of a market permits this luxury of choice. The relevant graphics are depicted in figures 3-1 and 3-2.

Figure 3-1 tells us that for each additional dollar spent a certain number of votes will be acquired; each dollar spent creates benefits while each dollar of financing becomes increasingly painful to increasing numbers of voters. The exact number of voters affected in their separate roles as beneficiaries and taxpayers determines the slopes and positions of the curves. In the case of the total votes-won curve, we suspect that the rate of increase in votes will be more than proportional at lower levels of

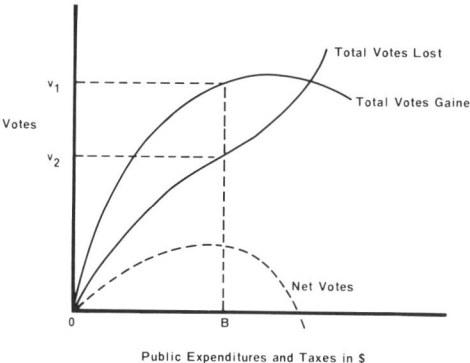

Figure 3–1
The Calculus of Votes and Budgets:
Simultaneous Choice

expenditure (highly elastic), while as spending mounts the votes won will become less than proportional as each additional dollar spent brings in fewer votes. On the other hand, as taxes increase, the number of votes in opposition will probably increase at an increasing rate. More people become taxpayers and each is taxed more. The rational Downsian government balances the marginal values (at v_1 and v_2) of these opposing tendencies. A government will continue to advocate spending as long as each added dollar brings in more votes than are lost. A budget size of OB will be chosen since net votes won will be greatest at that amount of expenditure and taxation.

Figure 3–2a and 3–2b depict another situation — one in which revenue and spending choices are divorced or unrelated. While this is more realistic, the logic of political choice remains as stated by Downs. In the instance of nonsimultaneous choice, governments spend without regard to taxation and tax without regard to expenditure. Of course, a balanced-budget requirement poses a different problem than one in which a balance of expenditures and revenues is not required. In any event, figure 3–2a, shows how governments might decide between two uses of a fixed sum of expenditures while figure 3–2b, illustrates a similar choice on the revenue side. The point is to balance the marginal votes won from each expenditure so that the total votes won will be maximized. Governments seek to enact revenue choices that minimize the number of votes lost. We should note that only rarely would a general-purpose government choose to spend all its money on one or a few programs, or choose but one or a few

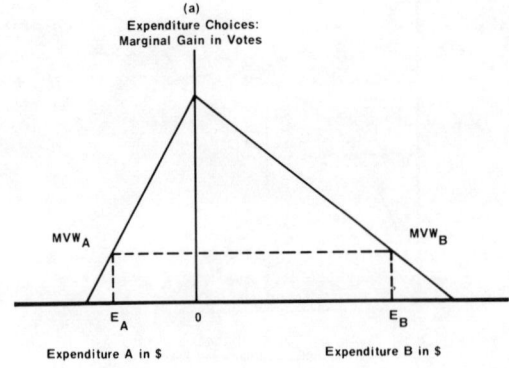

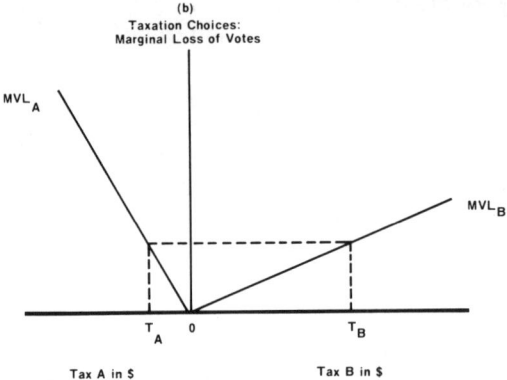

Figure 3–2a, b
The Calculus of Votes and Budgets:
Non-simultaneous Choices

sources of revenue. Some combination of expenditures and some combination of revenues will be selected. The logic is the same as that found in consumer and producer market choices.[5]

Perhaps because of the attractive competitive market analogue, Downs and others before him, including Lindahl, Hotelling, Bowen, Samuelson, and Tiebout, could view governmental choices as efficient, that is, citizen demands could be accurately honored.[6] Efficiency in fiscal matters is guaranteed by equating marginal costs and benefits; in collective choice this objective could be achieved by enacting or honoring the choices of the median voter/s. A plethora of empirical studies has followed but have not, for the most part, confirmed the theorem.[7] The problem remains, however, of the limited electoral opportunities for voters to directly express their choices in ways that politicians can understand and enact. A tendency to median consensus does exist in strong two-party systems, but, wherever multi-party systems and plurality rules prevail, equilibrium cannot be said to be as stable. Nor will an equilibrium necessarily conform to the choice of the median voter.

A major difficulty with demand-only analyses is found in the failure of the basic policy calculus adequately to consider uncertainty in responses to policy proposals of citizen-voters and politicians alike. Unlike consumers, voters do not engage in more or less continuous voting. Accordingly, governmental suppliers do not have continuous information to assess citizen responses accurately; in the short-run they are unable to know whether they have made popular choices or not. A firm can learn almost daily whether it is producing the right things in the right way and right quantities; only rarely are governments provided similar opportunities. And when governments learn it may be too late, for elections will have been either won or lost. While a firm may go bankrupt, it does not typically win or lose; instead, it increases or decreases its share of market sales and profits. Thus, while sales and profits of the firm are accurate indicators of wise and unwise choices, periodic voting is far less informative.

Interestingly, demand models tend to ignore changes in preferences and their distributions. The median-voter theorem does not account for changes in the distribution of voter preferences; it yields a short-run equilibrium outcome. Explaining vitally important substantive changes in individual preferences is arbitrarily delegated to psychologists.

In his justly renowned article "Why the Government Budget Is Too Small in a Democracy," Downs attempted to show the impact of voter information (pertaining to individual costs and benefits) on the size of the budget.[8] Perfect information of collectively imposed costs and benefits is supposed to produce a correct or efficient budget. While Downs is remembered for his contention that public budgets tend to be too small or suboptimal, he did, in fact, elaborate a complex typology of 25 subsets of varying types and levels of information reflecting nine basic states of *ignorance* or *information* — and their effects on budget size (see figure 3-3). Of the nine basic outcomes (that is, *correct, suboptimal,* and *supraoptimal* budgets), four are said to be suboptimal, one too large, one correct, and the remaining three indeterminate without additional knowledge of still other, unstipulated conditions. As the forthright title of the article suggests, conditions producing suboptimal supplies are said to be encountered most frequently.

The reason for this collective failure is simple: given the various states

	COSTS		
BENEFITS	Zero Ignorance	Partial Ignorance	Preponderant Ignorance
Zero Ignorance	"Correct" Size	?	"Too Large"
Partial Ignorance	?	"Too Small"	?
Preponderant Ignorance	"Too Small"	"Too Small"	"Too Small"

Figure 3–3
Budgetary Outcomes: Downsian Analysis

of rational voter ignorance regarding fiscal matters, the cost side is likely to be perceived while the *true* value of governmental output (public goods?) is apt to be seriously underestimated. Plausible argument rather than empirical data sustained the contention.

Buchanan and Tullock, and Tullock independently, claimed that the Downsian analysis was in error especially whenever benefits and costs are differential and majority rule is employed.[9] Their theory is the obverse of Downs's; that is, voters are more apt to exaggerate benefits and underestimate costs and, thereby, produce outsized budgets. Again, the alleged imbalance in perceptions was advanced in terms of theoretical plausibility rather than empirical data. In addition, logrolling, while generally defended as an efficient process, was shown to be inefficient (to oversupply) under a variety of conditions. If Downs had not adequately specified the role of logrolling, perhaps it was because it is so rare in direct large-N voting situations. Representatives are required before it can become an efficient process. Even then implicit logrolling will lead to coalitions of minorities and inefficient budgets.

Many of the theoretical differences between undersupply and oversupply theorists now seem attributable to an understandable failure to conceptualize adequately the nature of the goods involved in public production. Some of these differences can be reconciled by specifying the degree to which the goods are private, public, or some admixture. It is entirely possible that agreement might be forthcoming if one claims that pure public goods are underproduced by markets; that most pure private goods and transfers are always overproduced by governments; and that public and semipublic goods may or may not be produced in correct amounts by governments depending on the ratio of private and public attributes of the goods and the decision-rules. Then, too, demand theorists tend to exaggerate the importance of public goods in the formation of government and certainly overestimate their significance in the daily operations of ongoing polities.

Another difficulty concerns the relationship between the optimal size (as defined by the equalization of individual and social marginal benefits and costs) and the budget size actually selected by the political process. The correct budget size is indicated by the juncture of the total demand curve and the total marginal-cost schedule. There is no good reason, however, why the correct budget should be equal to the one adopted by the median voter/s. Whether it does depends on the distribution of voters. Figure 3–4 shows that the answer to the crucial question of the relationship between the optimal amount (as determined by cost-benefit considerations) and the quantity supplied in the political process depends on the shape of the vote-supply curve. If the vote-supply curve had the shape of the curve labeled P_1, the equilibrium level of expenditure would be e_1, which is exactly the amount required to meet the efficiency criterion. If the vote-supply curve were instead to follow the line of P_2, we can see that the expenditure would be confined to the level e_2, considerably less than the optimal amount. Conversely, if the supply were labeled P_3, the political equilibrium would be reached only after expenditures on the good in question considerably exceeded the efficient level.

Median-voter theories do focus on an important variable, namely, the distribution of voter preferences but seem unable to explain what determines the exact shape of the vote-supply curve. A partial explanation might focus on the manner in which the tax burden and the benefits of the given public program are distributed among the voters. Surely a demand-oriented theorist can accept the notion that the equilibrium level of expenditure on a public good for a single citizen is the level where his own share of the marginal benefit is equal to his own share of the marginal cost, as in market choices. It follows that the optimal supply for a given individual will be the same as the optimal supply for a society if and only if the percentage share of the total benefits which he receives is the same as the percentage share of the total costs which he must bear. A person who receives a disproportionately large share of the benefits will be in equilibrium only if the total supply of the good in question exceeds the optimal amount, while a person who bears a disproportionately large share of the

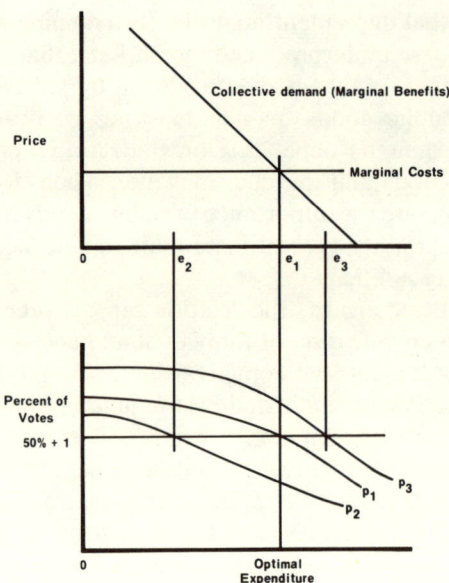

Figure 3–4
Demand and Supply of a Public Good

costs will want to see total expenditure fall short of the optimal point. When expenditure decisions are made by voting, then, the relationship of the political equilibrium supply to the optimal supply will depend on which type of voter is more numerous. But since most fiscal decisions are made in a complex political process rather than by direct voting these tendencies with respect to the distribution of costs and benefits must be considerably modified, a point to which we will return throughout these pages. Small, coherent interest-groups can shape the supply of publicly provided goods in ways quite foreign to the median-voter theorem. How spending could become excessive is not adequately explained by the theorem. Demand-based models, it would seem, overemphasize the extent of market failure and electoral efficiency and the importance of public goods and voting.

Spending Choices

Much of what we have said about the size of public budgets applies, *pari passu,* to the composition of budgets; in fact, much research really proceeds as though the two allocations were but one. Yet, it is possible and highly likely that the outcomes for efficiency need not be the same. An overall budget might well be deemed inefficient, yet particular program allocations be considered optimal or vice versa. Whereas it is impossible to actually determine whether a total budget is of the correct size, it does seem feasible to make some sound economic judgments with regard to specific programs. Before citing some illustrative studies it will be useful to enter a few more preliminary observations derived, primarily, from demand thinking.

We note at the outset that most citizens and officials are much more concerned with program allocations and especially those which most affect their own incomes than with budget totals. Such orientations make perfectly good sense under uncertainty and limited power to affect budget outcomes. Parochialism is further encouraged by a budgetary process that does not begin with a fixed or maximum level of expenditure. Without the latter constraint the problem of the size of the budget necessarily becomes a problem of accounting for program allocations. The size of the budget becomes an unintended outcome rather than a premise for program allocations. Simple addition of the component expenditures constitutes the budget; that process has been the principal way of composing public budgets in America. Accordingly, we might well have begun this essay with a discussion of program allocations and the logrolling that is so essential to their determination. Whatever the order of our discussion, we must explore the composition dilemma.

Whereas demand analysis of budget totals has been shaped by normative considerations, that is, explicit optimality properties — usually perfect information and the satisfaction of marginal requirements —analyses of program size have usually been much more empirically oriented. This is not to say that optimality rules are viewed as irrelevant but that, for some reason, analysts suddenly expand and alter their orientations to include legal and informal institutions, power, and a host of cultural variables or factors. We might begin, however, with an illustration of a nearly pure normative-demand model, the work of Edgar K. Browning on social insurance and intergenerational transfers.[10] Browning is able to show, using an analysis similar to Downs, that program allocations can be excessive. In a simple but imaginative model of majority voting on social-security expenditures, Browning showed that voters would overexpand social insurance even though informed about the consequences of their choices. He also maintained that voters are rationally ignorant of a large portion of the cost of social insurance and that this tendency exacerbates overexpenditure. Fiscal illusion is, as in Downs, an important element of the analysis. However, neither Downs nor Browning developed the role of government in promoting the illusions.

Earlier, Tullock claimed that majority voting tended to produce excessive public spending whenever private benefits could be obtained at the expense of all taxpayers.[11] Specific benefits and generalized taxation amount to transfers and possibly negative-sum games in which the gains of the winners are less than the losses of the losers. Generalized benefits and concentrated costs of taxation will probably produce the opposite outcome, meaning an insufficiency of public goods. Downs and Tullock agree on this point. The central problem in democratic fiscal processes is the element of coercion: majorities can inflict the costs of their preferences on others not in a position to exit from the game or contest. Less-than-unanimity rules accompanied by logrolling are the culprits. While this situation is generally descriptive of democracy, it is best and most clearly understood in the context of pork-barrel legislation.

But there is more to be said on who gets how much from the political system, and Downs said it: "Democratic governments tend to favor producers more than consumers in their actions."[12] This proposition vies with Downs's *rational-ignorance* theorem as the most famous and widely accepted generalization in public choice. In any event, because of widespread (and rational) voter ignorance as to the impact of issues on their personal welfare and the response of politicians to such limited and biased knowledge, the voter's producer role will dominate the consumer role. Most, if not all, of a person's income is derived from a single producer role, whereas a consumer's expenditures are spread over an enormous range of goods and services no one of which constitutes an overwhelming portion of all his or her expenditures. Accordingly, the voter is far more sensitized to work and personal income. In addition, most income-earners believe that they can affect their income more easily than the prices they pay in the market. Thus, producer interest-groups form more readily than do consumer organizations and exercise more influence. Successful politicians understand all this and act accordingly. They support special interests; publicize their support among interest-group members; solicit campaign funds from them; and logroll with other politicians representing still other interests.

Revenue Choices

In markets, individual spending and consumption are simultaneous and coordinated choices. Not so in the polity. Public-choice analysts must, therefore, explain governmental spending and revenue gathering as distinct processes at both the individual level of preferences and governmental level of policy making. While demand theorists have been aware of this separation of fiscal processes, they have not exploited the insight. The implications are enormous.

Downs and other demand-analysts recognize that the main problem for the voters is that they play two roles at once. On the one hand, voters have a general taxpayer interest in reduced spending, reduced inflation, and increased growth. Such an interest should focus on the overall size of the budget. On the other hand, voters are members of some interest group, usually a producer group. Accordingly, each voter has, as we have noted, a very intense stake in those particular spending programs that benefit that group. As in the market, everyone likes benefits and no one likes costs. But the market offers few opportunities to escape the dilemma, while the polity affords many such opportunities and thereby strengthens the incentive to free-ride. Thus, we see many glaring inconsistencies in beliefs, voting, and political action.

Demand models confront revenue dilemmas at the individual and governmental levels but are most successful in dealing with the former. While taxpayers are thought to believe that the best tax is no tax or one shifted to others, they do pay taxes. And politicians continue to enact still greater taxes. The explanation seems based on the notion that while taxes are unpopular, citizens do recognize that collective gains can be made and therefore agree to tax themselves in order to obtain various goods. Taxation is, then, treated as a voluntary exchange as it is by Wicksell, Lindahl, Bowen, Samuelson, and Musgrave.[13]

In this approach, resources are allocated in the polity in a manner analogous to their market allocation. Individuals buy publicly provided goods through taxes in accordance with benefits received and, as in the market, by equating marginal costs (tax shares) with marginal benefits. A major problem with this approach stems from the joint consumption of public goods, where joint also means equal consumption in spite of differential marginal values placed on goods by taxpayers. Since different taxpayers place different values on the same good the tax system or allocation of burdens must reflect these values. Unlike the market, the tax system should levy different prices on the same quantity of the good for each taxpayer and that tax price should equal the marginal valuation. While each citizen's total tax bill may be different, no single tax is in accordance with that citizen's preferences for each publicly supplied good.

The voluntary-exchange or demand theory of the revenue side of the budget is not terribly useful in explaining either individual taxpayer behavior or the tax policies (rates, bases, incidence, payment) that emerge from the political process. The major reason is simple: tax legislation is not a product of voluntary exchange. The essence of taxation is coercion. Having decided upon the level and allocation of public expenditures, democratically elected governments can determine the tax-prices to be paid by each citizen. To the extent that such governments must heed the votes of citizens there is some incentive to select the right expenditures and to provide them at least cost. That is the tentative lesson of demand theory.

Redistribution and Governmental Growth

Downs argued that equality of the franchise would induce governments to redistribute incomes from the affluent to the less affluent.[14] Coalitions are formed that use the state to benefit themselves at the cost of more numerous noncoalition members. Downs was careful to indicate that complete equality will not result, but downward redistribution will occur. Citizens have votes that are wanted by political parties. And governments have authority to enact public expenditures and levy taxes. So redistribution will take place. But it is limited because of uncertainty in policy formation, that is, governments may not know how best to redistribute without alienating unnecessary numbers of taxpayers. Then too, some members of the lower-income group may aspire to unequal higher incomes and thereby make their votes available to the upper-income coalition. Some sophisticated lower-income recipients may believe that redistribution will so impair the incentives to productivity that the GNP will be reduced or at least not increase at optimal rates. Finally, upper-income persons possess more political resources, including the incentives to make use of them. Their smaller numbers are more than compensated by their status, knowledge, wealth, et cetera.

More sophisticated demand-models have been provided, but they too encounter difficulties. Downs's model was unable to specify the actual redistribution outcomes, that is, who would gain how much. Later attempts such as those of Tullock and of Stigler improved the situation somewhat by contending, as in Tullock's case, that minimum-size coalitions for redistribution will form if vote trading is permitted under majority rule.[15] He also demonstrated the misallocation effects of such practices. Water-resource projects, and pork barrel more generally, are cases in point. Stigler, in his formalization of Director's Law, claimed that redistribution goes in quite different ways from those predicted by Downs. Instead of the classic downward redistribution, Stigler and Tullock independently predicted that the middle class would become the chief beneficiary of such government programs and that the contributors are apt to include both the upper- and lower-income recipients. Buchanan and Tullock argued, furthermore, that redistribution can and typically does result from almost any governmental action and policy. Downs seems to have viewed redistribution as a result of a more explicit and direct set of decisions on the part of both voters and governments.

These various demand-models emphasized the high costs of obtaining governmental benefits. Moreover, the costs of organization are such that the larger groups will find it more difficult to compete in redistribution struggles. Stigler was to enrich demand models with his theory of regulation, in which redistribution is achieved not by direct handouts from the government but by occupational groups obtaining differential market advantages from government under the guise of regulation in the public interest.[16] In effect, cartel services are provided by government to interested groups in exchange for power, status, income, and support. Stigler's theory of regulation provides an important bridge to the supply models discussed in the following section.

Demand models of redistribution are not without important implications for explaining the growth of government. All demand models predict increased growth of governmental expenditures; as noted, they differ only in identifying principle beneficiaries. Median-voter theories, as well as public choice more generally, contend that median voters — whether the middle or upper lower-class — prefer greater expenditures because benefits can be distributed to themselves while the higher taxes will be spread over the entire population with higher rates imposed upon the upper-income groups. Politicians have little trouble following the dictates of the median voter, so public expenditures grow. Self-interest among voters complemented by understandably skewed individual perceptions of benefits and costs ensures a distinct preference for greater public expenditures over greatly reduced benefits and minuscule reductions in individual taxes.

While this general explanation of redistribution and governmental growth has much to be said for it, the theory is deficient in accounting for the behavior of other members of the polity. Politicians and bureaucrats appear far more active and influential in deciding outcomes than demand theory suggests. Accordingly, we shift our attention to the roles they play in supply models.

Government as a Monopolistic Supplier: Supply Models

Dating the emergence of supply-based models is a difficult and possibly fruitless task because supply considerations have rarely been excluded from even the most demand-oriented theories. However, Downs moved far beyond the early analyses with a theory of the politician's behavior and later, but less successfully, of the bureaucrat and bureau. Shifts from demand to supply models may, perhaps, best be explained as responses to both theoretical difficulties and the unrelenting force of real-world developments. Casual observation of real-world politics suggests, among other things, that politicians and governments are not the passive creatures implied by the demand theorists of public choice and by interest-group theorists in political science. Politicians, bureaucrats, and governments have an enormous capacity to control and powerful incentives to decide their own fates. In order to survive, politicians and bureaucrats need not always keep their "ears to the ground" and "thumbs to the wind." Officials have considerable control over constituent demands and as governments they act not only as monopolistic suppliers but as the single most authoritative and powerful social institution.

Supply Models: A Thumbnail History

The dramatic growth of bureaucratic activity during the past twenty years has had a profound effect on theory building. The theories of collective choice advanced by Arrow, Black, and even Downs had no role for bureaucracy. Tullock and Niskanen were to have a significant part in writing the role of the missing actor.[17] One suspects, too, that ideological commitments or values had some role to play in sensitizing these two theorists to imperfect political competition as well as the unique power of government to control life. Such sensitivities doubtlessly encouraged scholars of libertarian economic proclivities to note and emphasize the allocative and technical inefficiencies and distributive inequities of politics. Demand models simply do not prepare one to recognize, let alone emphasize, these difficulties. Downs insisted that political competition made politicians responsive and responsible. Common sense has led many to question the fact and some the theory and logic.

In any event, explicit supply considerations began entering the literature about 1965 with the publication of Tullock's *The Politics of Bureaucracy* and, two years later, his *Toward a Mathematics of Politics*.[18] James M. Buchanan had contributed still earlier to these developments with a classic paper on "Social Choice, Democracy, and Free Markets" (1954),[19] and in the series of papers published in the mid 1960s under the title of *Public Finance in Democratic Process*.[20] Although the same author advanced some supply considerations in *The Demand and Supply of Public Goods* (1968), the title of the volume is misleading, since most of it is really about demand.[21] Niskanen's much cited *Bureaucracy and Representative Government* (1971), Randall Bartlett's impressive but little-noted *Economic Foundations of Political Power* (1973),[22] and Albert Breton's *The Economic Theory of Representative Government* (1974)[23] afforded a more complete theory of democracy than demand theory was or is able to attain. Others, notably, Stigler (1971), Tollison and McCormick (1981), Wittman (1973), Sirkin (1975), Peltzman (1976), Aranson and Ordeshook (1977), Rose-Ackerman (1978), Auster and Silver (1979), Mueller (1979), Wagner (1980), and Mackay and Weaver (1978; 1981), were all to make significant contributions to the realism of public-choice theories of government and politics.[24] Their analyses, some highly technical, were clearly inspired by theories of imperfect market competition and monopoly. Although these many contributions cannot be detailed in these few pages, some of the basic ideas can be summarized as they relate to the problem of fiscal behavior in and by the modern state.

One result of this recent interest in supply-side public choice is a richer, more complete, and realistic approach to politics than that afforded by demand analysis. The latter, as we have seen, was and remains fixated on the voluntary exchanges between citizen/voters and elective officials. The newer supply-side approach does not so much eschew the demand model as expand it to include bureaucracy and add to the complexity of relationships among citizens (beneficiaries, taxpayers, regulated), politicians, and bureaucrats. Certain of these relationships are considered to be not only important but crucial. These include a new emphasis upon regulation, authority, compliance, taxation; in other words, the political science tradition of treating the state as the embodiment of power and authority is revived by public choice. The state is now seen as a monopolist and possible exploiter rather than a neutral, responsive supplier of public goods. Figure 3–5a and 3–5b offer a schematic means for contrasting demand and supply models. The heavier lines indicate some of the new emphases in public-choice studies.

Private monopoly has been made an explicit benchmark for the analysis of government and in particular, bureaucracy. Various types of well-known monopolistic practices including all-or-nothing offers, tax share discrimination, and commodity bundling, are examined for their collective counterparts.[25] In addition, the power of government to set agendas

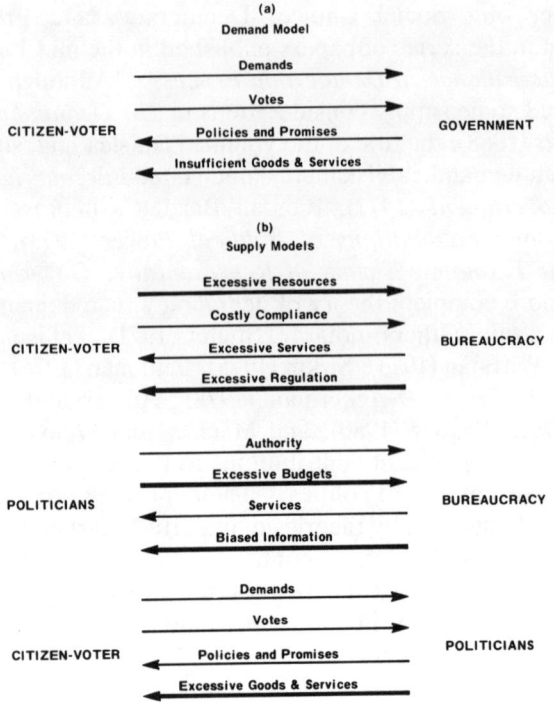

Figure 3–5
Basic Supply and Demand Models

and determine the rules of the game have become a major focus of research.[26] Government, then, is viewed as a monopolist, but a somewhat benevolent one following peculiar economic rules but highly rational political goals and strategies.

The Nature of Public Supply and Excessive Provision

The fundamental insight of the supply-siders is simple: monopolistic governments and their members pursue self-interests and no theory of democracy can possibly be maintained that does not take these interests into account. Richard Wagner put it well when he wrote, "It is contrary to reason and to history to expect that a monopoly position will fail to be exploited for the benefit of those in a position to do so."[27] Early theorists of supply tended to take the discovery too narrowly and assumed that governments had a singular and readily discerned interest that could be readily applied in devising positive theory. This simplistic understanding was soon rectified with the recognition that a government could have different objectives and that they might conflict. Accordingly, theorists began to consider the divergent objectives of different members or agents of government. As previously noted, both Tullock and Niskanen explored the situation and behavior of bureaucrats as distinct from those of elective officials, not to mention divergencies from the voters.[28] The various fiscal roles of legislators, executives, governmental employees, and such unique officials as city managers who are neither elected politicians nor civil servants were delineated and explored. Still other theorists, notably, Peltzman, Stigler, Posner, Hirshleifer, Lindsay, and Owen and Braeutigam were to concentrate on regulatory problems within a public-choice setting.[29] Choices to regulate, including the pricing of governmentally supplied utilities, are now discussed as political rather than purely economic decisions. Not unexpectedly, a small literature on political wage determination in bureaucracy has also emerged.[30]

In addition to viewing government as an interested but peculiar monopolist, supply-side theorists have insisted that governments do not respond to the same economic stimuli as private persons and organizations, that is, the stimuli of prices and price changes. In other words, governments do not necessarily buy less when prices rise or more when prices fall. In fact, under Keynesian precepts, government is advised to act in ways contrary to rational market behavior. Under any regime, governments do not observe the fundamental rule of allocation, that is, do not equalize costs and benefits at the margin. Governments are concerned with the *distribution* of benefits and costs because distributions shape the voting choices and electoral outcomes. Zero- and under-pricing of services is, of course, ubiquitous precisely because of these considerations.

Besides ignoring the marginal equivalence mandate, governments ignore the basic constraint on the financial choices of individuals, namely, income. While an individual's income determines possible expenditure, a government's expenditures determine the amount of its necessary income. To make things worse, under Keynesian rules a government can engage in deficit finance less as a matter of necessity than as a theoretical and ethical imperative.

This brief discussion of the peculiar economics of government cannot be completed without reference to a principle that is everywhere ignored by governments: *"Nobody spends somebody else's money as carefully as he spends his own."*[31] Voters, politicians, and bureaucrats are engaged in spending the money of others. And, since everyone is spending money on others as well as spending the money of others on themselves, a double inefficiency is incurred: spenders have little incentive either to economize or to provide the goods most valued by the beneficiary.

Traditional public finance and economics generally have maintained that marginal analysis *should* be applied to an analysis of the proper or correct role of government in the economy. Thus, it has been held that the expenditures of government should be carried to the point where the value of the last unit of all governmentally produced goods and services is equal, and the value of the last unit produced for the government sector is equal to the value of the last unit produced for the private sector.[32] Others have claimed that the government should spend until the value of the sums lost by taxation is equal to the value of the last unit bought by the government.[33]

Public choice, whether demand or supply oriented, has insisted that familiarity with actual political processes and historical patterns of expenditures suggests that the marginal calculus is rarely followed; indeed, it cannot be honored. The nature of the political product and the incentives of participants both work against the adoption of conventional economic advice. Furthermore, governments that might desire to apply the marginal calculus would encounter the prescriptive limitations of macroeconomic analysis itself. At best, macrotheory has progressed to the point where it can tell us what not to do and sometimes can inform us when it is necessary to reverse the direction of policy. It still, however, cannot tell the policy maker when he should act to prevent a change in economic conditions; what responses to a given act of government will be; or which course, among many possible, is the most desirable at a given time. The confidence generated when the Keynesian system of autonomous and dependent variables was first developed has long since been lost. A long overdue reappraisal is now taking place within macroeconomics. Complementary discoveries within public choice, not the least of which is the realization that the choice between alternative macro-policies is determined not by theoretical considerations but by the effects of those policies upon the careers of politicians and by the welfare of major economic interests, are of major importance.[34] Public choice has also been in the forefront in maintaining that there are no purely scientific criteria that can determine the proper level of government expenditures; at best, we might obtain some second-order efficiencies.

Rent Seeking and Redistribution

More recent treatments of income redistribution appear to offer improvements over the demand models previously cited. While not eschewing the insights of demand-based redistributive efforts by government, these newer theories include more participants, more complex institutions, and varied incentives in their models. The redistributive battle is now considered a major activity of the political process, and not simply a sideshow to the main act of public-good provision. Redistribution is not a direct, class-based conflict of one-way flows of wealth and income. Instead, as Stigler, Tullock, and many empirical investigators have observed, redistribution assumes many forms, directions, and patterns of incidence.

One of the first insights of supply-side public choice suggests that governments have no all-embracing scheme of redistribution in which each instrument of policy is finely tuned to the desired incidence. Much of redistribution is an unintended collective result of other intended individual activities and outcomes. Some redistribution stems from macro-policies, that is, expenditure and revenue decisions that are designed to counter the business cycle and not the redistributive desires of citizens. Still other policies are enacted to control markets but reduce market risks and thereby influence distributive outcomes. In fact, the recent literature on *rent seeking* appears to spring from such considerations. Rent seeking is now a deliberate strategy of nearly everyone. As an inclusive game for improving market shares, large investments in political activity now make considerable sense.

In a world such as ours, political participation becomes mandatory in the same sense that participation in a commons dilemma is obligatory. Individuals and interest groups attempt to improve their lot not simply by adjusting to each economic contingency; instead, they attempt to alter the rules to their own advantage. Demand models seem not to have made room for this strategy. In any event, the effort to seek rents depends on the relationship between costs and gains.

What appears to have happened over the past century is nothing less than a dramatic shift in the cost-benefit schedules of political action. The returns from political action have increased for many at a far greater rate than the mounting costs. Almost any economic policy can be challenged in the political arena and with a reasonable expectation of success.

Citizens attempt to obtain income and wealth at the expense of others, an observation made by both demand and supply analysts. This complex process has produced a number of interesting and even perverse consequences. While definitive estimates of redistribution are elusive, it is clear that 1) income and wealth are redistributed both vertically and horizontally; 2) almost every citizen is both beneficiary and donor; 3) significant transfers take place among members of the same income bracket; 4) lower-income groups have made significant gains during the past forty years; 5) total transfers, which are increasing, have not altered the basic distribution by very much; and, finally, 6) inequality prevails.

Supply-side analysts are apt to emphasize that rent seeking is very costly since the opportunity costs are enormous. They are also apt to stress the additional fact that rent seeking probably serves to make the better-off still better off and some of the poor poorer in a relative sense. And, worse, rent seeking is an essentially unproductive activity. If our economic fate depends less on productive market work than on wheeling and dealing in government halls, everyone will suffer.

Of course, everyone does not. The analytical problem is to determine which groups will gain the most and least, since all do not share equally. Unhappily, many of the answers are contradictory. Demand models tended to emphasize the downward flow of benefits from the rich to the poor. The more sophisticated models, whether demand or supply oriented, point to some limitations on the power and incentives of the poor to exploit the rich. These same models suggest that the middle class may be exploiting both rich and poor. Certainly, one can point to countless policies at all levels of government that were designed to aid middle income groups or to policies that were originated for the purpose of aiding the less well-off, but soon included the middle class as beneficiaries. The latter possibility may well be the political payment necessary to enact any redistribution to the low income strata. Such possibilities alert one to the fact that the substantial amounts allocated to the poor cannot be the products of the political power of the poor alone. Coalition efforts with other classes, altruistic impulses among higher income groups, and an historically increasing national income all have some role in explaining the success of the poor.

Different income and occupational groups tend to obtain their gains in quite different forms. Neither demand nor supply models have adequately considered this important policy choice. As noted elsewhere in this chapter, the rich tend to gain much of their rents through tax reductions, whereas the poor obtain their gains via welfare programs involving both cash income and benefits in kind. The middle class seems to derive its improvements from a combination of tax reduction and subsidies. Occupational groups seem to prefer or obtain market privileges such as tariffs, quotas, licenses, zoning laws, building codes, tax moratoriums, and preferential contracts.

But each form is also accompanied by the *quid pro quo* demanded by the politicians who enacted the laws and the bureaucrats who administer them. The regulated have found a means of increasing their incomes, but at a cost; the cost of regulation includes red tape, delay, petty decisions, and unreasonable requirements. The poor face humiliation, means tests, and often overbearing bureaucrats. Only the wealthy seem not to confront such personal relationships with government. Their checks come in the mail and their taxes are managed by lawyers and accountants.

Supply models have enriched our understanding of political redistribution beyond the somewhat confusing view of demand models which presumed that redistribution occurs from the rich to the poor and that producer groups are more powerful than consumer groups. Supply models correct the former error and integrate the Downsian view of producer power within a more complex rent-seeking model. Empirical evidence appears to support this newer view of redistribution.

Entrepreneurs, Policy Innovation, and Supplies

Collective goods do not emerge from the logic of rational, self-interested private action; if they are to be produced by collective action, political entrepreneurs must be willing to campaign on the behalf of the good. We owe this fundamental insight to Frohlich, Oppenheimer, and Young.[35] The earlier insight concerning the nature of public goods and free-riding was, of course, that of Olson.[36] The important point for us is the recognition not only of the activist role of the politician but the unique character of policy innovation in the public realm. Political and market entrepreneurs may have some attributes in common, but none is significant. Their situations, roles, and incentives differ in profound ways.

Market entrepreneurs innovate by inventing new products and services, offering better conditions or contracts, devising new sales techniques, et cetera. All this is accompanied by some personal risk or uncertainty. No such risk is imposed on the politician. The politician can promise new policies and fail in their delivery yet remain in office. Still, the political entrepreneur must win an election before the policy can be considered and enacted, whereas market competitors need not convince majorities to permit them to produce and retail an innovation. Paradoxically, once a policy is enacted it usually becomes exceedingly difficult to dislodge; a coalition of beneficiaries, resource suppliers, and bureaucrats will see to that end. The market knows no such powerful array behind the status quo. In short, innovation in politics is difficult because, as Friedman has written, "It is hard to start small, and once started, almost impossible to fail. That is why governmental intervention is at once so rigid and so unstable."[37] Perhaps Friedman's contention can be refined and extended: diffused losses and concentrated gains account for the initial success in securing the adoption of inefficient policies, whereas the diffused gains and concentrated losses that will result from reform account for the frequent failure of efforts to repeal policies.

But innovation does occur. What sort of innovation? And why? How can innovation take place in a political system with properties of the sort just outlined?

The kind of innovation that politicians offer is conditioned by their desire to remain in office or to achieve a still higher office. Such innovations are not apt, as W. Allen Wallis has observed, to be truly innovative; instead, the politician offers not a new product or service, but free access to one with which they are already familiar and whose price they cannot or wish not to pay.[38] In short, the politician is an innovator in redistributive schemes. Public provision of education in the nineteenth century is a fine example; publicly provided medical services is a singularly depressing example of a current effort at redistributive innovation. The first task of the politician is to discover a service in widespread demand which is increasingly burdensome for private persons to finance. Once such a large potential voting group has been located, the politician must devise a scheme that will transfer costs from the intended beneficiaries to third parties. And, ideally the regime's scheme must be such that the beneficiary knows he is a substantial beneficiary while the taxed are left unaware of their increased burden. Private market entrepreneurs are denied these opportunities; they must convince those who will benefit to pay and those who will pay that the benefits are worth the price.

This peculiar form of political innovation has serious consequences, many of them perverse. For example, the genuinely poor are less apt to benefit under such regimes, a distributive outcome that is not usually intended nor predicted by those who would aid the poor. The reason is simple: the genuinely poor lack most of the critical political resources that might compel the attention of politicians. The poor are neither numerous enough nor inclined to pursue political action, including the simple act of voting. Accordingly, the politician interested in redistributive innovations will turn to the better-off who wish to become still better off. The vast middle class is one such group according to Stigler and Tullock; the wealthy are another.[39] Sooner or later these groups manage to be included among the eligible for monies and services usually meant for the less well-off. A not unusual example: the removal of family income as a disqualification for low-cost student loans. Families earning over $40,000 per year and having offspring at Harvard and Stanford eventually came to qualify for these loans. Another program, unique to Oregon, began as a home and farm loan service (at half market interest rates) for veterans who had actually served during wars and were in need of assistance. The program then began making substantial sums available to nearly everyone who served whether during wars or peacetime and regardless of income. Public choice could have predicted both outcomes. This leads us into a more explicit consideration of the strategic elements of political entrepreneurship.

Although supply-side models have emphasized questions of the overall size and composition of budgets, there is a related literature stressing the strategic aspects of spending. I refer not to Downs' spending rule or Riker's minimal-size principle but to a variety of ad hoc generalizations concerning governmental spending as well as taxing proclivities.[40] Some have been rigorously generated as theorems, but many remain as informed but somewhat casual observations made in the context of general fiscal discussions. A few have been tested as ad hoc hypotheses.[41] Regardless, most, if not all, are probably consistent with one or another basic model of public choice.[42]

In spending money, governments want to purchase support, notably votes and campaign monies. The benefits that accrue from these expenditures will best ensure support if 1) the benefits are highly visible to the intended beneficiaries; 2) they are sufficiently large to make a difference to the beneficiaries; 3) they are received in the immediate present or short-run future and just before elections; 4) their flow is more or less continuous; and 5) they are given especially to those beneficiaries in a position to switch their votes. The loyalties of confirmed ideological opponents and supporters are less apt to be swayed by governmental spending.

Spending on highly visible goods for the visibly well-off must be at least partially concealed in order to avoid charges of favoritism. Accordingly, such spending must be accomplished in intricate if not devious ways so as not to anger others. This can be accomplished by the substitution of tax privileges, use of market controls (restricted entry), guaranteed loans, complex programs that conceal incidence, and culturally approved justifications including defense needs, stockpiling of strategic resources, and market failure.

If the spending is on the less well-off, legislators are well advised to confer goods and services rather than income; such an arrangement will satisfy many taxpayers and business suppliers. A large bureaucratic delivery system will be politically advantageous because it increases the number of persons beholdened to the program. Programs must also be encumbered by vast and complicated controls so as to satisfy taxpayers and create work for lawyers and bureaucrats. Again, justifications should reflect invariant but unfulfilled needs of the recipients.

Legislators, bureaucrats, and advocates of additional spending, whether for public goods or transfers, are also advised to adopt certain tactical measures that will increase the probability of enactment of the proposal/s.[43] For example, bureaucrats are advised to request less than the preferred amount/s in order to appear responsible and economy-minded. Additional funds can be subsequently gained through supplemental appropriations which have the further virtues of being quick, quiet, and unpublicized. Another popular tactic is to claim that the program is designed to meet a temporary condition. While bureaucrats prefer highly specified and not readily altered distributive formulas, they may have to concede more discretionary control to the legislators as a quid pro quo.

Recent constitutional spending-limitation proposals as well as tax limitation and budget balancing requirements would, if adopted, create a new and challenging set of circumstances for governments. While public-choice supply-siders are hardly in agreement, they do argue that each proposal has its separate virtues — virtues dependent upon the definition of or sources of fiscal irresponsibilty. In any event, these same theorists have yet to adequately explore the probable responses of government to enactments of their proposals. Increased skepticism about the possibilities of constraining self-interested and powerful political agents is a distinct likelihood.[44]

Interestingly, theorists who oppose these particular basic fiscal constraints are among those who have alerted us to governmental counterattacks. For example, Bennett and DiLorenzo and Penner have argued that the balanced budget requirement would simply induce governments to increase use of public corporations.[45] Promises of future spending programs, for example, could be offered in place of current income. Fiscally strapped governments might monetize the debt in order to lower interest payments. Conscription for military service might be substituted for a voluntary military in order to reduce the outlay for wages. Finally, since most balanced budget proposals contain an emergency clause, emergencies could become a way of life or simply pro forma responses on the part of government.

Others have maintained that a spending limitation will not succeed because governments can resort to all sorts of "off-budget" programs and "backdoor spending."[46] Guaranteed loans are an egregious example. Increased use of regulation will be employed to force the private sector to do that which in the public sector is prohibited.[47] Spending limitations on state governments have been easily circumvented by some legislatures. The state of Tennessee devised a formula to govern growth, but the formula itself was written by the legislature and is interpreted by the legislature. Spending has not been limited in any significant sense. Friedman, while a supporter of Jarvis-Gann, has noted that that particular tax limitation (property taxes) does nothing about halting the use of inflation as a tax by government.[48] And, worse, such tax limitation laws do nothing to correct the constitutional defect which prohibits the public from ever voting on the *total* budget of government. Our system is one which determines totals by treating each expenditure separately. Friedman also contends that balanced budget requirements at the state and local levels have not and cannot limit the growth of both expenditures and taxation. Similarly, he claims that tax limitations are but stopgaps and that they do not prevent all further growth. Many of the worst forms of government intervention do not involve much spending: often cited examples include tariffs, price controls, and regulation of industry. The regulators spend little, but in meeting regulations the regulated incur considerable costs.[49]

Although public choice has had something to say about the likely responses of government to these fiscal restraints it has had less to offer on the political feasibility of the proposals, that is, the probabilities that any of them might become law. One might have thought otherwise, since public choice is defined by some as the study of constitutions, decision-rules, and outcomes. Balanced budget requirements are typical at the state and local levels. Tax limitations are less so in one sense but not in another; the equal treatment provision of the Constitution provides a basis for all sorts of legal requirements that define tax law. Nevertheless, spending limitations are not apt to be popular among politicians and bureaucrats.

The scanty evidence which exists suggests that the property tax revolts of recent years have not slowed spending at the local level. In 1981, the *Wall Street Journal* cited a Census Bureau study showing property tax receipts falling by nearly $2 billion in the nation's 75 largest metropolitan areas while spending was increasing for schools, libraries, police and fire protection, and even parks. Supporters of tax limitations may find this disturbing, but it is all highly predictable: governments simply substitute other sources of revenue for the lost property tax. Increases in state and federal aid, boosts in other local taxes, and user fees more than made up for the drop in property tax income. In fact, overall direct local spending and taxes each rose by more than ten percent in 1979. And, in spite of all the misleading claims by the Reagan administration, federal expenditures and tax revenues continued to increase under that so-called conservative government.

Working Bureaucrats and Nonworking Bureaucracy

The role of voters in demand models has been explored and found to be exceedingly limited; they have voices but few choices. In turn, we examined the active role of politicians in supply models and showed how the nature of the political process makes it possible for the elected official to be much more influential than voters, even in the aggregate. We have now to consider the calculus and actions of the bureaucrats who actually provide services wanted and unwanted by citizens, authorized by the politicians, and financed by taxpayers. Theories of bureaucratic behavior and outcomes have proliferated during the decade since Niskanen's *Bureaucracy and Representative Government*. Niskanen's original model has been amended in important ways, but none so critical as to negate its basic approach.[50] We set forth the model without aid of mathematics or even elementary graphics and take but brief note of some of the suggested changes.

Like many brilliant innovations, Niskanen's theory is actually based on quite simple assumptions and reasoning. He argues that the bureaucrat and bureau are, like politicians and voters, self-interested and rational in their work. This orientation leads them to request and usually obtain budgets from their legislative sponsors that are excessive, that is, exceed the social optimum as defined by the equality of marginal costs and marginal benefits that would be achieved in a competitive market. Bureaucrats are able to overspend because, in part, their superior informational capacities enable them to identify a budget size that will equate total costs and total benefits and thus meet the electoral needs of the politician who wants to cover costs of whatever is provided. But the quantity preferred by bureaucrats is excessive because the additional costs, that is, costs beyond the social optimum, eliminate, in effect, the *consumer surplus* afforded at the optimum level of production.

The model provides a useful basis for understanding how bureaucrats can specify the positions and slopes of the relevant cost- and benefit-curves and "get away with it." Costs that are difficult to identify can be easily underestimated while vague and distantly received benefits, especially from public goods, can be significantly overestimated. Thompson[51] has questioned the assumption that legislators can be readily fooled by bureaucrats, while Breton and Wintrobe[52] have maintained that politicians can buy the relevant information. Accordingly, these critics argue that bureaucratic budgets are less outsized than envisaged in the Niskanen model; indeed, they may approximate the politically optimal levels. Others, including McKenzie and Tullock have set forth models that have bureaucrats more concerned with maximizing "waste" (their own salaries, perks, et cetera), than budget size and services.[53] The main outlines of the models are identical, but the levels of production are different in each, depending on the maximand/s set forth. McKenzie and Tullock think that most bureau budgets (quantity of service) are smaller than those predicted by Niskanen, yet larger than the quantity of services offered by a private firm operating under competition or even by a private monopoly. Ironically, then, the public monopoly, while self-interested and more powerful than a private monopoly, desires to offer the consumers more than would a private monopolist and, of course, at zero prices. Overproduction is, necessarily, a wasteful activity; too much of a good thing is generated! The resources could be better employed elsewhere.

Politicians and bureaucrats have different tasks and objectives in the Niskanen model. In this instance, the politicians rather than bureaucrats are thought to better represent the preferences of the voters. The reason: politicians must face voters who are taxpayers as well as beneficiaries, while bureaucrats face voters only indirectly and, in any case, as pure beneficiaries. Politicians are apt, therefore, to prefer lower levels of spending than are bureaucrats, but both sets of preferences are nonoptimal in the Paretian sense.[54]

The importance of bureaucracy in a democracy is difficult to exaggerate. Whether one is a poet or an economist, the fact of extensive bureaucracy cannot be denied, for it is felt in the impersonality of its treatment of citizens, the arbitrariness of its decisions, the boredom of its internal life, and the wastefulness of its allocations. Recent public choice has made this latter consequence a permanent element of modern political economy.

Obtaining Revenue: Strategies of Obfuscation

Demand models have contributed remarkably little to our understanding of taxation and, more generally, revenue choices of the state. Why this should be so is unknown; however, one might speculate that because citizen-consumers are, understandably, more concerned with voicing their producer interests than complaining about tax burdens, it has been necessary theoretically to reflect this imbalance in citizen attention. In any event, more recent public choice reflects a growing real-world concern with tax burdens, regulation, and inflation. Since citizens rarely picket to increase their taxes, one must assume that the only persons and organizations persistently interested in obtaining more revenue are governments and some liberal economists. Since governments are viewed as self-interested and rational, we should not be surprised that they develop strategies and tactics to maximize and/or assure their revenues. This assumption has only recently been made an explicit formal maximand in public choice primarily in the work of David Friedman and of Brennan and Buchanan.[55] The latter's *The Power to Tax* is a most important study focusing theoretical attention on the revenue activities of the state.

As Buchanan has shown, imaginative work of Amilcare Puviani, the turn-of-the-century Italian economist, is also especially relevant and useful.[56] In applying a Machiavellian approach to the fiscal activities of the state, Puviani assumed that the state wished to maximize its revenues while taxpayers preferred to minimize their sacrifices. The question, then, becomes one of their respective tactics. Puviani coined the term *fiscal illusion* to signify the means employed by the state to increase revenues without unduly annoying taxpayers. He did not examine taxpayer responses to state tax demands. In a sense, the state becomes a *price searcher*, that is, has the power to decide tax prices but is ignorant of the *optimal* tax burden. Optimal here means best from the perspective of the state. Puviani maintained that since increasing taxation reduces support, rational governments will attempt to conceal, obfuscate, disguise, or mislead the taxpayers into believing their burdens are less than they really are and/or that a different incidence prevails.

Although revenue maximization is a potentially useful axiom, its rigorous application and testing remains in infancy. Still, we can predict, with some confidence, that governments are more likely to pursue certain tax policies than others. For example, governments will tax those goods and services for which demand is more inelastic. When changes in price have little effect on consumption and production, a revenue-maximizing government may take easy advantage of the situation. Accordingly, we may expect to find not only substantial but increasing taxes on such goods as gasoline, salt, tobacco, and liquor. The political choice of whom to tax, the consumer or the producer, remains unexplored. Even when the economic effects are expected to be identical, political consequences may vary, for perceptions as well as incidence of the tax are germane. Perhaps, too, the actual manner of payment and the visibility of tax information are also important. In Oregon, liquor taxes are incorporated into the price, while in California, sales taxes are listed separately. On the other hand, gasoline taxes, while posted on the pumps, are not usually emphasized. We should also recognize, as do legislators and tax authorities, that taxpayers have varying capacities to avoid payment.

Wagner asserts that tolerance of the total tax bill is greater if a variety of levies and low rates are used.[57] This is due to the greater tax consciousness generated by high rates and the fact that with high rates the imperfections and the externalities that result from the tax law or administration become more significant to those who are taxed. We should not be surprised that politicians have shown considerable imagination in devising a bewildering array of tax instruments.

Many analysts argue that politicians satisfy liberal demands for a steeply progressive income tax by enacting nominally high rates on higher incomes but soften the impact and opposition of higher income taxpayers by enacting countless less visible exemptions, deductions, loopholes, and special treatment for various types of income. More generally, governments attempt to spread taxes as widely as possible and impose increases as gradually as circumstances permit. Increased burdens, thereby, become less perceptible, more quickly forgotten, or viewed as too small to warrant an organized attack or even resistance by individual taxpayers. For similar reasons, governments prefer to label social-security taxes as *contributions* or *premiums* designated by a misleading acronym — FICA (Federal Insurance Compensation Act). Still other taxes are earmarked for particularly popular programs.

In federal systems, higher levels of government manage to derive credit by enacting or mandating commendable goals and activities but leave tax choices and actual revenue gathering to the lower levels of government. Similarly, many local governments enact taxes that fall almost exclusively upon outsiders who happen to be nonvoters. Hotel and motel room taxes are favorite sources of local and state revenue.

When taxes "must" be increased, a favorite means is to attach reforms that supposedly correct outstanding and well-known inequities.[58] At the same time, legislators protect themselves by increasing the legal complexities of the tax laws. Lawyers and accountants may complain in public but profit, needless to say, from that complexity.

Although all of these tax tactics described by Puviani are important to taxpayer and legislator, alike, of far greater significance is the increasing use of inflation as a tax, the continuance of deficit financing, and an apparent inability to slow the growth of public expenditures and balance budgets. Contemporary governments prefer granting tax reductions to balancing the budget, because to do the latter means having to either increase taxes or decrease expenditures. Furthermore, reductions in tax rates can be compensated by increases in the tax base. It should be noted that increases in both base and rates can be and have been enacted repeatedly, as with social security. The power of 36 million recipients apparently exceeds that of 140 million taxpayers. The power differential reflects the fact that the former receive an average of $4,776 per year while social-security taxpayers made an average annual payment of $914.[59]

Inflation has a powerful attraction for legislators because increased revenues are automatically provided without the onus of having directly to increase taxes through public legislation. One estimate has the federal government gaining $1.65 billion in windfall revenues for every increase of one percent in the inflation rate.[60]

Some conservative politicians suggest, a la Puviani, that inflation-induced revenue problems can be overcome, as promised by the analysis underlying the so-called Laffer curve. The Laffer analysis may be expected to have considerable political appeal among both liberals and conservatives, for it maintains that tax rates can be reduced without a decline, and perhaps with an increase, in governmental revenues because of the positive impact of tax reduction on overall productivity. What is surprising is not the simple political appeal of the Laffer analysis but the fact that more politicians have not endorsed the idea and its policy implications.

Aside from the elaboration of Puviani tactics in the area of governmental spending, public-choice students have initiated more profound inquiries into the politics of taxation. David Friedman has set forth a model of revenue-maximizing governments and tested his results. The model is constrained by competition among nations and costless migration. With migration permitted, high taxes in a country are balanced by the attractiveness of the resulting low population density. Friedman shows that the countries with smaller populations have higher taxes. Friedman argues that the size and shape of nations will be such as "to maximize their joint potential net revenue and will approach from below the size which would maximize their potential gross revenue."[61]

A less quantitative, but much more ambitious and detailed theory of the revenue-maximizing Leviathan is set forth by Brennan and Buchanan.[62] The authors pioneer in their efforts to shift attention away from conventional normative theory in an attempt to develop more positive models. The effort, however, is hardly without normative interest, for the authors seek *authentic* tax reform and the book is suffused with *ought* questions. But their positive models hold interest because of their treatment of the state as a monolithic organization, a Leviathan. Recognizing this methodological departure from Buchanan's own earlier work, they contend that such an approach does yield significant empirical and normative results. The results are interesting but remain unchallenged because of the recency of publication. Aside from many particular insights on governmental organization and tax instruments, an important contention is that Downsian competition is insufficient to ensure that revenue-maximizing proclivities of the state are kept within bounds. The main limitation of the book stems from the assumption of monolithic state organization, since different agents of government do have different maximands and these are hardly consistent. As a result, different budgetary policies will be sought. Bureaucrats, for example, may value continuity or assurance of revenues at least as much as maximized revenues, while politicians must respond to demands for reduced taxation and different tax incidence. We must, after all, account for the fact that even now American governments rarely take more than a third of the national income as taxes.

Doing Good with Taxes: Social Loopholes

Our treatment of taxation suggests that the decision to tax is a most painful one for politicians. Yet they do devise new taxes and increase existing ones. Illustrations of how politicians are able to accomplish these otherwise painful acts and remain in office have been provided. Less apparent is the discovery by politicians that they can *do good* through taxation, or, more accurately, can do good by creating exemptions from taxation. The common designation is found in the clumsy and misleading expression *tax expenditures*.

Revenues lost through tax expenditures or loopholes have been estimated in excess of $150 billion per annum.[63] With high tax rates both taxpayers and politicians have found powerful inducements to avoid or reduce tax payments. Since tax payments are coerced and often unrelated to approved public uses, taxpayers may feel justified in escaping or reducing their "civic contributions." In any case, politicians have found a superior means to subsidize better-off citizens — that of tax loopholes. Just as benefits and beneficiaries have proliferated so have tax expenditures been liberalized. All sorts of *social good* can now be accomplished by creating *social loopholes* that reduce the taxes of those in a position to be heavily taxed. A taxpayer can reduce his income tax by preserving historical buildings, contributing to political campaigns, employing welfare recipients, insulating a home, purchasing a woodburning (polluting?) stove. The political logic of tax loopholes is not dissimilar to the political logic of subsidies: Congress defines income, defines ability to pay, views tax expenditures as superior to direct expenditures, and justifies loopholes by precedent. Astute as are Eismeier's observations and insights on taxes, they were preceded in another congressional context and era by the observations and insights of E. E. Schattschneider on tariff legislation and subsidies.[64] The logic of taxation loopholes and subsidies are identical because their net income effects can be identical. However, they are not identical in political appeal. Public choice might well address the question of their comparative electoral attractiveness.

A rather different, although not necessarily contradictory view of tax expenditures, is taken by Roberts and Wagner.[65] These authors look not at the taxpayer demand for tax loopholes, but the interests of the government in offering reforms that will close-up loopholes and do so under the guise of equity. Unlike Brennan and Buchanan, Roberts and Wagner argue that governments may be more interested in the maximization of their power than in revenue, a point alluded to earlier.[66] The argument, while imaginative, is fairly simple. Reducing revenues may actually increase citizen dependence on government and enhance the government's power. This is accomplished, according to Roberts and Wagner, by eliminating fringe benefits that go untaxed, itemized deductions, and the distinction between capital and income in current tax law. With some ingenious reasoning, the authors claim that successful reforms could create a greater role for government in the economy and increase demand for further government participation in such activities as health, mass transit, and public employment. The Roberts/Wagner and Eismeier theories become identical if one accepts the Roberts/Wagner contention that 70 percent of tax expenditures actually go to people with incomes of $50,000 or less. As Eismeier notes, tax expenditures are highly popular when they are provided to the middle and low income groups. Roberts and Wagner claim that the tax reformers have no intention of closing up these particular tax loopholes, only those benefiting the wealthy. Tax reformers, they say, will not advertise untaxed social-security benefits as a multibillion dollar loophole, nor publicize other income excluded from taxation such as military disability pensions, scholarships and fellowships, railroad retirement pay, disabled coal miners' benefits, veterans' disability compensation, sick pay, GI Bill benefits, and unemployment benefits. Liberal political scientists, suspicious of revenue-maximizing models in public choice, might have cause to reconsider models based on power maximization and their relationships with and implications for the venerable power-theories of Machiavelli, Lasswell, Catlin, Merriam, and other theorists.

Slow Growth, Retrenchment, and Taxpayer Resistance

Bureaucrats and politicians, not to mention public-choice theorists, are currently experiencing an apparently novel situation, that of fiscal retrenchment and persistent and widespread demands for economy from the electorate. How officialdom has and may be expected to respond appears to pose a new challenge for scholarship, so new that most public-choice theorists have yet to address, let alone adequately explain, the phenomenon. Demand models hardly prepare one to explain the changes, since they seem at such variance with normal theoretical expectations. Economic growth has slowed, inflation continues, noted liberal legislators have been defeated, taxpayer revolts have occurred, and state constitutional fiscal-limitation amendments have been proposed and sometimes adopted. Similar proposals have been initiated at the national level. These somewhat unexpected developments require explanation and that means rejection or revision of extant theories, whether demand or supply oriented. Interestingly, theorists of the latter persuasion may well have more explaining to do, since supply-siders — excepting perhaps Buchanan — have been highly pessimistic about achieving greater fiscal responsibility. We will begin with attempts at explaining taxpayer revolts, then consider governmental responses, and end with some suggestions pertaining to future work.

Among the earliest attempts to explain tax revolts was that of Buchanan and Flowers.[67] They examined sources of taxpayer *disequilibrium* and found them to include shifts in the subjective terms of trade or tastes, the divorce of expenditure and revenue choices, and the influences of inflation on taxpayer attitudes. All were considered relevant, but none was held to have explained the growing interest in tax reform that accompanies tax reduction. Since taxpayers are unable to adjust consumption to changing price ratios, as in markets, revolts are the only means of adjustment. But surely, this is incorrect; many taxpayers begin by cheating!

In 1979, Buchanan addressed himself to a different question — the question of the apparent success of California's Proposition 13 in being adopted (1978), whereas a previous ratio limitation (1972) had been rejected by voters. Now he was interested in explaining whether Proposition 13 could be interpreted without reference to changes in taxpayer attitudes and whether the answer to that question had any significance for other tax and spending limitation proposals. In brief, Buchanan argued that, while Jarvis-Gann could be explained without reference to changing taxpayer tastes, more general tax limitations would not be readily adopted in the future. The explanation of the former event rested on an unexpected application of the free-rider argument, that is, when confronted with an unusual choice between identifiable and measurable tax reductions and cuts in vague or generalized public spending, voters will obviously choose the former option. Future proposals that do not take advantage of the biased choice presented in Proposition 13 are not apt to enjoy the same success. If success is to be attained, a genuine change in taxpayer attitudes will have to occur. Given our fiscal institutions, the range for responsible action is extremely limited. A spending bias is inherent in those rules. We see the seeds, here, of the subsequent Brennan-Buchanan volume which seeks not changes in the rules of decision but in limiting the range of outcomes. Richard Musgrave took exception to the reform principles of Buchanan, but his diagnosis of the same revolt does not seem all that different.[68] Still, the animating spirits of the two lectures are distinct and at odds. Buchanan's distrust of political processes contrasts sharply with Musgrave's more sanguine partial reforms of specific sources of fiscal difficulties. Buchanan's abiding pessimism may be buttressed by the notable work of Ralph Miner and Miner and Chalice.[69] In these empirical studies of property tax measures, the authors were led to conclude that reform of taxes is exceedingly difficult and that widely shared interests suffer at the hands of minority exploitation, a not uncommon conclusion in either public choice or political science.

Fending Off Revolts and Maintaining Power: Uses of Crises and Off-Budget Devices

Rational governments may wish to honor citizen preferences, but when those preferences suddenly include demands for reduced spending and/or taxation, government is placed in a dilemma. Provision of public goods and services and their attendant spending programs are the raison d'etre of elective governments; limitation on those activities cannot be warmly greeted. A rational government or agency must either devise ways in which to ward off threats to its fiscal powers or, if unsuccessful, develop budgetary practices that minimize their revenue and/or power losses.

Governments do not sit idly by when the Jarvises are at large. State and local governments have responded quickly to the challenge by many means, including especially threats or predictions of dire social consequences stemming from reduced spending and revenues. Both politicians and bureaucrats are heard to lament reductions in the most widely used and popular programs. Educational cutbacks, police retrenchment, reduced highway and street repair, reductions in medical and social-security payments, and curtailments in park maintenance are among the threatened reactions. Of course, budgetary reductions in these and any other program are bound to arouse not only the direct beneficiaries and users, but those who supply necessary resources and the many administrators and other employees whose jobs are at stake.

A hue and cry will be heard from the liberal academic and intellectual worlds concerning *social needs* and *social imbalances*, et cetera. Direct and indirect government advertising will be increased to create a demand for government products where none had previously existed. Each plea will make some sense, because each program, in intent and fact, does some good for someone. Otherwise, how can the fear of being *cut out* be explained?

In spite of these scare tactics, tax reformers have succeeded in sensitizing taxpayers and politicians to tax issues and, on many occasions, have actually presented the issue to voters for their resolution. When voters are provided an opportunity to consider tax reform, governments respond in a number of ways. For example, issues may be confused by providing options that serve not so much to inform and expand options as to divide and conquer public opinion. When the voters of Oregon were confronted with a Jarvis-type proposal in 1979, the legislature offered its own reform, one that, in effect, created nine options for the voters but required a majority vote for enactment. Needless to say, support was widely dissipated and the original proposal as well as the legislative proposals were defeated.The actual wording of fiscal propositions provides further opportunities for obfuscation and confusion. The city of San Francisco, in an attempt to diffuse a recent attack on certain outrageously high public salaries ($21,000 for street sweepers), used double-negatives so that voters had to vote yes in order to express disapproval of the measure.

The discussion thus far has been premised on the notion that governments prefer to spend more and tax less — assumptions that fit both demand and supply models. Yet, governments are elected that profess a distaste for large public spending. Campaign promises are made to reverse prevailing trends. What do such governments do once elected?

Casual observation of conservative parties in power suggest that 1) they typically find it almost impossible to reverse increasing budgets; 2) at best they have occasionally slowed growth; and 3) they convey the impression of an active government successfully fighting governmental growth.

Presidents, governors, mayors, and others almost always impose a hiring freeze and enforce a cutback in the number of agencies through consolidation. They also hire more consultants and part-time employees who are not officially counted as full-time workers. Such measures do little to hold down governmental spending because the size of the bureaucracy is not the key to budget growth. While such orders and enactments sound good to loyal followers and uninformed citizens, they pose little threat to the existing bureaucracy; no one will be fired. Those who die, resign, or otherwise leave the public service will not be replaced, at least for the time being. More trivial examples include President Carter's ban on limousines for a few top officials and President Reagan's ban on office redecoration. Reagan's sixty-day freeze (1981) on *pending* regulations merely put off a decision on a promised but as yet unrealized massive deregulation. Proposed abolition of various unpublicized small agencies such as the Tea Tasting Board (by Nixon and Carter) and the Council on Wage and Price Stability (by Reagan) save few funds and are merely symbolic actions soon forgotten by voters. Such agency cutbacks offend no one for none had an important constituency.

Far more important than these rather patent tricks are the efforts of governments to maintain and increase their power even when revenue flows may be reduced. Off-budget fiscal activities including loan guarantees worth nearly $200 billion in fiscal 1980 testify to the ingenuity of politicians and bureaucrats who crave the best of two worlds: extra benefits for constituents without the extra pain of higher taxes. As budget pressures mount, the attractions of political credit allocation, that is, government loan guarantees and other future commitments and liabilities, can only rise. Such policies have enormous political appeal because they hide ultimate costs. The wasteful activities of Amtrak and student loan programs are but two convenient illustrations. Worse, the obvious waste may be the least of the total costs. Because loan guarantees are really subsidies, and subsidies are designed to encourage something, that something may be overproduced. America's housing inflation is surely a by-product of FHA, just as the cheapening of American higher education has been fostered by student loans and other financial guarantees to education. Because the market test of risk and productivity is reduced or even eliminated, the political allocation of capital is inherently inefficient. Vast sums of scarce capital can be channeled into projects that are unwanted and would fail in the market. When capital is wasted on unproductive uses, there is less capital for productive ones. Unfortunately, politicians can advance their careers by deciding who gets how much credit, tempting some to believe that they are superior to the market.

The laws authorizing many social programs specify that their beneficiaries have *entitlements* to payments in perpetuity according to various formulas. The social-security program is a classic case. Railroad retirement, federal pensions, unemployment benefits, child nutrition measures, food stamps, Medicare and Medicaid, and state and local government transfers, are others. Several of these allocations and entitlements are now tied to changes in the consumer-price index or to changes in census data. Because of these budget requirements, budgets are said to be largely *uncontrollable*; whether they are seems almost irrelevant because Congressmen act as though they are and, thereby, protect recipients as well as themselves as *donors*.

Unfortunately, public choice has not had much to say about the possibilities of reforming entitlements. We do not know the political possibilities of rewriting the formulas, placing limitations on available funds, or eliminating program/s. What little we know suggests that the latter option is impossible, the second nearly impossible, and whatever chances for reform do exist pertain to marginal alterations of formulas. Once more we have reason to believe that passionate minority coalitions of beneficiaries will overcome indifferent majorities of taxpayers.

Governmental power can also be enhanced under reduced budgets by increased use of regulatory instruments and justified by the police powers of the Constitution. In other words, the police power and and the budget are interchangeable or substitute means for the control of private resources.[70] Limits on spending, for example, do little to alter the incentives of government to expand. As Wagner points out, majority coalitions will only intensify their redistributive efforts under current institutional arrangements. Government may be expected to mandate more private activities because the costs of regulation, while high for businesses, are quite low for government.

Underlying these many fiscal gimmicks for fending off tax and spending revolts is the discovery that it may not be stability politicians and bureaucrats seek but instability and crises. Economic and social stability does not increase the demand for governmental services.[71] Roberts argues that governments seek an optimal amount of instability. If officials generate too much instability, other political entrepreneurs may succeed in displacing them, but, if they fail to produce the optimal amount, they deny themselves jobs, budgets, status, power, and excitement. Unemployment and inflation are crises to be manipulated rather than terminated. Ironically, we find Roberts, the ex-writer for the *Wall Street Journal*, in agreement with Michal Kalecki, the deceased Polish Marxist economist.[72] Their disagreements — not to be minimized — center on the specific incentives pursued by government. In any case, those who would deny that government has a stake in instability must explain how so many good and well-intentioned policymakers have generated results inconsistent with their goals. Are they misinformed or interested in power?

Unfinished Tasks: A Research Agenda

Although this review-essay is lengthy, it has hardly begun an inventory of a burgeoning literature on the fiscal tendencies of modern states. I have not included a substantial technical literature which deals with concepts of public-sector equilibrium, nor have I considered various theories and empirical studies that purport to examine relationships between specific public institutions and fiscal behavior. The former was not included because much of that work is really more concerned with establishing technical conditions of optimality than describing actual public choice. The second area of inquiry has not been discussed because of its own very considerable scope. Adequate treatment of the policy effects of institutions would require a paper at least as long as this one.

While further research on the impact of political institutions will not generate the aesthetic rewards of pure model-building, it may be far more useful during the coming decades. The choice of fiscal and monetary policies as well as the constitution-building advocated by Buchanan should be more usefully influenced by theory and research that is grounded in actual fiscal institutions or settings.[73] The essentially normative work on fiscal federalism, electoral systems, tax principles, cost-benefit analyses, and related themes all need to be reconsidered in the light of public-choice *principles* and findings. Not only must we gain a better grasp of the economic effects of political institutions, a task begun long ago by conventional public-finance, but we are in urgent need of theories that enable us to better predict and understand which institutions and policies will be chosen in which political process. While we have come a long way, we have a long way to go.

Notes

1. Duncan Black, *The Theory of Committees and Elections* (Cambridge: Cambridge University Press, 1958); Anthony Downs, *An Economic Theory of Democracy* (New York: Harper, 1957).
2. Eric Lindahl, "Just Taxation — A Positive Solution," in Richard A. Musgrave and Alan T. Peacock, eds., *Classics in the Theory of Public Finance* (London: Macmillan, 1958),

pp. 168–76, first published in German, Lund, 1919; H. Hotelling, "Stability in Competition," *Economic Journal*, 39 (March 1929):47–51; H. R. Bowen, "The Interpretation of Voting in the Allocation of Economic Resources," *Quarterly Journal of Economics* 58 (February 1943): 27–48; Black, *Committees and Elections*.

3. Carolyn L. Weaver, *The Crisis in Social Security* (Durham: Duke University Press, 1982).

4. Downs, *An Economic Theory of Democracy*.

5. Richard E. Wagner, *The Public Economy* (Chicago: Markham, 1973).

6. Lindahl, "Just Taxation"; Hotelling, "Stability in Competition"; Bowen, "Voting in the Allocation of Economic Resources"; Paul A. Samuelson, "The Pure Theory of Public Expenditure," *Review of Economic Statistics*, 36 (November 1954): 386–89; Charles M. Tiebort, "A Pure Theory of Local Expenditures," *Journal of Political Economy*, 64 (October 1956):416–24.

7. Thomas Romer and Howard Rosenthal, "The Elusive Median Voter" unpublished paper, Carnegie-Mellon University, 1978.

8. Anthony Downs, "Why the Government Budget Is Too Small in a Democracy," *World Politics*, 12 (July 1960):541–63.

9. James M. Buchanan and Gordon Tullock, *The Calculus of Consent* (Ann Arbor: University of Michigan Press, 1962); Gordon Tullock, "Some Problems of Majority Voting," *Journal of Political Economy*, 67 (December 1959):571–79.

10. Edgar K. Browning, "Social Insurance and Intergenerational Transfers," *Journal of Law and Economics*, 16 (October, 1973): 215–37; Edgar K. Browning, "Why the Social Insurance Budget is Too Large in a Democracy," *Economic Inquiry*, 13 (September 1975):373–88.

11. Tullock, "Some Problems in Majority Voting," pp. 571–79.

12. Downs, *An Economic Theory of Democracy*, p. 297.

13. Knut Wicksell, "A New Principle of Just Taxation," in Richard A. Musgrave and Alan T. Peacock eds., *Classics in the Theory of Public Finance* (London: Macmillan, 1958), pp. 72–118; Lindahl, "Just Taxation"; Bowen, "Voting in the Allocation of Economic Resources"; Samuelson, "Public Expenditure"; Richard A. Musgrave, "The Voluntary Exchange Theory of Public Economy," *Quarterly Journal of Economics*, 53 (February 1938):213–37.

14. Downs, *An Economic Theory of Democracy*.

15. Gordon Tullock, "The Charity of the Uncharitable," *Western Economic Journal*, 9 (December 1971):379–92; George J. Stigler, "Director's Law of Public Income Redistribution," *Journal of Law and Economics*, 13 (April 1970):1–10.

16. George J. Stigler, "The Theory of Economic Regulation," *Bell Journal of Economics and Management Science*, 3 (Spring 1971):3–21.

17. Gordon Tullock, *The Politics of Bureaucracy* (Washington, D. C.: Public Affairs Press, 1965); William A. Niskanen, Jr., *Bureaucracy and Representative Government* (Chicago: Aldine-Atherton, 1971).

18. Gordon Tullock, *Toward a Mathematics of Politics* (Ann Arbor: University of Michigan Press, 1965).

19. James M. Buchanan, "Social Choice, Democracy, and Free Markets," *Journal of Political Economy*, 62 (April 1954):114–23.

20. ———— *Public Finance in Democratic Process* (Chapel Hill: University of North Carolina Press, 1967).

21. ———— *The Demand and Supply of Public Goods* (Chicago: Rand McNally, 1968).

22. Randall Bartlett, *Economic Foundations of Political Power* (New York: The Free Press, 1973).

23. Albert Breton, *The Economic Theory of Representative Government* (Chicago: Aldine, 1974).

24. Stigler, "The Theory of Economic Regulation"; Robert D. Tollison and Robert E. McCormick, *Politicians, Legislation, and the Economy* (Boston: Martinus Nijhoff, 1981); Donald Wittman, "Parties as Utility Maximizers," *American Political Science Review*, 67 (June 1973):490–98; Gerald Sirkin, "The Anatomy of Public Choice Failure," in R. D. Leiter and G. Sirkin, eds., *Economics of Public Choice* (New York: Cyrco Press, 1975); Sam Peltzman, "Toward a More General Theory of Regulation," *Journal of Law and Economics*, 19 (August 1976):211–40; Peter H. Aranson and Peter C. Ordeshook, "A Prolegomenon to a Theory of the Failure of Representative Democracy," in R. Auster and B. Sears, eds., *American Revolution: Papers and Proceedings* (Tucson: University of Arizona, 1977); Susan Rose-Ackerman, *Corruption: A Study in Political Economy* (New York: Academic Press, 1978); R. D. Auster and Morris Silver, *The State as a Firm* (Boston: Martinus Nijhoff, 1979); Dennis C. Mueller, *Public Choice* (Cambridge: Cambridge University Press, 1979); Richard E. Wagner, "Boom and Bust: The Political Economy of Economic Disorder," *Journal of Libertarian Studies*, 4 (Winter 1980):1–37; Robert J. Mackay and Carolyn L. Weaver, "Monopoly Bureaus and Fiscal Outcomes: Deductive Models and Implications for Reform," in Gordon Tullock and Richard E. Wagner, eds., *Policy Analysis and Deductive Reasoning* (Lexington, Mass.: Lexington Books, 1978), pp. 141–66; Robert J. Mackay and Carolyn L. Weaver, "Agenda Control by Budget Maximizers in a Multi-Bureau Setting," *Public Choice*, 37 (1981):447–72.

25. Mackay and Weaver, "Agenda Control by Budget Maximizers."

26. Charles R. Plott, "Axiomatic Social Choice Theory," *American Journal of Political Science*, 20 (August 1976):511–96.

27. Wagner, "Boom and Bust" p. 2.

28. Tullock, *The Politics of Bureaucracy;* Niskanen, *Bureaucracy and Representative Government*; Niskanen, "Bureaucrats and Politicians," *Journal of Law and Economics*, 18 (December 1975):617–43.

29. Sam Peltzman, "Pricing in Public and Private Enterprises: Electric Utilities in the U.S.," *Journal of Law and Economics*, 14 (April 1971):109–47; Peltzman, "Toward a More General Theory of Economic Regulation"; Richard A. Posner, "Theories of Economic Regulation," *Bell Journal of Economics and Management Science*, 5 (Autumn 1974):335–58; Jack Hirschleifer, "Comment" on Sam Peltzman, "Toward a More General Theory of Regulation," *Journal of Law and Economics*, 19 (August 1976):241–44; Cotton M. Lindsay, "A Theory of Government Enterprise," *Journal of Political Economy*, 84 (1976):1061–77; Bruce M. Owen and Ronald Braeutigam, *The Regulation Game* (Cambridge: Ballinger, 1978).

30. Melvin W. Reder, "The Theory of Employment and Wages in the Public Sector," in Daniel Hamermesh, ed., *Labor in the Public and Non-Profit Sectors* (Princeton: Princeton University Press, 1975); ch. 3, George J. Borjas, *Wage Policy in the Federal Bureaucracy* (Washington, D. C.: American Enterprise Institute, 1980).

31. Milton and Rose Friedman, *Free to Choose* (New York: Harcourt, Brace, Jovanovich, 1980), p. 31.

32. Hugh Dalton, *Principles of Public Finance* (1922; reprint ed., New York: Augustus M. Kelly, Publishers, 1967).

33. Richard A. and Peggy B. Musgrave, *Public Finance in Theory and Practice*, 3rd ed. (New York: McGraw-Hill, 1980).

34. Richard E. Wagner, "Economic Manipulation for Political Profit: Macro-Economic Consequences and Constitutional Implication," *Kyklos*, 30 (1977):395–40.

35. Norman Frohlich, Joe A. Oppenheimer, and Oran R. Young, *Political Leadership and Collective Goods* (Princeton: Princeton University Press, 1971).
36. Mancur Olson, Jr., *The Logic of Collective Action* (Cambridge: Harvard University Press, 1965).
37. Milton Friedman, "Introduction" to Mary Bennett Peters, *The Regulated Customer* (Ottawa, Ill.: Green Hill Publishers, 1971), p. IV.
38. W. Allen Wallis, *The Overgoverned Society* (New York; Macmillan, 1976).
39. Stigler, "Director's Law of Public Income Redistribution"; Tullock, "The Charity of the Uncharitable."
40. D. G. Hartle, *A Theory of the Expenditure Budgetary Process* (Toronto: University of Toronto Press, 1976).
41. Edward R. Tufte, *Political Control of the Economy* (Princeton: Princeton University Press, 1978).
42. William D. Nordhaus, "The Political Business Cycle," *Review of Economic Studies*, 42 (April 1975):169–90; Bruno S. Frey, *Modern Political Economy* (New York: John Wiley & Sons, 1978).
43. Aaron Wildvasky, *How to Limit Government Spending* (Berkeley: University of California Press, 1979).
44. Rudolph G. Penner, "The Nonsense Amendment," *New York Times*, 28 March 1982, p. 1.
45. Penner, "The Nonsense Amendment"; James T. Bennett and Thomas J. DiLorenzo, "Underground Government: Subverting Constraints on Public Sector Expansion," *Journal of Social, Political and Economic Studies*, 6 (Fall, 1981):219–33.
46. James T. Bennett and Thomas J. DiLorenzo, "How the Government Evades Taxes," *Policy Review*, 19 (Winter 1982):71–89.
47. Wagner, "Boom and Bust."
48. Milton Friedman, "The Limitations of Tax Limitation," *Policy Review*, 5(Summer 1978):7–14.
49. Murray L. Weidenbaum, *Business, Government, and the Public* (Englewood Cliffs, N.J.: Prentice-Hall, 1977).
50. Niskanen, "Bureaucrats and Politicians."
51. Earl A. Thompson, review of *Bureaucracy and Representative Government* by William A. Niskanen, *Journal of Economic Literature*, 11 (September-December 1973):950–53.
52. Albert Breton and R. Wintrobe, "The Equilibrium Size of a Budget Maximizing Bureau," *Journal of Political Economy*, 83 (February 1975):195–207.
53. Richard D. McKenzie and Gordon Tullock, *Modern Political Economy* (New York: McGraw-Hill, 1978).
54. Hans van den Doel, *Democracy and Welfare Economics* (Cambridge: Cambridge University Press, 1979).
55. David Friedman, "A Theory of the Size and Shape of Nations," *Journal of Political Economy*, 85 (1977):59–77. Geoffrey Brennan and James M. Buchanan, *The Power to Tax* (Cambridge: Cambridge University Press, 1980).
56. Buchanan, *Public Finance in Democratic Process*.
57. Wagner, *The Public Economy*.
58. Ralph E. Miner, "Some Observations of the Political Economy of Property Tax Reform," *Public Choice*, 17 (Spring 1974):49–62.
59. Musgrave and Musgrave, *Public Finance*.
60. Paul Craig Roberts, "Idealism in Public Choice Theory," *Journal of Monetary Economics*, 4 (1978):603–15.

61. Friedman, "Size and Shape of Nations."
62. Brennan and Buchanan, *The Power to Tax*.
63. Theodore J. Eismeier, "No End to Loopholes," *Journal of Contemporary Studies* (Winter 1981):39–50.
64. E. E. Schattschneider, *Politics, Pressures and the Tariff* (New York: Prentice-Hall, 1935).
65. Paul Craig Roberts and Richard E. Wagner, "The Tax Reform Fraud," *Policy Review*, 9 (Summer 1979):121–42.
66. Brennan and Buchanan, *The Power to Tax*.
67. James M. Buchanan and Marilyn Flowers, "An Analytical Setting for a Taxpayers' Revolution," *Western Economic Journal*, 7 (December 1969): 349–59.
68. Richard Musgrave, "Tax Revolt," *Social Science Quarterly*, 59 (March 1979):697–703.
69. Miner, "Political Economy of Property Tax Reform"; Miner and Chalice, "Representation, Redistribution and Group Size" (Paper delivered at the 1975 Annual Meeting of the Public Choice Society, Chicago, April 3, 1975).
70. Richard E. Wagner, "Limiting Government Budgets: The Misplaced Emphasis," *Policy Report*, 1 (Octover 1979):1–7; Brennan and Buchanan, *The Power to Tax*.
71. Roberts and Wagner, "The Tax Reform Fraud."
72. M. Kalecki, "Political Aspects of Full Employment," *The Political Quarterly*, 4 (October/December 1943):322–31.
73. James Gwartney and Jonathan Silberman, "Distribution of Costs and Benefits and the Significance of Collective Decision Rules," *Social Science Quarterly*, 26 (December 1973):568–78.

Comment by Margaret Levi

Who is unaware of the fact that the behavioral assumption of public choice is flawed, that the model tends to oversimplify reality, that many of the questions public choice can authoritatively answer are trivial, and that many, too many, of the most intelligent proponents of public choice suffer from a libertarian, conservative, or an out-and-out right-wing bias? Dennis Mueller in his account of the literature attempts to differentiate between positive and normative public choice,[1] a distinction often blurred in practise. Yet, despite its weaknesses, public choice, that is, the application of neoclassical economics to nonmarket behavior, has significantly advanced the capacity of social scientists to explain certain kinds of political action within modern democratic polities. Anthony Downs, Mancur Olson, Gordon Tullock, James Buchanan, and William C. Mitchell himself are among those who have helped create and popularize the need for more rigorous models than political scientists are traditionally apt to favor. Although, as Mitchell admits, we are still some distance from a satisfying empirical theory, it is at least partially his purpose in his excellent survey, and certainly mine in my commentary, to lay the basis for such a theory. Thus, I shall not address the normative questions Mitchell raises: suboptimal provision of public goods; the optimal size and composition of budgets; appropriate constitutional arrangements for a democratic fiscal policy; or even the maldistribution of taxes and their benefits. Rather, I intend to emphasize the necessary components of a theory capable of explaining variations in fiscal policies among polities and over time.

Mitchell differentiates, describes, and critiques demand and supply models of fiscal policy. It is the former that receives the severest trouncing, one it richly deserves. Since Mitchell designates Anthony Downs " . . . the pre-eminent theorist of the late 1950s and early 1960s," his *An Economic Theory of Democracy* will be used as the focal point of this discussion.[2] It is, after all, a major contribution to the tradition of public choice and to democratic theory in general.

What Mitchell makes abundantly clear in his critique is the relationship between pluralist theory and the Downsian approach. Downs is a sophisticated pluralist. He posits competitive parties seeking votes rather than a totally passive and unitary state. He raises the dilemma of rational ignorance as well as arguing that citizens are more likely to organize in their role as producers than as consumers, and he recognizes the conditions for and existence of coalitions. Thus, he makes room in his model for unequal influence among citizens. Nonetheless, he seems to assume an open political system in which citizens can be *heard*.[3] The actors who compose the state seem, in this view, to have but one goal, to be reelected, and they have but one viable means, to respond to the citizens who will vote for them or, perhaps, will help them financially.[4] Once in power, they will try to maximize revenues, but vote-seeking remains the major constraint on their behavior.

The problems with the demand model are the same problems that beset pluralism. In themselves, the pluralist dimensions of his argument are not damning. If Downs and his followers had succeeded in producing a causal theory of fiscal policy processes, all would be well. Unfortunately, they have not and cannot. The reason, for which Mitchell rightly and roundly takes Downs at least to task, is his identification of politics and markets. Downs proceeds as if taxing and spending choices are made simultaneously, which they are not. He treats the state as if it were a firm receiving immediate feedback through sales (or lack of sales), which it does not. Most important, he assumes that the basis of state power is voluntary exchange, which it is not. Downs has fundamentally misunderstood both politics and the state. Although Downs seems to understand that power is distributed unequally throughout the society, the basis for inequality still seems to lie more in the lack of interest on the part of citizens than in institutional obstacles or unequal political and economic resources.[5] Of course, he was not able to take into account the collective-action problem as made famous by Mancur Olson several years after the publication of Downs's seminal book.[6] Even so, he indicates no sense of the complex political process that must be incorporated, if simplified, into any adequate model. Finally, for Downs the state itself remains a black box to which parties and bureaucrats turn and from which policies emanate. It has no autonomous existence. Downs has treated the state as an institution without interests of its own and without the ability to push those interests, and he ignores the fact that state power is rooted in its coercive capacity. Consequently, we are left with a model that can account for very little of the reality of fiscal policymaking.

The advance of supply models is precisely the rediscovery of the state as an important actor in the political process. The emphasis on self-interested individuals who compose the state, on government as a monopoly, on revenue-maximization as an axiom, on the nature of the actual constraints on policymakers, and on the relationship between bureaucrats and policymakers permits more rigorous and successful theorizing than hitherto. Mitchell obviously prefers this approach, and for good reason. However, by not sufficiently pointing out the important shortcomings of this model as it has so far been developed, he fails to facilitate the development of a positive theory to the extent he might otherwise.

In contrast to the pluralist predilections of demand theorists, supply theorists emphasize the exploitative tendencies of the state. This is a crucial corrective. Nonetheless, Mitchell and those he cites make too much of this exploitation. Although they discuss collective action, the constraints of elections, logrolling, bargaining, and institutional restraints, they offer no real model of constraints. Surprisingly, these writers fail to understand the relevance of transaction costs, an increasingly important concept in political economy ever since the publication of Oliver Williamson's influential book.[7] Transaction costs are " . . . not only the costs of forming and enforcing contracts (including seeking information from market transactions), but also the costs of delineating and policing exclusive rights (including those of institutional arrangements such as legislative enactments.)"[8] The most important in the consideration of fiscal policy are the costs of measuring and monitoring compliance to policies. Transaction costs ultimately refer to the costs involved in the authoritative allocation of valued resources, one of the classic definitions of the role of the state. The notion of transaction costs offers a means to theorize about constraints by helping to clarify the conditions under which the state is in fact powerful and those under which it is not. It also illuminates the nonexploitative role of the state in defining property rights and arbitrating conflicts over them.[9]

What all this suggests is that a theory of fiscal behavior of the modern democratic state must in fact be a theory of the state, capable of explaining variations in state policies. Public-choice scholars have done this to some extent, but they have been limited by the limitations of neoclassical economics.

Economic historian Douglass C. North is one scholar who offers the seeds of such a theory. He treats the ruler as a discriminating monopolist engaged in rent seeking, a perspective Mitchell advocates (although Mitchell seems to believe it illuminates only the behavior of the modern state whereas for North it is the sine qua non of all societies). For North the state is composed of principals and agents who compete with each other and with subjects for the division of society's resources.[10] He begins with the Hobbesian premise that without the state to enforce contract and property rights there can be no economic exchange or growth. However, the state exacts a price for the benefits it provides. In particular, rulers attempt to maximize revenues (as does everyone else in this model), but their marginal cost calculations include transaction costs, that is, the costs of measuring and monitoring revenue extraction. This includes the proviso that the ruler take into account the power of their subjects to resist or strike bargains with alternative rulers in premodern societies and with alternative political parties in democratic polities.

I have also attempted to construct a model of state policymaking.[11] Following North, all states are institutions that control sufficient force to tax, police, and defend the population of a given territory. The ruler is the actor (or set of actors) whose position as head of state enables him or her to make its policies, of which the most important are those affecting its property rights. Starting with a hypothesis that all rulers are predatory, that is, they will try to maximize their personal wealth and/or power, I propose a model that focusses on the constraints on the ruler. Significant differences in state policies will primarily reflect differences in the bargaining power of agents and constituents vis-à-vis the ruler and in the transaction costs of the ruler, particularly his measuring and monitoring costs.

In this model, state policies are the outcome of an exchange, a complex transaction between the ruler, his agents, and his constituents. I assume that the ruler is rational in that he will attempt to achieve his ends in the most efficient manner possible. I argue that he is also self-interested and will make policies on the basis of a calculation in which his own ends are paramount. An analytical distinction exists between the ruler's private interest and the public good (or, indeed, the good of anyone else). Sometimes the two will overlap; it is just as likely they will not. Randomness of ends characterizes public-choice models in general; in the case of rulers this implies a diversity of potential objectives. Even so, every ruler will maximize wealth and/or power, for whatever the ruler's ends, wealth and power are necessary to attain them.

In applying this model to fiscal policy, the focus must be on the ruler's choice of a revenue production system, particularly how revenue collection is organized and what revenues are collected from whom. Moreover, in order to understand fiscal policy in modern democracies, it is necessary to have a model that can equally well explain fiscal policy chosen in other kinds of regimes and in other historical periods. In particular, the mode of production, that is, the property rights, organization of production, and organization of exchange, is a crucial variable in this regard.[12] The structure of property rights affects the distribution of economic and political resources, which are major determinants or relative bargaining power. The organization of production has further effects on resources as well as on the capacity of the producing population to organize. Finally, the extent to which a society uses exchange affects monitoring, measurement, and enforcement of revenue-production schemes. Weber[13] and Ardant[14] both emphasize that role of the market and particularly a market economy in determining forms of state agency.

A deductive and testable theory of the state requires a more sophisticated view of constraints than public choice or neoclassical economics have so far mustered. For this it is necessary to combine the behavioral assumptions of rational choice with the macrohistorical and macrosociological contributions of Marxists and Weberians.[15] Only through such an unconventional marriage will an adequate model of fiscal policy emerge.

Notes

1. Dennis Mueller, *Public Choice* (New York: Cambridge University Press, 1979).
2. Anthony Downs, *An Economic Theory of Democracy* (New York: Harper and Row, 1957).
3. This is an important element in the famous statement on the components of democracy as provided by Robert Dahl, *Who Governs?* (New Haven: Yale University Press, 1961).
4. The person who makes this important addition quite clearly is Timothy Bates, *Economic Man as Politician* (Morristown, N.J.: General Learning Press, 1976).

5. Mitchell points out that the important work in this area is from Gordon Tullock, "The Charity of the Uncharitable," *Western Economic Journal* 9 (December 1971): 379–92; and George Stigler, "Director's Law of Public Income Redistribution," *Journal of Law and Economics* 13 (April 1970): 1–10.

6. Mancur Olson, *The Logic of Collective Action* (Cambridge: Harvard University Press, 1965).

7. Oliver Williamson's *Markets and Hierarchies* (New York: Free Press, 1975).

8. Steven Cheung, *The Myth of Social Costs* (London: The Institute of Economic Affairs, 1978), p. 53.

9. For an elaboration of this theme, see Margaret Levi and Douglass C. North, "Towards a Property-Rights Theory of Exploitation," *Politics & Society* 11, no. 3 (1982): 315–20.

10. The most important recent statement is in his *Structure and Change in Economic History* (New York: W. W. Norton, 1981). Also, see Douglass C. North and Robert Thomas, *The Rise of the Western World* (New York: Cambridge University Press, 1973).

11. "The Predatory Theory of Rule," *Politics & Society* 10, no. 4 (1981): 431–65.

12. For an elaboration and empirical use of this definition, see William Brustein, "A Regional Mode of Production Analysis of Political Behavior," *Politics & Society* 10, no. 4 (1981): 355–98.

13. Max Weber, *Economy and Society*, ed. Guenther Roth and Carl Wittich (New York: Bedminster Press, 1968).

14. Gabriel Ardant, *Histoire de L'impot*, 2 vols. (Paris: Fayard, 1971).

15. See Levi, "The Predatory Theory of Rule," pp. 431–35.

4 A MARXIST THEORY OF THE STATE

Stephen Resnick and
Richard Wolff

Introduction

There is not one Marxian approach to social analysis; there are several. The last two decades attest to an intensifying debate about diverse Marxist theories. One of the more important points of debate concerns the relationship between the state as an institution and the rest of the social system in which it exists. This is an important point for Marxists for several reasons. States seem to have become relatively more powerful institutions within generally capitalist societies during this century. In those societies, it has often been argued that proper state policies can successfully prevent basic social change, particularly change toward socialism or communism. They can do this by helping to foster a profitable capitalist environment or by the actual repression of threats to that environment. In so-called Third World countries, the state looms large as an institution providing dominant leadership in terms of overall social development. Finally, Marxists generally recognize that in the socialist countries the state typically exercises great influence on the direction and pace of social development. For these and other reasons,

Marxist theorists have been provoked to make a variety of efforts to explain what states are, why they persist, what they do, and how they are changing.

One Marxist theory with many adherents explains the state as the creature of economic forces in society.[1] In this view, the state functions as an *executive committee* for managing the common interests of those who own and/or control the economic forces of production in any society. Such owners/controllers of the economy, the *ruling class(es)*, are shown to utilize their dominant economic power to bend state policies to meet their needs, above all their need to retain their ownership and control of the economy. Like any executive committee, the state has two basic functions: to arbitrate disputes among the ruling classes whose interests it represents and to secure those interests against challenges from the ruled classes or ruling classes of other societies.

As with most theories, Marxist and non-Marxist alike, this particular theory exists in both crude and quite sophisticated versions. Across all versions, however, a common method or logic of analysis is at work. The logic is deterministic. The state is approached as socially determined by the economy: it is caused, maintained, and governed by the particular structure of the economy. The state is understood as a class state in the sense that the economic class structure determines the predominant goals and limits of state power and action. From the standpoint of such a Marxist theory, for example, any state's claim to be democratic is tested and judged by asking whether economic ownership and control are democratically distributed across the population. If not, the claim is rejected.

Historians, political scientists, and other researchers who approach social analysis by means of this kind of Marxist theory have produced a complex body of knowledge about the state as it exists within both capitalist and noncapitalist societies. Needless to say, that knowledge is different from the knowledge produced by researchers working with different theories. For example, a theory which holds that the state and politics are independent of economic forces would produce a very different specific analysis of state policies and actions. Similarly, a theory that reverses the Marxist determinism previously discussed (that is, makes the state determine the economy) would produce its own particular knowledge of what its practitioners choose to study.

The particular theoretical approach we propose to use is pointedly non- or even anti-determinist. It is that kind of Marxist theory which rejects any proposition that one aspect of society is any more determinant of other aspects than they are of it.[2] Thus, we do not think that the state may be explained as the creature of the economy, nor the economy as the creature of the state. Both determinisms are unacceptable. Moreover, we do not think of the different aspects of society, such as state and economy, as independent of one another. The kind of Marxist theory we use underscores its particular approach to social analysis by means of the term *overdetermination,* a term increasingly current in the debates among alternative Marxist theories in recent years.[3] Our particular analysis of the state and its place in society grows out of and depends on this *overdeterminist* Marxist theory.

General Approach

As we understand it, Marxist theory approaches society as a set of distinct processes structured in a particular relationship to one another. To simplify matters, we group these processes into four sorts. Natural processes are those involved in the physical, chemical and biological changes which ceaselessly characterize human life and its environment. Economic processes are those involved in the production and distribution of goods and services designed for consumption or for further production. Political processes are those involved in the ever-changing lines and patterns of authority exercised among people living in groups. Finally, cultural processes are those involved in the endlessly innovative ways that people devise to produce meanings: writing, reading, painting, and praying are examples.

Marxist theory begins with the insight that any one of the infinite variety of processes in society is influenced by all of the others. For example, any one economic process in a society is shaped both by other economic processes and by the many other natural, political, and cultural processes affecting that society. However, the words *influenced, shaped,* and *affected* do not go far enough to convey exactly what Marxist theory means by the idea that each social process is determined by all the other social processes. Thus the word *overdetermination* is necessary to reach the precision we seek. Each process in society — natural, cultural, political, or economic — is overdetermined by all the others. Literally, each process in society is understood as a site produced by the combined interaction of the influences exerted by all the other processes. Thus, no social process can be understood as the determining cause or determined effect of another; each social process is rather overdetermined by all the others.

Cultural processes, such as thinking, are complexly overdetermined by natural processes (for example, nerve cell chemical changes, atmospheric shifts) interacting with economic processes (for example, price increases, deepening unemployment) and with political processes (for example, legislative enactments, police activities). Political processes, such as voting, are complexly overdetermined by all the other political as well as the cultural, natural, and economic processes in the social environment. There is no basis for the argument that any one process, say, price increases, is *more* important or determinant in influencing, say, voting patterns than any other process. Any such argument would require a prior condition: the economic process would have to be conceived of as existing independently of all other processes so that we could identify its particular effect upon voting. We could then measure the *amount* of influence exerted by, say, physiological versus economic processes on voting patterns. This procedure, however, is ruled out because the effectivity of the economic process only exists as the combined result of the determinations of all other processes. Therefore, there is no way to disentangle the effectivities of the economic from, for example, the physiological on voting processes. Since all such processes are conceived to exist as sites, their mutual dependence or effectivity rules out the possibility that any one process is *more* or *less* determinant in its effectivity than any other. Instead, Marxist theory proceeds to make sense of the different ways other social processes participate in overdetermining the particular process being analyzed, such as voting in the example already given.

The Marxist concept of overdetermination carries some particular implications for a Marxist analysis of the position of the state in society. To argue that each particular social process is overdetermined by all the others means that the existence and all the qualities of that process are overdetermined. As noted, each process is nothing other than the site of the interaction of the determinations exerted by all the other processes. But these determinations are very different depending on the different processes from which they come. For example, the determinations of someone's voting that come from his or her participation in the job market will likely be different from the determinations coming from his or her religious activities; and these will be again different from the determinations coming from his or her sexual propensities. Marxist theory presumes that these economic, cultural, and physical processes will exercise different determinations on the political process of voting; it presumes further that these different determinations will push and pull the process of voting in conflicting directions.

The overdetermination of each social process means that it is composed of conflicting pressures: it is in this precise sense contradictory. The consequence of being overdetermined is that each social process is itself contradictory, the site of the conflicting effects of all the other social processes. From the standpoint of the Marxist theory at work in this discussion, every social process — natural, political, cultural, and economic — is understood as overdetermined and contradictory. In the example of the political process of voting, its overdetermination carries the implication that it is a contradictory process (whose conflicting pushes and pulls will be only partly felt and understood by the voter).

Overdetermination and contradiction imply change. The pushes and pulls embedded in the existence of each distinct social process produce its unique pattern of change. As it changes, a social process also changes the determinations it exerts on all other social processes which further changes them. And this in turn changes the overdeterminations of all processes on one another. The general result is a ceaseless change characterizing each social process and the social totality. Indeed, one reason we refer to the different aspects of society — the natural, cultural, economic, and political — as so many *processes* is to underscore the ceaseless change which overdetermination and contradiction produce in each aspect. This idea, that everything is always changing, is basic to Marxist theory; it can be rendered more precise by means of the concepts of overdetermination and contradiction.

Another implication of the concept of overdetermination is the problem it presents to anyone seeking to use it to explain a social process such as voting. If voting is overdetermined in different ways by all the different natural, economic, political, and cultural processes in society, where is analysis to start, and how can it ever complete an explanation of a particular process, such as voting? Analysis can start with any particular process or subset of social processes and from there proceed to weave its particular explanation of the overdetermined interaction among all social processes. However, this point of entry into social analysis has its own effects on the explanations thereby produced: where one starts influences the explanations one generates and the conclusions one draws. In a parallel fashion, whether one proceeds from a determinist or overdeterminist approach decisively shapes one's explanation of any aspect of social life. As we understand Marxist theory, not only is its approach overdeterminist, but it also has a distinctive entry point. It starts from one particular economic process which it defines as the class process. From there, Marxist theory proceeds to construct its particular knowledge of societies, past and present, as the ever-changing interaction of the class process and all the other social processes that overdetermine the class process.

The problem of completing any social analysis has, for Marxist theory, no solution. That is, no Marxist analysis can ever claim to be complete nor accept any other theory's claim to be so. First, it would take any analyst more than a lifetime to describe the totality of interactions of social processes. Second, the totality would be changing all the while the analysis was proceeding. Both of these considerations render any analysis incomplete and efforts at final completeness rather pointless. This is in no way distressing. Incomplete social analyses are the only sort people can produce, and producing them is itself a cultural process exercising its particular determinations on all the other processes of social life. These determinations are the reward and goal of social theorizing; they range from the personal feelings of satisfaction on the part of producers and consumers of such theories to the political effects of the various theories.

So far we have characterized Marxist theory as operating with certain basic notions of overdetermination, contradiction, and the ceaselessness of change in the set of processes that comprise the social whole. However, our reference to Marxist theory's distinctive entry point into social analysis as the class process requires some brief elaboration before we launch into our Marxist explanation of the relation between state and society. Marx means something very specific when he talks about class in his major theoretical work, *Capital*. First, he means class as a particular social process defined as the production of surplus labor.[4] His reasoning begins as follows: in all communities of human beings, naturally given materials are transformed to meet certain goals of the community. Human labor, the exertion of brains and muscle, transforms nature into objects thought to fulfill certain human needs. One portion of this labor Marx calls *necessary* in the sense that it is the amount necessary to sustain those direct producers performing this labor. The remaining portion he calls *surplus* to emphasize that it exceeds necessary labor and that it is destined for purposes other than the sustenance of the direct producers.[5]

These other purposes concern the particular social form in which surplus labor is produced. Marx distinguishes several different forms: primitive communism, ancient, slave, feudal, capitalist, and a few others. Each form has its own particular economic, political, and cultural qualities that distinguish it from the other forms. Surplus labor is then the portion of total labor devoted to maintaining that particular social form in which the surplus labor is produced. The class process and the various forms it may take are, following the logic of this theory, overdetermined by the other processes of the society in which the class process occurs. Some of these processes occur naturally as, for example, rainfall; they require no allocation of surplus labor (or its products) to be reproduced over time. Other processes, such as passing of certain kinds of knowledge from generation to generation, occur within interpersonal relationships that likewise require no allocation of surplus labor to be reproduced. However, some of the processes which participate in the overdetermination of the class process can only be sustained by means of allocations of portions of surplus labor.

For example, if a particular form of surplus labor production, say that characterised by Marx as the slave form, requires the maintenance of a legal system to enact and enforce laws sanctioning human chattel property, then a portion of such surplus labor will typically be allocated to support that system. If another form of the class process is determined in part by institutionalized religious practices, a portion of the surplus labor produced in that form will typically be allocated to sustain religious practitioners and to defray the materials costs associated with their practice. If some form of the class process requires a credit extension institution presiding over quanta of loanable funds, a portion of surplus labor will typically need to be allocated to sustain such an institution. In sum, surplus labor produced in one or another form of the class process is that portion distributed to those individuals who perform certain other social processes whose existence is required if that form of the class process is to endure. In the absence of such a distribution, that form of the class process would cease to be overdetermined, and, hence, would cease to exist. The class process would then change its form.

All the myriad social processes that combine to overdetermine any particular form of the class process are so many conditions of existence of that class process. The surplus labor portion of total output is that portion devoted to securing the conditions of existence of the given form of the class process. The distribution of this surplus to those members of society whose activities secure these conditions of existence is itself one condition of the existence of the class process of producing surplus labor.

We may now add a refinement to our definition of class as the entry point of Marxist social theory. Marx works with two closely intertwined and interdependent notions of class. The first we may term, following Marx, the *fundamental class process;* it refers to the process of producing surplus labor in one or another particular social form. The fundamental class process implies two fundamental class positions: those who perform the surplus labor and those who receive it directly from the performers. In Marx's work, the form of the fundamental class process labelled primitive communism involves the positions of performers and receivers being united in the same persons: a single, fundamental class social arrangement. Marx is, however, much more interested in the other social forms of the fundamental class process (feudal, slave, capitalist, et cetera), where the performers are different people from the direct receivers of surplus labor.

Marx's second notion of class refers to the social process of distributing already produced surplus labor to those individuals whose activities secure conditions of existence of the fundamental class process. We call this distribution of surplus labor the subsumed class process. It also implies two subsumed class positions: the distributors and the receivers of surplus labor. People occupying either subsumed class position are sustained by means of the surplus labor produced in the fundamental class process; they perform no surplus labor themselves.[6]

For Marxist theory, both the fundamental and subsumed class processes are overdetermined and indeed participate in overdetermining each other. Hence they are contradictory and changing. Their contradictions sometimes take the form of conflicts over the quantitative dimensions of the fundamental class process (division of the working day between necessary and surplus labor) or the quantitative dimensions of the different shares of surplus labor received by the different subsumed classes. Such contradictions may also take the form of conflict over the form of the fundamental class process itself as, for example, a conflict over capitalist versus communist forms. Such conflicts are what Marxist theory means by the term *class struggles*.

We are now in a position to summarize the general approach of the Marxist theory at work in this discussion. We begin any social analysis by specifying the particular forms of the fundamental and subsumed class processes existing in the society in question. We proceed to construct an understanding of how those class processes are overdetermined by, and participate in the overdetermination of, all the nonclass processes in that society. There is no determinism at work in this construction; class is not the determinant of culture, nor politics the determinant of economics. Overdetermination is the rule in our theoretical elaboration. Explaining any social process amounts, then, to specifying its overdetermined contradictions and hence its unique pattern of change or development. Our research into the available empirical materials is informed by this Marxist theory, while such research in turn has its determining effects on the theory itself. The result is one particular Marxist body of social knowledge that is different from alternative knowledge developed in different ways from different entry points. Our Marxist knowledge is also different from other knowledge in terms of its particular effects on where it exists and contests with other distinctive social theories.

A Concept of the State

Our discussion will consider the state in a society such as the United States today, in which the most widely prevalent form of the fundamental class process is capitalist. The capitalist form involves several distinguishing characteristics: the products of labor take the form of commodities; the ability to do work (labor power) itself becomes a commodity exchanged in a market; and surplus labor is realized by capitalists in the form of surplus value. We propose to construct a Marxist class analysis of the state in capitalist society.

The state is a site in society. It is quite literally a subset of different social processes collected together under a single institutional umbrella. The state is the place where a variety of social processes are performed. The aim for us is to specify what these processes are and how they relate to the other social processes not performed in and by the institutionalized state. We ask in particular how the state's set of social processes interact with the class processes within capitalist society.

We begin by illustrating the various sorts of social processes usually performed by states in capitalist society. States intervene in natural processes, such as seeding clouds to make rain; breeding animals threatened with extinction; altering the chemical compositions of air, water, and soil; converting water power into electricity; and so forth. Of course, the state is not the only institutional site where these natural processes are performed. And indeed, the same can be said for the economic, political, and cultural processes performed in and by the state in capitalist society.

The state performs certain political processes. It establishes rules of social behavior in the community, typically by the design and legislative enactment of laws and public policies. It adjudicates disputes over the interpretation of such laws and policies, typically by means of judicial and administrative procedures. It administers public policies and enforces laws and judicial judgments, typically by means of executive directives, police and military proceedings. These political processes discharged by the state share the common objective of securing particular authority-relations among members of the society and with other societies.

The state engages in a variety of economic processes. It controls, at least in part, the quantity of money in general circulation. It provides incomes via transfer payments to designated members of society. It taxes individuals and enterprises, lends to and borrows money from them, and both employs persons and buys commodities. It may itself produce commodities for the market. It regulates different aspects of enterprise activities.

The state conducts many cultural processes. It usually manages much of the formal education process. It maintains museums and usually a variety of offices charged with producing and disseminating officially endorsed interpretations of political and other social events (in some capitalist societies such offices include state-operated mass media). The state is thus the site and organizational form of a set of cultural processes which produce meanings for the society.

Most of the social processes performed in and by the state are also performed at other sites in the society. The cultural process of education, for example, may also be produced in the household as a matter of interpersonal communications among family members. Education also occurs in the private firm in various forms, as through the sale of educational services as a commodity by private schools. Similarly, the state's political process of policing typically coexists with policing performed at other social sites: in troubled neighborhoods as residents rotate a patrol function among themselves, or in enterprises whose employees include security personnel. Similarly, the economic processes performed by the state include many also performed at other social sites: borrowing money is done by individuals and enterprises, controlling the money supply is done by institutions accepting demand deposits, and producing commodities is hardly an economic process limited to the state. On the other hand, the state is often the exclusive site of some social processes. Maintaining a full-time military force, manufacturing legal tender, allocating airspace for aircraft traffic, and rendering final legal judgments (supreme courts) are examples of social processes usually exclusively performed in and by states.

It is important to keep in mind that social processes have been and are continually shifted from one site to another in society. Currently, several processes produced within the state are under attack. It is argued (often by the Republican Party) that certain nonstate sites in society, for example, the household and private enterprise, are the proper places for the production of goods and services currently provided by the state. A struggle may even occur within the state over this issue: some state officials push for the reduction or elimination of particular social processes provided by the state, while others resist such changes and may call for an expansion of such processes.

Marxist theory approaches the state as a site in society by specifying the particular social processes performed at and thereby defining that site. This is indeed how Marxist theory approaches any other social site chosen for analysis. Household, family, enterprise, school, two-person love relationship, sports team, and individual are examples of other sites in society understood as particular subsets of social processes. Any relationship in society is such a site, whether formally institutionalized or not. We distinguish one site from another precisely in terms of which particular social processes constitute each one. Thus there will be differences between states in different capitalist societies according to which social processes are or are not performed by them. There are other differences between processes in capitalist and those in noncapitalist states, but these two are analyzed by Marxist theory in terms of the specific social processes performed by and thus defining such different states.

The particular subset of social processes that defines the state in a particular capitalist society is overdetermined by all the other processes in the society. This is a premise of Marxist theory. It means that each constituent process of the state is overdetermined not only by the other processes performed by the state but also by all the other processes in the society no matter at what site they may occur. The interactions among sites such as state, individual, family, and enterprise are analyzed by means of the Marxist concept of the overdeterminations of the social processes that constitute each of these sites. It follows that Marxist theory must reject the proposition that any of these sites or indeed any social process is independent of another; overdetermination links them all. At the same time, since each social process is uniquely overdetermined by all others, it can never be reduced to the effect merely of another social process or subset of social processes. By logical extension, each social site is a unique composition of social processes, not reducible to the effect merely of another social site. The state, in Marxist theory, is not reducible to an effect of the economy or any part of the economy. Rather than being determined by the economy or a particular economic class, the state is a specific subset of social processes overdetermined by all the other political, natural, and cultural, as well as economic, processes in the society.

State and Class

In capitalist society, most commodities are produced by capitalist enterprises. The adjective *capitalist* refers to the predominant form in which surplus labor is produced in such enterprises. This form involves the direct producers performing necessary and surplus labor for capitalist employers in exchange for wages. Employment is conditional: only if the direct producers produce more value than capitalists have to spend on their wages will they be employed. *More value* — what Marx calls surplus value — is the particular form taken by surplus labor in the capitalist fundamental class process. In order to exist, this capitalist form of the fundamental class process requires the existence of all the natural, political, economic, and cultural processes which overdetermine it.

Some of the conditions of existence of the capitalist fundamental class process are performed in and by the state. To sustain the state employees who perform these processes and to pay for the materials they need to perform them, a portion of the surplus value produced in capitalist enterprises is distributed to the state. Thus, in addition to being the site of many other social processes, the state is also the site of a subsumed class process. State employees constitute a subsumed class by virtue of their receipt of a share of surplus value, predominantly in the form of taxes. To a limited degree in capitalist societies, the state also includes the fundamental class process: certain state employees directly produce and others directly receive surplus value in connection with state production of commodities. However, the United States is a capitalist society in which the state is prevented from producing commodities, from directly producing surplus value itself, to a far greater degree than in most other countries.[7] Therefore, we will proceed in this discussion without further consideration of state commodity production. We will focus instead upon the state as a site of a subsumed class process.

The state performs processes that are conditions of existence of the capitalist fundamental class process. The state performs natural processes that permit and shape, that is, participate in the overdetermination of, the capitalist fundamental class process. For example, state agencies dig, dredge, and clean harbors, thereby facilitating trade, extending markets, and contributing to the reproduction of the capitalist fundamental class process. State agencies, often linked to military activity, produce new chemical compounds whose formulation is made known to capitalist enterprises, enabling them to realize production economies, market altogether new commodities, and generate greater profits. State agencies operate various public health programs affecting population growth, length of productive life, worker absenteeism: all factors directly related to the profitability and hence viability of capitalist enterprises and the capitalist fundamental class process. The directors and actual performers of all these natural state processes require personal incomes to reproduce such processes; in addition, the state agencies in which they perform require funds to purchase the capitalist commodities, for example, buildings, equipment, and raw materials necessary to perform these processes. They receive incomes and funds as distributed shares of surplus value produced within the capitalist fundamental class process; they are a subsumed class.

The state performs certain economic processes which likewise require subsumed class payments to the state. To prevent rapid price inflation, state employees must monitor private banking practices and monopolistic tendencies throughout the economy. The incomes of such monitors and the costs of the facilities they require are defrayed by means of subsumed class payments to the state. The typical existence of masses of unemployed workers in capitalist societies often results in state policies of retraining, relocating, or simply minimally sustaining them for parts or all of the duration of their unemployment. The processes of retraining, relocating, and minimally sustaining what Marx calls this "reserve army of the unemployed" all require subsumed class payments to the state to cover personnel and income maintenance costs. States typically build means of transportation, communications networks, and public works which condition the profitability and development of capitalist enterprises in innumerable ways: parts of the costs of this infrastructure are defrayed by means of subsumed class payments to the state (other parts are often recovered by charges made for use of the infrastructure by capitalist enterprises and others).

The political processes performed in and by the state have attracted the most analytic attention, which has not infrequently tended to reduce the state to a purely political site in society. By contrast, the Marxist theory at work in this discussion cannot make such a reduction. The capitalist state passes laws in its legislatures and maintains administrative and judicial bureaucracies to enforce them. To take one area of law, we can consider the enactments establishing private property in the means of production. There can clearly be no capitalist enterprise in the absence of the political processes of legislation, administration, and judicial decision which secure the rights of private property in the means of production. Such processes are political conditions of existence of the capitalist fundamental class process and their various costs require subsumed class payments to the state to perform them. Military and police forces perform the process of securing noninterference from potential (or actual) disrupters — foreign or domestic — of the fundamental capitalist class process. The typically enormous costs of the personnel and materials needed to perform these processes are likewise defrayed out of subsumed class payments to the state charged with maintaining military and police forces.[8]

Public education is a major cultural process performed in large part by states in capitalist societies. Such education provides conditions of existence for the capitalist fundamental class process by systematically disseminating certain conceptions of the meaning of life, work, politics, justice, goodness, and so forth. The dissemination of such meanings is a condition of existence of the capitalist fundamental class process in the sense that workers, for example, have to understand the world in certain ways if they are to be satisfied with their condition as workers. Such understanding also affects their productivity on the job. If workers thought that justice required any surplus value they produced to be theirs, their acceptance of the capitalist fundamental class process in which such surplus passes rather to capitalists would be problematic. That in turn would jeopardize the reproduction over time of that fundamental class process. If workers believed that the good life required and deserved, as a matter of basic human right, the distribution of produced goods and services according to individual human need — rather than purchasing power — the existence of the capitalist fundamental class process would be similarly jeopardized. Public education is a state-run cultural process designed to disseminate those particular concepts and meanings whose wide acceptance is a condition of existence of the capitalist fundamental class process. And this costs money, subsumed class payments to the state.

All of these processes may affect capitalist enterprises in contradictory ways. For example, the state's provision of public education involves paying salaries to teachers, building schools, and buying materials. These economic processes affect labor, capital, and consumer goods markets both directly and indirectly. The net effect of the demand by the state for materials and by its employees for consumer goods may be to raise the prices of these commodities, depending on the nearness to full capacity of the commodity-supplying capitalist enterprises. A similar effect may be felt in the labor market, depending upon its closeness to full employment. If prices and money wages do rise as a result, then costs to enterprises will rise and profits will be less than what they would have been otherwise. This same spending by the state and its teachers can also be an important condition of existence of capitalist profits since the value of capitalist commodities is not realized until they are sold. The economic processes involved with providing public education may well facilitate this surplus value realization. In addition, mass public education may enhance the productivity of the mass of workers. This in turn tends to reduce the prices of commodities and thus the costs to capitalist enterprises. Their profits will be higher than they would be otherwise. However, taxes on profits, destined in part to support public education, result in less profits available for capital accumulation, salaries of managers, dividends, acquisition of the stock of other enterprises, et cetera. This may constrain the future profits of the enterprise. Even if the state sells bonds or prints money rather than raises taxes to cover the costs of public education, the possible resulting higher interest rates and/or prices of commodities still may adversely affect enterprises' profits. They do so by increasing costs of debt (finance) and of commodities. This example just begins to outline the different and contradictory ways any state process, such as education, can affect capitalist enterprises. Indeed, we could extend this example of education to all such state processes. In so doing we would show how the profits of all capitalist enterprises are overdetermined by such state processes.

Many of these social processes can be combined, depending upon the political environment, in an attempt to affect capitalist enterprises in particular ways. Specific fiscal and monetary policies may be developed with the hope of either stimulating or constraining the economic activity of such enterprises. To succeed, these policies often require accompanying political and even cultural changes in and by the state. Particularly relevant examples of this were provided by the Roosevelt, Johnson and, more recently, Reagan administrations. The political reforms of these particular administrations were every bit as important as the economic policies pursued.

Any actual state-run activity is not a political or economic or cultural or natural process but rather a specific combination of all or most of these processes. We have separated the distinct processes so far only to explain them clearly. To analyze the state in capitalist society requires, in Marxist theory, understanding state policies and actions as specific combinations of these processes. For example, when a branch of the U. S. military builds a naval base somewhere in, say, Central America, the construction and maintenance of that base involves many different state-run social processes. Natural processes are involved — utilizing engineers and personnel trained in the natural sciences — to make changes in land and water conditions appropriate for such a base. Other natural processes are involved as well, whether intended or not: possible air and water pollution with secondary effects on fish and animal life, crop-growing conditions, and so on. The construction and maintenance of the naval base involves complex political processes as well. Not only is the security of the capitalist fundamental class process in the United States presumably enhanced thereby, but likely also that of the particular government which granted the United States permission for the naval base. Since the Central American government is itself a state subsumed to the fundamental class process(es) in its country, the U. S. naval base provides political conditions of existence for them as well as for the capitalist fundamental class process in the United States. State-run cultural processes come into the picture as naval personnel feel the need to produce a flood of press releases, white papers, and research reports presenting the U. S. government's theory of what is occurring in Central America, why a U. S. naval base is appropriate, what its social consequences will be, et cetera. This theory will be systematically presented to the mass media in the United States and across the world. In different ways, these media will then reproduce this theory, which thereby becomes part of the educational process occurring in this and other societies. Teachers in schools will teach it. And in repressive periods, the state might perform various police and judicial processes to enforce the dissemination and teaching of its theory and the banning of any alternative theory.

The naval base's construction and maintenance include economic processes as well. First, there is the subsumed class process involving the allocation of U. S. tax revenues to the base. Second, there will be purchases of commodities made in the United States, both base equipment and consumer goods for U. S. personnel. Such purchases will likely also involve the process of developing a taste for U. S. goods in the local population thus furthering the export market for U. S. goods. Production technologies used at the base will thereby be introduced into the society around the base; the same will likely apply to banking, communication, and transportation technologies. The local purchases by the base and its personnel will expand local markets, stimulate local production, and change local labor markets, wage rates, tax revenues, and credit conditions.

It would be misleading, therefore, to reduce the complexity of foreign naval-base building and maintenance to only one of the sorts of processes involved. More than political processes are included; there are also natural, economic, and cultural processes inextricably woven together with the political to constitute the state action. Foreign policy by a state involves all of these processes. The economic and noneconomic policy of the state may include the distribution of aid, loans, and military support to foreign countries as well as the passing of laws regulating trade, immigration, and foreign investment. Treaties between states involve all these processes. Foreign policy may also include searching for and maintaining access to cheap raw materials for capitalist enterprises, opening up markets for such enterprises and for their capital, preventing foreign enterprises and their capital from having easy access to such markets, resisting potential and actual threats from communist states or movements, protecting the national honor, et cetera. Foreign action by a state can even be a form of bringing together different domestic classes in the face of foreign threats, be they from other capitalist societies or from noncapitalist ones.

The same complexity applies to any other state actions: setting an annual state budget, passing a law, operating a community college, changing a central bank rediscount rate, launching a space mission, et cetera. The state is a site in society, the locus of a specific subset of the full set of processes which together comprise society. Each activity performed by the state is then a subset of the subset. Combine all its activities and you have what Marxist theory means by the state; combine the state with all the other sites and you have what is meant by the social totality, society as a whole.

It follows that Marxist theory is inconsistent with and opposed to any other theory which reduces the state to merely a political institution or which explains the state as the effect merely of one or another kind of social process. For Marxist theory, the state as a social site is a subset of many different social processes. For Marxist theory, the state is also overdetermined by all other social processes; it is not determined only or mostly by economic processes.

The Marxist theoretical approach to understanding the different processes in the state and the complex overdetermination of the state begins in studying all state employees as a subsumed class. Class concepts are our entry point, but class processes are neither dominant components of the state nor dominant determinants of what states do. For Marxist theory, the focus of interest in the complex and overdetermined state is its relation to fundamental and subsumed class processes. What distinguishes Marxist theory from others is its entry point of class along with its notions of social process, overdetermination, and contradiction.

We use Marxist theory because its focus on class strikes us as precisely what is needed, as well as badly lacking, in alternative social theories. It is needed, in our view, because basic social change is on the human agenda as a solution to the complex problems confronting us. It is needed, further, because other efforts at, and theories of, social change have not gone far enough in grappling with the class aspects of society and hence of social change. Marxists share with others many ideas about, and struggles for, social change, but they are unique in their focus on the class aspects. The logic is simple: without theoretical and practical attention to these class aspects of social change, such change as does occur will take unwanted forms, frustrating the hopes embedded in those changes. Marxist theory focuses on class precisely to increase the likelihood that social changes realize such hopes. Class is not any more important than other aspects of social change; it is rather the theoretically neglected, underestimated, and often utterly lacking aspect. Marxist theory is in large part the effort to begin to remedy this situation.

Contradictions in the State

As a subset of social processes, the state is a site of all sorts of contradictions by virtue of the overdetermination of each of its processes. The state is the site of all manner of pushes and pulls emanating fom the totality of all social processes. We may illustrate the contradictory nature of the capitalist state with some particularly significant examples.

As a subsumed class, state functionaries receive a share of the surplus value produced in the capitalist fundamental class process. But theirs is only one share; other capitalist subsumed classes claim their shares. Bankers receive a share, called interest payments, in consideration for the condition of existence they provide (credit) to capitalists. Landlords receive a share, called capitalist rent, in return for providing the land under the factories and office buildings of capitalists; access to privately owned land is clearly a condition of the latter's existence as capitalists. Another share is allocated to owners of shares of stock in capitalist corporations; called dividends, this share also secures certain conditions of existence of the capitalists. One such condition is the access by capitalists to use of the means of production owned by stockholders in the form of their shares. Another condition is the access of capitalists to equity markets, that is, their ability to raise capital by issuing new shares of stock. To be able to do this when survival requires it, a corporation must maintain the stock-market value of its shares; this is done in large part by maintaining a solid record of dividend payments. Still another claim upon surplus value emanates from corporate managers. They are not themselves productive workers; they do not participate in the capitalist fundamental class process producing commodities. Rather they perform processes that are conditions of existence of commodity production. For example, managers purchase new means of production and labor power (accumulation) and organize and discipline the productive labor force, exerting all sorts of authority in the factory or office by means of rules, punishments, and direct commands. For performing such economic and political processes — accumulating capital and establishing and enforcing worker behavior patterns — managers receive a share of produced surplus value. Such accumulation and behavior are conditions of existence of surplus value production; the managers accomplishing them are a subsumed class.

These are but some of the many subsumed classes making claims upon the surplus value which accrued initially to capitalists. The state's share, chiefly in the form of taxes, will be larger or smaller in relation to the shares captured by other subsumed classes. There is, in short, a competitive struggle among subsumed classes for relative shares of surplus value. That struggle displays some of the contradictions in the state.

Suppose that the capitalist state succeeds, for whatever reasons, in snaring a very large share of surplus value by a rapid increase in tax rates.

Corporations forced to pay these higher taxes are then left with less surplus value with which to meet the other subsumed classes' claims.[9] Such a corporation might inform its creditors that it cannot pay interest payments, or its landlords that it cannot pay rents, or its shareholders that it must cut dividends, or its managers that it must reduce their salaries and departmental budgets. Each of these subsumed classes will fight back. Creditors will threaten that if not paid, they will never again provide credit. In other words, they threaten that unless given their share of surplus value, they will cease to provide a condition of the capitalist's existence, thereby jeopardizing it. Similarly, the landlords threaten eviction proceedings. Shareholders threaten to sell off their holdings, which would depress the market prices of the corporation's shares and thus undermine its ability to raise capital by issuing more shares. Finally, managers threaten to decrease their purchases of new machines and labor power or to work less hard or move to other concerns if paid less; that is, they threaten not to perform their functions, thereby undermining the accumulation of capital and workforce discipline which are conditions of existence for the production of surplus value.

Each of these subsumed classes might well come to resent the state's grabbing a larger share of surplus value at its expense. Capitalists, under the pressures of this resentment, and perhaps also occupying some of these subsumed class positions themselves, might also be offended by higher taxes. All classes might well begin to campaign for a cut in taxes, especially taxes on corporations, or for a cut with the same level of state services being delivered. A cry might rise up across the land that government is too big, taxes too high, state productivity too low, freedom threatened, et cetera.[10] State functionaries, sensing that their share of surplus value is under attack, would likely counterthreaten. With any lesser tax revenues, they would argue, military security would be compromised, or the educational level of the workforce would be reduced, or other state-performed conditions of existence would be undermined. Each subsumed class uses the threat that it might not reproduce a condition of existence of the capitalist fundamental class process to maintain and, if possible, increase its share of surplus value. Of course, even if taxes on corporations are reduced, there is no guarantee that one or more particular subsumed class distributions must increase as a result. So, for example, a reduction in corporate taxes does not necessarily imply that corporate capital accumulation and thus employment must rise. Instead, corporations may redistribute the surplus value to higher dividends, salaries of managers, acquisition of other companies' stock, et cetera. There is no guarantee of increased investment because of societal laws, beliefs, et cetera that effectively prevent the state from directing corporations to spend their profits in particular ways.

Contradictions in the state arise as various subsumed classes simultaneously seek to reduce taxes and to increase state support for their respective social positions. Banks in difficulty seek state financial support at the same time as they seek to reduce the taxes from which such support might come. Stockholders seek reduced corporate taxes to free surplus value for more generous dividends; at the same time they seek greater government orders for the corporations whose stock they own, orders made possible by tax revenues. Landlords support reduced taxes at the same time as they pressure the state to pump mortgage financing into the construction industry to enhance the demand for and thus the value of their land holdings. The state is the site of contradictory pushes and pulls from the competing subsumed classes in the society.

The state is the site of other contradictions that stem from capitalists themselves. Confronted by the various claims of their various subsumed classes, capitalists may well seek to appease all of them at the expense of tax payments to the state. They will then join in the cry to reduce government, but in all likelihood will simultaneously call for more government spending on the particular commodities they happen to produce. Thus, munitions producers will couple their pressure for tax reduction with that for greater military spending. Construction companies demand tax reductions but without any reduction in government construction projects. Agribusiness wants lower taxes but no lowering of farm subsidies.

The state is the site of still other contradictions coming from a clash between capitalists and the productive workers performing their surplus labor. The former want to save money by abolishing occupational health and safety regulations that hurt profitability. The latter want more health and safety inspectors to make the law genuinely effective in improving the job environments of workers. Capitalists want reduced taxes on corporations; workers prefer tax reductions in middle and lower personal incomes. Capitalists want legislation outlawing strikes; workers seek the extension of unemployment benefits to strikers.

There is one particular kind of contradiction in the state that may usefully serve to summarize much of the argument we have developed to this point. Capitalists sometimes react in a special way to all the subsumed class demands on the surplus value they receive from their productive workers. Instead of playing them off against one another, paying one a larger share to the extent another can be satisfied with a smaller share, capitalists move instead to alter the portion of total labor that is surplus. That is, they seek to reduce the share of total output paid to productive workers in the form of wages and thereby enlarge the quantity of surplus value available for distribution to the various subsumed classes. In this effort, capitalists pressure the state for various policies designed to lower wage levels: reducing or eliminating legal minimum wage levels, stimulating immigration to increase labor supply, reducing student loans to force students into the labor supply, reducing retirees' social-security benefits to force them into the labor supply, and so forth. Productive workers, through unions and otherwise, fight back by pressuring the state to reject such policies. These workers might seek to have the state lower taxes on corporations so as to ease pressure on their wage levels. Alternatively, these workers might push for state policies to nationalize banking. The logic of this is quite simple: state banking could mean lower interest payments by corporations, thereby freeing surplus value for payments to other subsumed classes without adding pressure on wages.

There are innumerable ways besides those listed for capital to affect the quantity of surplus value via its influence upon state activities. As we demonstrated earlier, the state through its various political, economic, and cultural processes can affect directly and indirectly the profit rate of corporations. For instance, accelerated depreciation allowances, public road systems, mass public education, foreign policy, et cetera are all ways to affect the cost of capital and labor power to corporations. These different ways are implemented at different times depending on class and nonclass pressures. It is even quite possible for higher taxes to the state to produce a particular pattern of state policies that so enhance corporate profits that increased distributions can be made to all other subsumed classes. In this case, higher taxes *and* higher dividends, interest payments, capital accumulation, et cetera are possible because of the particular way state policies overdetermine the corporate profit rate.

The contradictions in the state so far discussed have been class contradictions stemming from the subsumed class process in the state and from the capitalist fundamental class process to which the state is subsumed. But class contradictions are hardly the only ones in the state. It is also the site for contradictory pushes and pulls concerning its policies and actions that stem from all the other economic, political, natural, and cultural processes that it performs. State policies on religion, water fluoridation, voting procedures, tariff agreements, and so on are also pushed and pulled in various ways by citizens with different religious, ecological, political, and economic positions. Any citizen occupies not only one or more class positions in society, but also a great variety of other economic, political, and cultural positions. The citizen is himself or herself a contradictory site in society; it follows that the pressures he or she exerts on the state are contradictory too. Some of these pressures stem from class positions; others stem from nonclass positions.

To generalize, we may say that the contradictions necessarily overdetermined in any social site imply that the pressures of that site on any other will also be contradictory. Citizens pressure the state in contradictory ways and vice versa. It is only the particular Marxist concern with class that has led us in this discussion to focus on the state's class contradictions. In capitalist states such as the United States, class contradictions refer to the state's position as subsumed to the capitalist fundamental process, a position which affects everything else that the state is or does.

Implications of This Marxist Theory

A basic change in the nature of the state and in its relations with the rest of the society in which it occurs requires a basic change in its position as a subsumed class. There is a tradition in Marxism that distinguishes between basic changes that are reforms and those that are revolutions. We might interpret that tradition as follows: a reform of the state is a change in its position as a class subsumed to the capitalist fundamental class process. A revolution of the state is a change which partly or entirely eliminates its status as a class subsumed to the capitalist fundamental class process. Some changes in the state will be judged as neither reformist nor revolutionary.

This last sort of change in the state may be illustrated by several examples. An election in the United States which replaces Democrats with Republicans in the White House and Congress is highly unlikely to involve either reform or revolution in the state. The state will retain its subsumed class position. Such changes as may occur will be more or less limited to alterations in tax rates, to relatively minor alterations in spending for the different social processes performed by the state. No challenge will be mounted to the subsumed class position of the state, its task of securing certain conditions of existence of the capitalist class process. Nonclass changes in the state — that is, changes in its religious, political and other policies — will be limited by the commitment to maintain its subsumed class position. The changes of faces and policies usually produced by U. S. elections will not basically alter the state, however much particular groups may benefit or lose economically, politically, or culturally from such limited changes.

It need not be different if the new faces and policies are labelled socialist or communist or anything else. The analytic question for Marxist theory remains the same: do the changed faces and policies basically change the state as a subsumed class in capitalist society? If they do not, their accession to state power involves neither reform nor revolution, whatever the particular changes in state policies they produce. If the state's position as a subsumed class is basically altered, it remains to ascertain whether it is a reformist or a revolutionary alteration.

An example currently receiving wide attention around the world may illustrate our argument. In certain countries during the twentieth century, changes in states have occurred through electoral and/ or military means that have been widely considered reformist and/or revolutionary. Socialist and communist governments in Eastern Europe, Scandinavia, China, Africa, Latin America, and elsewhere have been so considered. We propose to examine the question of the reformist or revolutionary changes in their states from the vantage point of the Marxist theory developed in this discussion.

Typically, such changed states took a series of steps to nationalize private property in the physical means of production. They did this to varying degrees, but in all cases a sizeable portion of previously privately owned means was nationalized, with or without compensation to the former owners depending on each country's particular history and conditions. The state had changed its position as a subsumed class. It was no longer dependent merely on the tax portion of surplus value for its existence as a performer of certain conditions of existence of the capitalist fundamental class process. If it had nationalized banks, the state was henceforth the agency extending credit for which it received the subsumed class payment of interest in addition to the taxes it levied. If it had nationalized all or much of the land, it added rent payments from capitalists to its other subsumed class receipts. If it had nationalized portions of the privately owned shares of capitalist enterprises, then it added dividend payments to its subsumed class receipts.

The point is that such states as undertook this sort of change did alter their subsumed class position. Their alteration took the historically important form of a greater or lesser *extension* of their subsumed class position into areas previously restricted to private ownership (of money, land, stock, et cetera). This strikes us as clearly a reform in and of the state. Such a reform will have far-reaching social effects. Capitalist enterprises will function differently when they borrow and rent from, and pay dividends as well as taxes to, a single state. Such a state will display a different pattern of class and other contradictions from the sort of pattern we discussed earlier as appropriate to the U. S.-type capitalist state. The society in which such a state exists will display a different dynamic than one in which the state is limited to subsumed class payments in tax form.

But the question remains: however altered by the extension of its subsumed class position, has the state in any sense eliminated its subsumed class position? Only an affirmative answer would qualify the changes involved as revolutionary alterations of the state. However, despite the enormous volume of both Marxist and non-Marxist literature on the subject of state changes in these countries across this century, this question still lacks an answer.

Socialists and communists who insist on the most profound theoretical and practical differences between them nonetheless share the identification of the nationalization of means of production with the demise of capitalism. Social democratic politicians in Scandinavia and official pronouncements from Moscow share the view that capitalism weakens and vanishes in proportion to the state's take-over of formerly privately owned means of production. We would argue that such viewpoints evade rather than answer the basic question. By asserting the end of the capitalist fundamental class process as equivalent to the nationalization of the means of production, they need not, and do not, go on to analyze what the fundamental class process is that remains when the state extends its subsumed class position.[11] Hence they collapse reform and revolution into one undifferentiated theory of state change, which is probably why social democrats and communists see eye to eye on this matter.

But neither the logic of Marxist theory nor empirical research into the concrete histories of the countries whose states have so extended their subsumed class positions supports the collapsing of reform and revolution into one another when state changes are analyzed. Suppose that a state in capitalist society is so changed that not only does it extend its subsumed class position to all formerly privately owned means of production, it also takes over the fundamental class process of producing surplus labor. The state would then be both the direct receiver of produced surplus labor and the subsumed class receiver of distributed shares of that surplus labor. Different branches or offices of the state would then play the different roles of capitalist and various subsumed class positions. Payments would flow among them in ways perfectly analogous with those in the private institutions in a U. S.-type capitalist society. Of course, such a state directly involved in the fundamental as well as the subsumed class processes would develop differently from one occupying a far more socially restricted position. But the question remains: is the state no longer subsumed to the capitalist fundamental class process?

We would venture to answer no. The state may own all the means of production; it may employ productive workers and receive the surplus they produce; it may then distribute that surplus to its various branches that provide the conditions of existence of the surplus labor production. None of this implies that the fundamental class process is not still capitalist. Some examples from the United States may help to underscore this point. In the United States, the government owns, as nationalized property, large tracts of land. Some of these it leases to capitalist firms (in oil and gas production, in agriculture, et cetera) who must pay rent to the state which thus occupies an extended subsumed class position. It gets both taxes and rents from such firms. The U. S. government also lends money to capitalists; hence it gets interest payments from them. U. S. government-pension funds own large blocks of shares in U. S. firms. U. S. government agencies (for example, the Tennessee Valley Authority) also produce commodities for sale and receive surplus value from their productive employees in the process.

Capitalism in the United States is not weakened by these aspects of the state, these extensions of its subsumed class position, and even this occupation of a fundamental class position (in the TVA case). Similarly, the question is whether the state in a society like that of the Soviet Union presents us with a revolutionary, as opposed to a reformist, change. The answer hinges on how we would analyze the fundamental class processes currently existing in the Soviet Union and on the Soviet state's relation to them. If these fundamental class processes did not include the capitalist form or did so only to a socially minimal degree, we would conclude that the Soviet change of state was indeed revolutionary as various of its defenders and critics alike claim. But since the Marxist theoretical tradition has yet to produce developed analyses of what the communist fundamental class process involves and how it influences the position of the state within a society that was predominantly communist, we cannot answer the question.

What distinguishes this theory of Marxism from other Marxist and non-Marxist theories, however, is that we raise this question in a particular way and consistently refuse to reduce changes in state and class to mere patterns of ownership of means of production. We also believe it useful to emphasize the question of the fundamental class process in the determination of whether any given state change is revolutionary.

One implication of this theory is that even if a law is passed vesting ownership of the means of production in the performers of surplus value, we would still raise the question of the revolutionary nature of such state action. Suppose under such a law workers now own the means of production and receive a so-called social dividend for distributing the means to their users. These workers now occupy two class positions: in the fundamental class as performers of surplus labor and in the subsumed class as receivers of dividends for providing a condition of existence of this surplus labor. Suppose in addition the means are distributed to state enterprises that exhibit the following class structure: the same workers who own the means produce the surplus labor, they are supervised by state-managers, and the surplus labor is received by the state directors of such enterprises. It is quite possible that this surplus labor could be still appropriated in capitalist form despite the fact that workers, the proletariat, own the means of production. However, there has been a significant change in the structure of the state. State officials occupy the fundamental class position as receivers of surplus labor and the subsumed class position as managers of state-run enterprises.

Another implication of this Marxist theory of the state is a particular view of the likely effectiveness of citizens' efforts to change state policies and structures. Any change produced in the state will have effects, including effects on the various fundamental and subsumed class processes in the society. Persons using this Marxist theory to produce social analyses must then continually assess and reassess the likely effects of the various changes being pressed on the state by all sorts of groups in society. For example, women's groups who produce changes in state support for women seeking abortions will thereby produce changes throughout the society, including class changes. Different changes will flow from altered state policies on the environment, race relations, minimum wage rates, and public education. One major goal for Marxist theory is to specify the social effects of these different changes with particular reference to their effects on the various fundamental and subsumed class positions in the society.

Another goal is to specify the conditions that overdetermine how successful any particular effort to change the state is likely to be. The desire to change the state can hardly suffice to determine such a change; the desire requires organized actions under certain social conditions if it is to succeed. Marxist theory seeks to specify, for example, whether any particular proposed change in the state would undermine its provision of a condition of existence of the capitalist fundamental class process. If so, the expectation would be that capitalists and others with whom they might ally would fight strenuously against such a change. By contrast, proposed state changes that leave intact the state's effectivity as the performer of social processes providing the conditions of existence of the capitalist fundamental class process would be less opposed or perhaps endorsed by capitalists.

From assessments such as these, whereby Marxist theory produces its particular class knowledge of the social conditions for, and effects of, different state changes, the Marxist practitioners of the theory draw practical conclusions. Doing such Marxist theory is one determinant, among many others, in the overdetermination of the strategic and tactical decisions taken by Marxist organizations concerned with the transformation of society, with special reference to its class structure. This Marxist theory precludes certain views sometimes found in other Marxist theories. For example, adherents of this theory could not reject practical efforts to alter state policies on the grounds of some supposed irrelevance of the state or its different branches to class change, including revolutionary change. Nor could adherents of this Marxist theory take the opposite tack and propose a practical attitude toward the state that imagines that changes in it would necessarily produce a social transformation including revolutionary alteration of the class structure. This theory's commitment to overdetermination as against the determinism of this or that aspect of society, such as the state, precludes precisely either of these two views found in alternative Marxisms.

One final implication of this Marxist theory of the state may be briefly mentioned to illustrate its explanatory powers. While the state may be the social site where certain conditions of existence of the capitalist fundamental class process are produced, it need not always be the site where they are produced. That is, what the state does may at other times be done at other sites. For example, mass education is only sometimes a state activity. While such education is clearly a condition of existence of the capitalist fundamental class process, it need not always, or ever, be done in and by the state. Currently in the United States, large parts of mass education of children are being shifted to nonstate sites: enterprises which sell education as a commodity in the market and other subsumed classes outside the state (for example, parochial schools). Similarly, local police functions formerly performed by state employees are increasingly being performed instead by private security enterprises selling protection as a commodity. Proposals are currently receiving serious attention in the United States to shift from publicly run mass pensions (social security) to a much greater reliance on private pension systems.

The logic of this Marxist theory insists that the conditions of existence of the capitalist fundamental class process be reproduced, not that the state need be the only site for their reproduction. Thus, the size and sorts of processes performed in and by the state will vary across the history of capitalist societies — and noncapitalist societies as well. No necessary trend to bigness or smallness is inscribed in this theory. Indeed, what Marxist theory would suggest is that a major determinant of expanding versus shrinking states would be capitalist perceptions of whether their conditions of existence would be more securely reproduced by the state versus alternative social sites. In the 1930s the U. S. state appeared to be the social site of last resort, so it grew. In the 1940s the state was needed to provide military security in a world war; it grew. In the 1960s the maintenance of social peace in the face of demands by black Americans, women, poor people, and others, and another war, this one in Vietnam, combined to make for another growth spurt in the state. By contrast, the 1950s, the later 1970s, and the 1980s have been periods when capitalists oppose growth in subsumed class payments to the state, preferring to see their conditions of existence reproduced at other social sites.[12] The state shrinks; its relative position as a site in society is curtailed. Presumably, Marxist strategies for social change would have to alter with the kind of social changes involved in differing relative positions of the state in capitalist society.

Conclusion

This Marxist theory of the state produces a complex knowledge of the position and history of the state in capitalist society. It is a knowledge which recognizes and elaborates the state as an overdetermined, contradictory site in society. It is a knowledge which focuses upon and emphasizes the relationships of the state to the fundamental and subsumed class processes in the society. It carries far-reaching implications for the practical activities of Marxist adherents to the theory.

Alternative theories produce their alternative knowledges of the state; they make sense of the state differently. Their theories help to shape different practical attitudes of their adherents toward the state. Indeed, our struggle in theory against those theories — our critiques of them — is a part of our practical struggles. That is, we seek changes in the state which we theorize about that are opposed to, and by, the changes sought by adherents of the theories we oppose. To paraphrase Marx, life is struggle, with the struggles in theory complexly interwoven with, and interdependent on, the struggles in practical activity.

Notes

1. A version of this theory can be found in G. A. Cohen, *Karl Marx's Theory of History: A Defense* (Princeton: Princeton University Press, 1980), especially pp. 216–248.

2. The relationship between the state and the economy is but a variation of a broader theme in Marxist theory: what is the relation between the base (the economy or *mode of production*) and the superstructure (all the noneconomic or nonproduction aspects of society). A predominant tendency within Marxism has been to affirm the determinance of the base over the determined superstructure. This has its sophisticated version arguing the dominance of noneconomic aspects in noncapitalist societies as determined in the last instance by the base. A full and critical discussion of economic determinism within Marxism can be found in Stephen Resnick and Richard Wolff, "Marxist Epistemology: the Critique of Economic Determinism," *Social Text*, forthcoming in 1983. One of the first expositions of a nondeterminist (or overdeterminist) approach is Louis Althusser, "Contradiction and Overdetermination," in *For Marx*, trans. Ben Brewster (New York: Vintage, 1970). Also see Raymond Williams, *Marxism and Literature* (Oxford: Oxford University Press, 1977), pp. 75–127.

3. This term is borrowed from Althusser, "Contradiction and Overdetermination." Also see Resnick and Wolff, "Marxist Epistemology."

4. The class process is one "in which unpaid surplus-labour is pumped out of direct producers." Karl Marx, *Capital*, vol. 3 (New York: International Publishers, 1977), p. 791.

5. See Marx, *Capital*, vol. 1, p. 217, and vol. 3, pp. 632–633. He defines there new categories for Marxian theory.

6. A full elaboration of fundamental and subsumed class processes can be found in our article, "Classes in Marxian Theory," *The Review of Radical Political Economics*, 13 (Winter 1982). Perhaps a simple example will make clear the relationship between fundamental and subsumed classes. Suppose an individual performs ten hours of labor, five of which are assumed necessary to sustain the labor effort of this individual. The remaining five hours are received by, say, a different individual. The fundamental class process refers then to those two individuals who occupy different class positions depending upon whether one is a performer or receiver of surplus labor. The five hours of surplus labor is embodied in products which are now distributed (the subsumed class process) to other individuals who secure the social conditions for this production. Officials of the state may receive, say, one hour for providing political, economic, and cultural processes necessary for the existence of surplus labor. Managers in the work place may receive one and one half hours for the process of supervision — one of their tasks being to insure that the actual labor is performed. Owners of tools may receive two hours of labor for providing their owned means of production to the fundamental class of receivers of surplus labor who, in turn, combine them with the performers of labor. Finally, one half hour of surplus labor may be distributed to merchants who purchase the items produced by the ten hours of labor and sell them in the market place. In general, we can summarize the above class relationships in a simple formula:

$$SL = \Sigma \, SC$$

where SL is the produced surplus labor and $\Sigma \, SC$ is its distribution to all the subsumed classes who quite literally make this production possible. As the text suggests, we can differentiate among different societies by specifying a different formula for each. For example, a capitalist society could be summarized as: $CSL = \Sigma \, CSC$ where the new letter C refers to the capitalist value form in which surplus labor is produced and distributed.

Our particular conceptualization of subsumed classes is influenced by Marx's class analysis in volumes 2 and 3 of *Capital*. He there carefully analyzes merchants, managers, owners of common stock, bankers, landlords, state officials, and monopolists as capitalist subsumed classes if they are recipients of extracted surplus value. He then demonstrates how the sum of all these claims to surplus value (ΣCSC in our formula) equals surplus value (CSV).

7. One economic argument often advanced is that state production of commodities is inherently inefficient. The claim is that resources would be more efficiently used by private, as compared to public, enterprises. A related argument is that state commodity production would threaten private enterprise and open the door to socialism. Since socialism is identified with the end of democracy, any attempt to extend the state's economic powers in such a direction is viewed with great antipathy. What this amounts to is that various cultural processes in the United States, some of which are provided by the state itself in the form of public education, produce a particular knowledge of *state* commodity production whose effect is to restrict that production.

8. Because of the quantitative importance of, and political controversy associated with, the military budget, we might mention here that the cost of providing this political process involves an economic process, namely military weapon production. In the United States, such production is typically accomplished in capitalist enterprises whose commodities (military goods) are sold to the U.S. state or to foreign states: their prices influence the subsumed class payments to the state.

9. Parallel to our analysis of the state, a corporation is also conceived of as a site in society. It too exhibits a complex class structure. For example, individuals who sit on the boards of directors of such corporations receive and distribute surplus value to various subsumed classes. These individuals participate in the fundamental capitalist class process as direct receivers of surplus value; they occupy the fundamental capitalist class position. Their receipt of surplus value depends upon the provision of processes both internal and external to the corporation. As the text argues, they must distribute (the subsumed class process) the received surplus value to managers, owners of the corporation (stockholders), creditors, state, landlords, et cetera. We can think of the directors and managers as constituting the internal fundamental and subsumed class structure of the corporation (conceived of as a site) and the rest as subsumed classes external to the corporation. If we call surplus value SV, its distribution to corporate managers SC_I, its distribution to all other subsumed classes excluding the state SC_{II}, and its distribution to the state SC_{tax}, then a summary equation specifies clearly the distribution among the three subsumed class groupings:

$$SV = SC_I + SC_{II} + SC_{tax}.$$

For a given SV, higher SC_{tax} must diminish either or both of SC_I and SC_{II}.

We should also add that any individual may occupy more than one class position. So, for example, individuals who sit on the board of directors, and thus occupy the capitalist class position, will likely occupy various subsumed class positions as managers, stockholders, et cetera. In this case, they would appear on both sides of the equation and receive income in their subsumed class position(s).

10. Proposition 13 in California and 2½ in Massachusetts are particular results of such a *tax revolt* as are the recent, rather dramatic, federal corporate-tax reductions.

11. The equating of nationalization of means of production with socialism is conditioned by a particular form of essentialist reasoning. The origin of socialism is reduced to the nationalization of the means of production. This approach takes what we refer to as only *one* of the conditions of existence of capitalism, the private ownership of means of production, and argues that a struggle over such ownership will necessarily lead to a struggle over the fundamental class process. This approach is far different from what we have here presented.

12. Current economic theory plays an important role in contributing to the shift of several processes to social sites other than the state. One tendency in economic theory, currently predominant in the Reagan administration, understands the state to be the prime cause of several social problems in the United States. Inflation, low growth of productivity, breakup of the family, creeping socialism are all traced ultimately to the ubiquitous interference of the state in the free market system. It follows that the solution is to reduce state interference by economic and cultural reforms. The effect is to reduce its size and interference. Private enterprise, family, and individual become the proper sites in the society to carry on several former state activities including welfare, pensions, environment control, education, and health maintenance. The reasoning in this approach is essentialist: it identifies the state as the ultimate cause (essence) of societal problems. The essentialist political policy implemented follows logically from the essentialist theory advanced.

Selected Bibliography

Althusser, Louis, *For Marx,* trans. Ben Brewster (New York: Vintage, 1970), Chs. 3, 6, and 7.

Balibar, Etienne, *On the Dictatorship of the Proletariat,* trans. Grahame Lock (London: New Left Books, 1977).

Baran, Paul A. and Paul M. Sweezy, *Monopoly Capital: An Essay on the American Economic and Social Order* (New York: Monthly Review, 1966).

Bettelheim, Charles, *Class Struggles in the USSR: First Period, 1917–1923,* trans. Brian Pearce (New York: Monthly Review, 1976) See also subsequent volumes of this work.

Cohen, G. A., *Karl Marx's Theory of History* (Princeton: Princeton University Press, 1980).

Draper, Hal, ed., *Karl Marx and Friedrich Engels: Writings on the Paris Commune* (New York and London: Monthly Review, 1971).

Gramsci, Antonio, *Selections from the Prison Notebooks,* trans. Quintin Hoare and Geoffrey Nowell Smith (New York: International Publishers, 1971), part II, section 2.

Holloway, John and Picciotto, Sol, eds., *State and Capital* (London: Edward Arnold, 1978).

Lenin, V. I., *The State and Revolution,* many editions.

Lukacs, Georg, *Lenin: A Study on the Unity of his Thought,* trans. Nicholas Jacobs (Cambridge, Mass.: MIT Press, 1971).

Mandel, Ernest, *Late Capitalism,* trans. Joris De Bres (London: New Left Books, 1975), Ch. 15.

Marx, Karl, *Capital,* 3 vols. (New York: International Publishers, 1977).

Miliband, Ralph, *Marxism and Politics* (Oxford University Press, 1977).

Moore, Barrington, *Social Origins of Dictatorship and Democracy* (Boston: Beacon Press, 1966).
Moore, Stanley W., *The Critique of Capitalist Democracy* (New York: Paine-Whitman, 1957).
O'Connor, James, *The Fiscal Crisis of the State* (New York: St. Martins Press, 1973).
Pashukanis, E. B., *General Theory of Law and Marxism* (London: Ink Links, 1978).
Poulantzas, Nicos, *Political Power and Social Classes*, trans. Timothy O'Hagan (London: Verso Editions, 1978).
Resnick, Stephen and Wolff, Richard D., "Classes in Marxian Theory," *The Review of Radical Political Economics*, 13 (Winter 1982): 1-18.
Resnick, Stephen and Wolff, Richard D., "Marxist Epistemology: the Critique of Economic Determination," in *Social Text*, 6 (Fall 1982): 31-72.
Sweezy, Paul M., *The Theory of Capitalist Development* (New York: Monthly Review, 1956).
Sweezy, Paul M. and Bettelheim, Charles, *On the Transition to Socialism* (New York and London: Monthly Review, 1971).
Williams, Raymond, *Marxism and Literature* (Oxford: Oxford University Press, 1977).
Wright, Erik Olin, *Class, Crisis and the State* (London: Verso Editions, 1979).

Comment by Andrzej Brzeski

For a crisp and definite — indeed, definitive — version of the Marxist theory of the state, one can look to Lenin. "According to Marx," we read in *The State and Revolution*," the state is an organ of class *rule,* an organ for the *oppression* of one class by another; it is the creation of 'order,' which legalizes and perpetuates this oppression by moderating the conflict between the classes." This is as clear as can be. Add the fundamental, incontrovertibly Marxist idea that *"the existence of classes* is only bound up with the *particular historical phases in the development of production"* (letter to Weydemeyer), and the conception of the nature and evolution of the state within the larger scheme of *historical materialism* becomes complete.

Political institutions merely serve as a prop for the existing social and economic arrangements (*social relations of production*), which, in turn, are determined by technology and organization, broadly conceived (*forces of production*). The causality, although not always direct and transparent, is inevitable; it matters little whether the state, that is, the sum total of political institutions, is a part of the *base,* or *superstructure* — a moot doctrinal issue, but devoid of real significance. Ultimately, or as Marx put it, *"in der letzten Instanz,"* the various forms and processes shaping man's social existence, depend on, and change according to, the development of his productive powers.

This view — reducing the state to an epiphenomenon of class, and, in the last count, production — is straightforward and in harmony with the logic of Marxism. It also is quite crude and in obvious conflict with historical experience. Marx himself, in thinking along such lines, failed the test of history; he was convinced that capitalist democracy was ephemeral — "only the political form of revolution of bourgeois society and not its conservative form of life" (in *The Eighteenth Brumaire of Louis Bonaparte*). He stuck to this conviction stubbornly throughout the heydays of European parliamentary order. Some of his followers (for example, Kautsky, Austro-marxists) did recognize the weakness of the theory of the state. So do also various self-professed Marxists of our day. The political realities of contemporary capitalism are too difficult to ignore; *bourgeois democracy* — welfare statism, business regulations, judicial social activism, environmentalism and the like — cannot convincingly be explained in stark Marxist terms *à la* Lenin. Therefore, much of the recent Marxist writing (for example, by Bowles, Gintis, Weiskopf, Wright) on the state and related matters tends toward reinterpretation and reassessment. Some writers "question . . . traditional Marxist theory," and ascribe to the state a sui generis autonomy. They even envisage the prospect "that liberal democracy may well be radically transformed . . . toward an instrument, however imperfect, of popular power."[1] Apparently, the neo-Marxists are discovering . . . Eduard Bernstein. With time, some might even stumble upon, say, Max Weber.

But regardless of new insights and doubts, severing one's attachment to Marxism is rarely easy. For many, Marxism is admittedly more than a theoretical orientation. It is an existential creed and a way of life. Stephen Resnick and Richard Wolff demonstrate in their contribution the intellectual perils of such a commitment. In the spirit of the eleventh thesis on Feuerbach, the two writers conclude *their* version of the Marxist theory of the state with a solemn declaration of activism: "our struggle in theory against those [other] theories . . . is a part of our practical struggles." Presumably, the "practical struggles" which are alluded to are against capitalism, imperialism, et cetera — all legitimate Marxist causes. Furthermore, the writers are no doubt earnest about trying to contribute to

Marxist theory. Yet, recognizing the inadequacy of main-line Marxism in its treatment of the state, Resnick and Wolff try to finesse the point by resorting to conceptual and analytical innovation. "There is not one Marxian approach to social analysis," they insist, "there are several." And, surely, in the huge Marx-Engels oeuvre, one can find passages to justify every conceivable interpretation of Marxism; Marx's well-known quip: "I am not a Marxist," could be richly supported with quotations from his own writings. Alas, what Resnick and Wolff have to say on the unsettled subject of the state is not very enlightening. Theirs is a pseudo-Marxist pseudo-theory.

Even the underlying epistemology — something that greatly preoccupies the writers — is blatantly at variance with their avowed Marxism. Their position has more in common with Kuhn's paradigm-switching than with the critical realism of *praxis*. "Alternative theories, produce . . . alternative knowledges (sic) of the state," we are told. But then, what precisely *is* the knowledge resulting from the writers' "particular theoretical approach?" Stripped of a rather awkward terminology, the pickings are embarrassingly slim.

Resnick and Wolff stress that their approach "is pointedly non- or even antideterminist." Wary of oversimplification, they emphatically deny "that the state may be explained as the creature of the economy . . . [or] the economy as the creature of the state." This is common sense, and I, for one, fully agree. Still, the open-ended view of the relationship between the state and the economy offered by the writers yields no theoretical implications. *Overdetermination*, a concept borrowed from Althusser, and crucial to the argument, boils down to a platitude: everything depends on everything. If this be so, we can have little hope of understanding anything. Reflecting on universal interdependence makes good dialectics; it is of no help at all in gaining specific knowledge about the world. If, as Resnick and Wolff approvingly note, "Marxist theory begins with the insight that any one of the infinite variety of processes in society is influenced by all of the others," it can at best end in statistical regressions. Unless used to formulate hypotheses — back to determinism! — and a way to test them, this would be a very limited kind of knowledge, a low-level empiricism. Few, least of all a Marxist whose main interest is in society's *laws of motion*, would be satisfied. Not surprisingly, Resnick and Wolff are not.

In their quest for a different sort of knowledge, they reintroduce a little order into the infinity of interacting, often contradictory processes. The state, as a special *site* — a terrible term! — at which these processes intersect, is considered in relation to the *class process*, that is, to the arrangements under which surplus value is appropriated and redistributed in a society. On the one hand, the state performs a variety of functions, including those necessary for the preservation of capitalism. In return, *qua subsumed class* — another awful term! — it receives a part of the redistributed surplus value. Reforms, including policy changes and revolutions, inasmuch as they affect the state, are simply changes "in its position as a class subsumed to the captalist fundamental class process." There are "all manner of pushes and pulls emanating from the totality of all social processes" to determine the outcome. But even so, short of a hope for the effects of the writers' good "struggle in theory," no predictable direction of change emerges from the discussion. What remains of Marxism is a focus on conflict and change, but the nexus of the state with civil society and, more fundamentally, with production is vague, and the presumption of inevitability of progress is gone.

Even the centrality of the *class process* is tentative. "Class is not any more important than any other aspects of social change," Resnick and Wolff concede. Then why not forego the sterile speculations of pseudo-Marxism altogether? So far the latter have shed no light on the state and its policies.

Note

Samuel Bowles and Herbert Gintis, "The Crisis of Liberal Democratic Capitalism: The Case of the United States," *Politics and Society*. Vol. 11, No. 2 (1982), p. 93.

5 WHITHER (POSITIVE) POLITICAL ECONOMY? ONE READING
Warren J. Samuels

Introduction

Larry Wade has produced a remarkable collection of essays on the dominant approaches to political economy. This concluding essay explores areas of agreement and disagreement among the three approaches and the direction in which *positive* political economy may, and perhaps should, proceed. Although I share Wade's suspicion that a fully satisfactory or unequivocal synthesis of all approaches to political economy is probably impossible, I will suggest certain lines of thinking which could, problematically, facilitate some useful progress in that direction.

Wade's own essay is notable for his demonstration of the myopia, if not hubris, of an apolitical Keynesianism which failed to appreciate the complexities of politics applicable to the contest of economic stability

---

The author is indebted to Allan Schmid and Elizabeth Johnston for comments on an early version of this chapter.

(itself not a simple matter) with other objectives. This point also applies to both the neoclassical and public-choice approaches and is reinforced by William C. Mitchell later in the volume. Wade also properly stresses both the importance of the Madisonian emphasis on conflict resolution as the principal social-control role of government and the complexities of political vis-à-vis economic liberalism.

The essay by L. Jay Helms is a straightforward statement of the applied neoclassical welfare-economics approach to public finance, an approach which I subsequently will refer to as Pigovian, even though it shares with public-choice theory the notion of Pareto optimality. Helms's essay is useful, first, for identifying what the neoclassical, or Pigovian, approach does and does not cover and, second, for distinguishing the mainstream Pigovian from the public-choice approach.

The essay by Mitchell is a useful summary of the nature and central strands of the public-choice approach. His distinction between demand- and supply-based analyses, which perhaps ought not to be pushed too far (in light of the concept of overdetermination discussed below), is a helpful integrative and analytical tool. Especially noteworthy is his relatively nondogmatic, if not substantially nonideological, account of public-choice theory. It constitutes a major step toward a more positive public-choice theory and political economy.

This last point also applies to Stephen Resnick and Richard Wolff's interpretation of the Marxian approach to political economy. Whether because of, or despite, their respective right-wing and left-wing ideologies, both public-choice and Marxian theories make positive contributions to political economy. Resnick and Wolff's overdeterminist approach to Marxian political economy is a useful complement to the neoclassical and public-choice approaches. Moreover, it may contain the germ of successful future synthetic efforts. The neoclassical approach leaves us with the problems of (1) having to determine (a) which of each pair of reciprocal externalities is to be considered the putative policy problem and (b) which of a ubiquitous set of such putative problems government is to attempt to *solve* and (2) studying how political processes work out answers to (1). Public-choice theory correctly points to the array of competing demands on government and to the complex behavior of government officials and other employees in seeking their own objectives in a complex network of kaleidoscopic interrelationships. Accordingly, the notion of overdetermination can help place the complex phenomena and processes of government, and the interactions of government with other institutions and processes, in robust and unbiased perspective.

It should be obvious to any student of political economy that these essays by no means exhaust the field. As examples of other principal sources, I call attention to the work of such diverse writers as Charles Lindblom, Kenneth Boulding, Frederick Pryor, John Kenneth Galbraith, James Willard Hurst, Robert Solo, Randall Bartlett (whose work is mentioned, but not fully treated, in Mitchell's essay), and institutionalists in the tradition of John R. Commons.

Two other preliminary points are worth mentioning. First, it should be obvious that each of the three principal approaches to political economy discussed earlier — neoclassical, public choice, and Marxian — is heavily ideological and normative. But it also is true that each has been a source of hypotheses useful for more positive, scientific inquiry. This should not be surprising; Joan Robinson has emphasized that economics has been both a vehicle for ideology and a method of scientific investigation.[1] This does not mean, of course, that ideology is to be taken for science.

Second, although thirty years ago Bushrod Allin, Frank Knight, and Howard Ellis argued as to whether group choice is a part of economics, that is no longer an issue.[2] Whether political economy be understood as the study of group or collective choice, or the interrelations between legal and market (and perhaps other) processes, and so on, political economy now has an indisputable, and even honorable, place in scholarly work in the social sciences, yes, even in economics. Of course, the argument three decades ago was misleading. Institutionalists, Marxists, and neoclassical economists did treat group choice, the latter frequently without so designating their work. At least one subsidiary issue, of course, does remain viable: the probative value of juxtaposing so-called voluntary market exchange to so-called coercive group action, a consideration which raises the question of rival discursive systems to which I turn below.[3]

It should be appreciated that political economy, like economics, has at least three coordinates of meaning. Political economy is an attempt at knowledge, a vehicle of social control, and, as a mode of psychic balm, a means of setting minds at rest; that is, political economy includes both explanation-understanding and rationalization-legitimation. This being the case, the future of political economy inescapably is complex and multidimensional. In this essay I will concentrate on positive political economy, that is, political economy as an attempt at knowledge (explanation-understanding), fully recognizing, and indeed stressing, the difficulty, if not impossibility, of isolating such a version of political economy from the normative forms it typically takes.

Two Normative Discursive Systems of Political Economy

The neoclassical and public-choice approaches to political economy represent two variants of one, and the Marxian approach a second, discursive system. These may be designated the *productivity* and the *exploitation* discursive systems.[4] Each expresses a set of images internal to the structure of thought and analysis. Explication and analysis founded upon either one tends to give effect to the understanding of the world embedded in the respective discursive system. The fact that more than one discursive system exists reflects the multifaceted nature of a socio-economic reality amenable to varying interpretations and the existence of multiple perspectives from which interpretation can be conducted. The existence of two discursive systems thus reflects selective perception; further selective perception can be exercised within each discursive system. Furthermore, work within each discursive system is directed much more at elaborating, and thus reinforcing, that system than at objectively and open-mindedly analyzing the actual political economy.

What I have designated the discursive system of productivity has three facets: market, productivity, and harmony. This mode of thought takes as given the market as the framework of analysis and the locus of determination of a priori proper economic categories and quantities. The market — its operation and performance — is given paramount normative standing. Closely intertwined therewith are the ideas that distribution is in accordance with productivity as determined in the market and that, absent undesirable government interference, the market can achieve equilibrating and optimizing individual adjustments to stimuli and an harmonious integration of individual behavior. It assumes as given whatever (minimal) government action is necessary in order to have a market economy.

One variant of the productivity discursive system is, in Helms's terminology, the neoclassical or, in mine, the Pigovian (after the approach to welfare economics of Henry Sidgwick, Alfred Marshall and, especially, Arthur Cecil Pigou). This approach stresses the promarket presumption of the productivity discursive system, maintaining that markets generally work effectively. However, it does open the door for government corrective action by focusing on market failure of one kind or another. Notwithstanding its generally promarket orientation, the distinctive psycho-dynamic character of the Pigovian variant is reformist. Pigovians tend to be willing to use government in various ways, including redistribution policies, within the aegis of a predominantly market economy.

The second variant of the productivity discursive system is, in Mitchell's terminology, the public choice or, in mine, the Paretian. Its basic logic is affirmatively to reinforce the case for the market, negatively to finesse Pigovian activism by government, and to articulate, using essentially market-based criteria of performance, what it perceives as the irrationality and failures of government decision-making and policies. Whereas the neoclassical, or Pigovian, variant uses a restricted, but professionally safe (say, vis-à-vis a liberal reformist or Marxian), welfare criterion, the public-choice, or Paretian, variant introduces a negative, or skeptical, view of government and of the efficacy of politics.

It should be apparent that both the neoclassical and public-choice theorists of political economy use the concept of Pareto optimality. The difference, broadly speaking, is that whereas the Pigovian, or neoclassical, analyst begins with that concept and proceeds to explore opportunities for corrective action (not limited to a more fully specified definition of rights) consequent to perceived failures of the market to realize the requirements of Pareto optimality, the Paretian or public-choice analyst asserts the overwhelming predominance of opportunities for voluntary exchange and of Pareto optimality and the coercive and problem-generating character of government so-called corrective action. Pareto optimality is the core concept of both variants but is used differently with regard to establishing a posture applicable to policy. It should be no surprise that the literature on both sides includes, in addition to technical work, quasi-theological tracts attempting to erect impregnable intellectual fortresses in defense of each position.

This last point is also true, of course, of the exploitation discursive system of which Marxian economics and political economy is the best known and most highly developed variant. The Marxian discursive system, insofar as it constitutes a critique of capitalism, focuses on the market as a vehicle of exploitation, the power structure which governs exploitation, the conflictual character of capitalism, and government as a corrupted agency for organizing and administering exploitation.

Clearly, these two discursive systems, or these three approaches to political economy, represent normative constructions of reality. Although each has positive (nonnormative) elements, the distinguishing characteristic of each resides in its normative portrayals. Thus each is heavily, albeit usefully, ideological. Each provides a normative definition of reality and specific values to serve as a guide to, and a critique of, policy. But by providing a political economy laden with ideology, each predetermines the issues, values, and objectives of both analysis and policy. Each makes political economy a mode of social control, which is ironic in the case of the neoclassical and public-choice approaches, especially the latter with its ostensibly libertarian orientation.

Toward a Positive Discursive System of Political Economy

There exists the possibility, indeed the rudiments, and the desirability, of a positive (nonnormative) political economy. This would attempt to describe, explain, and understand the nature, causes, and consequences of government decision-making and policy actions. It also would attempt to analyze and predict the likely substantive performance consequences, under varying assumptions or conditions, of alternative institutional arrangements, including varying specific government policies, vis-à-vis the abstract and formal consequences of efficiency and exploitation analysis. These analyses can be used to help identify the variables usefully researchable in particular settings (for example, regarding neoclassical economics, competition, number of alternatives, and ownership; and regarding public-choice theory, transaction costs and their distribution).

A positive political economy would attempt, insofar as is possible, to hold ideology and normative formulations in abeyance, to disengage the ideological engine which hitherto has driven, so overwhelmingly, each normative approach or discursive system.

A positive political economy would recognize and give the necessary effect, without either celebration or denigration, respectively, to the vital and interrelated roles of market and nonmarket modes of interaction, market and government specifically, and market mechanism and power structure; the Madisonian reality of power and conflict; methodological individualism and methodological collectivism (as distinct from their respective normative counterparts); and the factors governing the structure of opportunity sets as well as choice within given opportunity sets.

A positive political economy would study the entire social valuational process, including but not limited to the market, which governs the meaning of welfare in the lives of the actual actors who comprise the political economy. It would include, therefore, considerations of (re)distribution as a subject both predictable and important. It also would recognize that there is more to government than can be realized through the market analogies advanced by public-choice theory, which tends to make invidious comparisons between market activity and politics, and by

Marxian theory, which tends to have its own myopia about market and government.

One does not have to be dedicated to either market or government to conduct positive political economy.

The development of a positive political economy is facilitated by the circumstance that the normative approaches to political economy do have positive components. In some cases these elements exist in their respective normative approaches relatively untouched by surrounding ideology. In others, the normative elements can be filtered out so that the basic positive elements can be examined relatively independently of the ideologies which hitherto have governed their distinctive perceived identities.

It is possible, therefore, to identify tentatively certain areas of agreement or convergence. One concerns the economic roles performed by government. Marxian political economy identifies several such roles: the institutionalization, legitimation, and reproduction of the economic system, including the structure of social relations of production; the facilitation of private capital accumulation; the arbitration of disputes among dominant groups; and the securing of the interests of dominant groups against challenges from dominated groups and from dominant groups in other societies. Surely such is not entirely precluded (however it might be reworded) by the public-choice approach, which recognizes that in the market economy (bourgeois system) it is in the self-interest of dominant groups (or would-be dominant groups) to control government so as to have government perform these functions both per se and in a manner consonant with their interests. (*Groups* may or may not include *classes*.)

Second, although they each contribute to the myth system of society, both public-choice and Marxian political economy consider it important to debunk and demythicize. One concept which they both subject to such treatment is the so-called public interest approach to explaining politics.

Third, both public-choice and Marxist political economists have concentrated on identifying and interpreting problems of public spending and taxing in the liberal welfare state with which each is so uncomfortable. Although their diagnoses and preferred remedies tend strongly to differ, there are (as Wade notes) common points in their analyses. One involves the separation between tax and spending decisions. Another involves the tensions between the demands for service and the cost of service rendered by the state. Still another is the existence of bureaucratic nontax resources.

Fourth, both public-choice and Marxist political economists have been more realistic than the standard model (and perhaps unduly caricatured) neoclassical and Keynesian (or Samuelsonian "neoclassical synthesis") economist with regard to the limits of government power both in general and in the pursuit of particular policy goals.

Fifth, given their different respective negative attitudes toward government in a market economy, the Marxist and public-choice political economists more or less share an understanding of government as essentially an exploitative phenomenon. Closely related, both approaches center on conflict between groups as an engine of socioeconomic change. Both also articulate this conflict as involving the social organization of production through the (re)definition and (re)assignment of property rights.

It should go without saying that there are enormous discursive, or paradigmatic, differences between public-choice and Marxist political economists as to the way in which they develop such ideas. My point here is that, if one is willing to try to transcend the ideological components of their respective analyses, one can identify, as a matter of positive analysis, points and areas of objective research such as those just listed. Even if one were to deny the existence of these areas of agreement, the case for a positive political economy would remain unaffected. Indeed, a positive political economy could take advantage of differences as to areas of research interests and as to how theory identifies and organizes institutional and performance variables. A positive political economy can acquire content from each approach. If there are areas or points in common, fine, but any such common material is likely to be small in relation to what a positive theory requires.

A positive political economy would examine, without attempting to pass judgment, the impact of nominally private, market economic activity on government and the impact of nominally government activity on the structure, operation, and performance of the market. The performance of the market would be seen as partially a function of power structure, rights, governmental definition and assignment of rights, and the contest to control and use government to define and assign rights in order to promote certain interests rather than others. Government would be seen as an object of capture and use and as an arena in which the contest over rights (and other modes of securing and defending economic interests) and, ultimately, social structure, income, and wealth is fought. Analysis would recognize differential access and exposure to government and its consequences.

A positive political economy would recognize that most theories of government and of the economic role of government are so many normative attempts to structure and channel the use, or agenda, of government, whatever they nominally may claim to be asserting.

A positive political economy would enable analysis to transcend certain common conceptions of the economic role of government which underlie, often only implicitly, most thought and analysis on the subject. These include (1) the exogenous black-box approach, which posits a somehow preprogrammed, perfectly operating government which does not have to make subjective decisions; (2) the approach which considers government to be a neutral extension of private choice, involved in choice but imposing no direction of its own in aggregating preferences; (3) the view that government is an instrument of the powerful, serving their interests even when seemingly catering to the demands of the masses; (4) the opposite view that government is an instrument with which to countervail the power of the powerful; and, inter alia, (5) that government is a source of waste if not evil or (6) that government is a source of progress.

A positive political economy would unhesitatingly and objectively, insofar as is possible, study the play of power in economic and political affairs and, especially, as will be discussed, where economics and politics come together. Among other things, decisions will be seen to be a function of power structure, *and* power structure will be seen to be a function of decisions. The working rules of law and morals will be seen to govern the distribution and exercise of power, *and* the distribution and exercise of power will be seen to govern the development of the working rules of law and morals. Values will be seen to depend on the decision-making process, *and* the decision-making process will be seen to depend on values. The distributions of income and wealth will be seen to be a function, in part, of law, *and* law will be seen to be, in part, a function of the distributions of income and wealth. Power will be seen to have its way in both politics and economics.

A positive political economy would identify law and market as two interactive, or recursive, systems of social control, each with subsystems similarly functioning, each operating separately, and together, to channel and integrate behavior on certain terms and not others.

A positive political economy would pay attention, in addition to power, to the knowledge and psychology dimensions of the political economy, including the processes of the formation of personal identities and preferences and the selection of leadership in the economy and polity. A positive political economy would consider conflict, along with power and power play, a *natural* condition requiring study and explication.

A positive political economy must treat several subjects in a manner quite different from past normative approaches. The latter generally have taken initial entitlements, the structure of rights, as given. It is only on that basis that ostensibly determinate solutions to problems of analysis and policy have been reached. Although it is widely appreciated that there is no unique Pareto-optimal solution, because each such solution gives effect to a particular configuration of rights, policy analytic closure typically is reached by identifying *the* Pareto optimal solution as if that were not the case. This is done by making some (often implicit) selective assumption as to rights. A positive political economy would be less interested in identifying the formal conditions of static equilibrium and substantive optimality solutions and more in the dynamics of rights redefinitions and reassignments, definition of commodities, and, inter alia, the determination of individual utility functions and social preferences, all of which underlie market valuation and individual adjustment as a mode of welfare realization. Distribution — of power, income, and wealth — would have to be given a truly central place in political economy.

In addition, both partial static equilibrium solutions and the limiting practice of working out determinate solutions will have to be transcended. Although it is fundamentally characteristic of the scientific mentality to seek determinate answers to questions, such a procedure can only be question-begging in a world of general equilibrium, ubiquitous interdependent relations that is studied in a partial equilibrium way. There is a widespread tendency to let partial equilibrium solutions serve as proxies for general equilibrium solutions. Thus, in matters of political economy as well as economics per se, conclusions of optimality and of government action constitutive of interference and distortion are reached. But the partial static analysis on which the conclusions rest takes the structure of rights as given and therefore cannot properly be addressed to questions of legal change of legal rights and cannot do so without introducing implicit selective normative premises as to whose interests are to count as rights.

A general equilibrium approach to questions of political economy would examine the processes both of working out optimizing adjustments by individual actors and revisions of the structure of rights and other actions of government of economic significance. It is in this connection that Resnick and Wolff's development of the concept of overdetermination may be especially useful. Traditional political economy generally has postulated the economy and the polity as separate entities, each existing independent of the other. Overdetermination, or a general equilibrium or interdependence approach, stresses that they are not separate and independent; rather, each is seen as the combined result of the other and of still other social processes. The economy and the polity are what they are not independently, preexistently, or exogenously determined but because of mutual interaction. There are deep legal elements in nominally nonlegal processes and deep nonlegal elements in nominally legal processes. *Public* and *private* are not mutually exclusive, closed categories. Economic performance is the product of mutual determination, not of the economy as an abstract, separate entity alone. Not only is there interdependence among institutions and processes, but also individual institutions and processes have no absolute independent existence and identity. They are formed within the overdetermination, or general equilibrium, process. Following such a procedure would make analysis more complex and difficult and would tend to preclude reaching premature closure through narrowly *determinate* analytic solutions. Such a procedure would permit the introduction of fewer implicit normative premises as to whose interests count in the definition of economy or polity used in analysis. But such would be more consonant with the nature of political economic reality. Such a view, of course, challenges certain traditional practices of science, certain predispositions of the practitioners of pro- and antimarket ideology, and the strict economic (dialectical materialist) determinism of certain Marxists. In any event, there is nothing particularly or conclusively Marxist about overdetermination and nothing particularly or conclusively anti-market about general equilibrium. Both are analytical tools.

(Brzeski's appropriate complaints about overdetermination emerge from a deterministic, rather than a conditionistic, approach to Marx. Clearly there are multiple levels of possible abstraction regarding the ties of the state with the mode of production (economic foundation). Moreover, although hypotheses suspend overdetermination for analytical purposes, they do so only tentatively, incompletely, and problematically, much as does partial equilibrium in relation to general equilibrium analysis.)

There is an infinitude of questions whose exploration such an approach would facilitate. One of the most subtle is that of the senses in which state power may (or may not) be said to increase in the event of a change in policy, for example, in the case of a redetermination and reassignment of rights.

In pursuing the development of a positive political economy, at least to the extent that such is possible, a number of questions can and must be asked of the hitherto dominant normative approaches. How much politics does each approach explicate? How much politics does each include? How much politics does each justify or condemn? Are causal chains being carried back far enough? What fundamental issues and processes are begged? I think that it will be found that each approach has an incomplete view of what politics and economics is all about, what governments do, fundamental legal-economic problems and processes, and the causes and consequences of government. Such incompleteness is due in part to the vastness and intractability of political economic phenomena but also in part to the superimposition of ideological myopia. Each traditional approach to political economy tends to practice premature closure, introduce selective normative premises, and involve considerable wishful thinking. Still they have made valuable contributions to knowledge.

One further major issue must be raised. Each traditional approach to political economy has been not only normative and ideological but also, each in its own way, *activist*. As Wade suggests, and as the other principal papers illustrate, theory-building in political economy, as well as in economics generally, has involved the practical tasks of legitimation, clarification of objectives, and the identification, assessment, and selection of tactical possibilities of policy. Each traditional approach to political economy has comprised an attempt to describe, explain, and interpret so as to influence if not directly channel policy, to influence action. Each approach is nominally Marxist insofar as it perceives the problem of the intellect to be changing, not merely studying, society; or perhaps it would be better to say that there is nothing exclusively Marxist in that well-known position of Marx's. These approaches have contributed to, indeed served as, social control by attempting to limit and channel change in a Madisonian conflict world. The actual political economy is an artifact capable of redesign and redirection. Each approach has constituted attempts to do just that. The focus of each approach has been on what ought to be done. Each portrays reality in a manner considered consonant with that purpose. Description, explanation, and understanding for their own sake have been of lesser importance than providing a framework for channeling activism. Each has had a practical policy orientation. Each has proceeded from an implicit, if not explicit, belief that the proof of analysis is in its policy relevance, its service as a guide to, if not sole determinant of, policy. The ultimate desire is for policy relevance. As Klein unabashedly states, theory is perforce good only if it leads to sound public policy.

Policy significance *is* of critical importance. It is one respect in which theory, and indeed all knowledge, is meaningful.

One objection to this view is that policy soundness, as a test of policy relevance, or for that matter policy relevance itself, is tautological with the normative or ideological premises of analysis. Policy implications are prefigured — and given normative stature — by the assumptions of analysis. (And, of course, it is sometimes perceived that certain analysis is designed and conducted in a manner calculated to support particular preconceived policy positions or orientations.)

Another objection to this view is that much analysis, particularly within the neoclassical and public-choice approaches, is formal and nonoperational. A semblance of policy relevance is achieved only by the intrusion of implicit selective normative premises (in addition to those which generate the approach itself) as to whose interests count.

As Mitchell seems to acknowledge, there are no purely scientific criteria that can determine the proper policy, for example, the correct level of government spending or assignment of rights. As Klein and Levi seem to agree, both the neoclassical and public-choice approaches often deal in trivia.

A positive political economy will have to reach an uneasy position with regard to the proclivity to be policy relevant, or activist. I personally am ambivalent. While I fully understand and appreciate that one of the uses of knowledge is for purposes of action and control, I also believe that knowledge is valuable for its own sake. I do not believe that policy relevance or activism is the sole raison d'etre of political economy research and analysis. Indeed, I believe that the desire for policy relevance, coupled with, or giving vent to, the engine of ideology, has preempted the pursuit of that very knowledge which would enrich and strengthen the making of policy itself. At any rate, to call for a positive, nonpolicy activist political economy is not to call for the termination of normative, policy activist political economy. To do so would be to exercise static partial equilibrium unrealism, for the policy activism of political economy is one of the forces in the political economy itself. This, of course, raises the fundamental question of the respective force of ideology (ideas) and power, and of their interrelations, which cannot be summarily dismissed by a self-conscious positive political economy.

Political economy in the future must, inevitably, draw on the hitherto existing approaches to political economy. It also must draw on the social sciences (and other investigatory disciplines, for example, linguistics) other than economics and politics, as well as on past work in those disciplines which have largely been filtered out of professional consciousness. Most especially there must be an attempt somehow to integrate the political and the economic, to focus on the *legal-economic* nexus. Economics must be seen always to be the vehicle of politics, meaning by politics the structure and operation of power, but economics must be seen always to have impact on politics. Political economy is, among other things, the study of the points and processes of those relations; normative political economy with the objective of channeling as well as understanding, and positive political economy with the objective of understanding. We know, in various senses, a great deal about the political economy, but there is much more that we do not know, much of which we have only stylistic perceptions, and very little that we truly understand, perhaps especially the factors entering our love-hate relationship with government.

Notes

1. Joan Robinson, *Economic Philosophy* (Chicago: Aldine, 1962).
2. Bushrod W. Allin, "Is Group Choice a Part of Economics?", *Quarterly Journal of Economics,* 67 (1953): 362–379; Frank H. Knight, "Is Group Choice a Part of Economics? Comment," *Quarterly Journal of Economics,* 67 (1953): 605–609; Howard S. Ellis, "Further Comment," *Quarterly Journal of Economics,* 67 (1953): 609–613; and Bushrod W. Allin, "Reply," *Quarterly Journal of Economics,* 67 (1953): 613–614.
3. Knight, "Group Choice," pp. 607–608.
4. Warren J. Samuels, "A Critique of the Discursive Systems and Foundation Concepts of Distribution Analysis," *Analyse & Kritik,* 4 (October 1982): 4–21.

Index

Adams, John, 17
Agriculture, and primacy of land, 29–30
Allin, Bushrod, 159
Aranson, Peter H., 87
Arrow, Kenneth, 32, 38
Auster, R. D., 87

Bartlett, Randall, 19, 87, 159
Beard, Charles, 11
Bennett, James T., 96
Bentham, Jeremy, 48
Bentley, Arthur, 11
Bergson-Samuelson social-welfare function, 50, 56
Bernstein, Eduard, 153
Black, Duncan, 72
Boulding, Kenneth, 159
Bourgeois democracy, 153
Bowen, H. R., 72, 76, 83
Bowles, Samuel, 153
Braeutigam, Ronald, 89
Brennan, Geoffrey, 100, 102
Breton, Albert, 87
Browning, Edgar K., 81–82
Brzeski, Andrzej, 152–155, 167
Buchanan, James M., 20, 71, 78, 85, 86–87, 102–103, 105–106, 114
Budget
   competitive vote-maximizing parties and, 74–80
   constitutional spending limitations on, 96–97
   entitlements in social programs and, 109
   fending off taxpayer revolts in, 106–110
   fighting government growth in, 107–108
   size of, 77–78
   spending choices in, 80–82
   taxpayer revolts and, 97–98, 105–106
Bureaucracy, in supply models, 98–99
Burton, John, 21

Calhoun, Daniel, 12
Capital (Marx), 126
Capitalist state
   characteristics of, 128–129
   class and, 131–132
   complexity of combinations of processes in, 135–136
   contradictions in, 140
   fundamental class process in, 144–145
   Marxist demystification of, 16–17
   political processes in, 133
   public education in, 133–135
   social processes in, 129–130
   surplus value and taxation in, 138–140
   unemployment in, 132–133
   wage levels in, 140–141
   worker ownership of means of production in, 145–146
Carter, Jimmy, 6, 108
Census Bureau, 97–98
Class
   capitalist society and, 131–132
   fundamental class processes on, 127, 144–145
   Marx on, 126
   state and, 131–137, 154–155
   struggles in, 128
Coase, R. H., 21
Commons, John R., 159

INDEX

Commune, 15
Communist Manifesto (Marx), 15
Communists, 143, 144
Competitive economy, 35–38
　assumptions of, 36
　consumption externalities in, 41–45
　distributive equity in, 48–51
　production with large fixed costs in, 45–48
　technological externalities in, 41–42
　vote-maximizing parties and budgets in, 74–75
Congress, 7, 66, 104
Cost, in classical economics, 30
Credit policy, and recessions, 8
Cultural processes
　in capitalist society, 133–135
　overdetermination and, 123–124
　state and, 129–130

Dahl, Robert, 11
Debreau, Gerard, 32, 38
Demand
　public choice models based on, 72–85
　redistribution and governmental growth and, 85
　rent seeking and income redistribution in, 91, 92, 93
　unitary governments in, 73
　utility and, 31
Democracy
　liberal, and control of political power, 18
　Marx's notion of, 15–16
DiLorenzo, Thomas J., 96
Downs, Anthony, 71, 73–78, 81–82, 83, 84, 85, 86, 95, 114, 115–116

Economic processes
　Madison on political system and, 16
　public choice and institutional focus on, 21
　state and, 129, 132–133
Economics
　group choice in, 159
　neoclassical public finance and, 28–30
　primacy of land in, 29–30
　professionalization of, 2–3
Education
　capitalist societies and, 133–135
　state and, 130, 147
Eisenhower, Dwight D., 7
Eismeier, Theodore J., 104
Ellis, Howard, 159
Engels, Friedrich, 15, 16, 154

Entitlements, 109
Excise taxes, 52
Expenditures
　constitutional spending limitations on, 96–97
　property tax revolts on, 97–98
　second-best taxation and, 51–59

Feudalism, 16
Flowers, Marilyn, 105
Foreign policy, 136
Freud, Sigmund, 16
Friedman, David, 100, 102
Friedman, Milton, 93, 97
Frohlich, Norman, 93
Fundamental Theorems of Welfare Economics, 29, 38, 39

Galbraith, John Kenneth, 70, 159
Gintis, Herbert, 153
Government
　autonomy of national policy of, 5–6
　budgets and fighting growth of, 107–108
　classic economics on, 3
　economic stimuli and distribution of benefits and costs by, 89–90
　focus on long-term structural forces by, 8
　political theory models of, 10–11
　private monopoly and, 87–88
　pursuit of power in, 3–4
　recognition and response lags in recessions by, 7–8
　transaction costs and, 116–117
　utility functions and compromises in, 6–7
　see also State

Hamilton, Alexander, 17
Hedonism, 48
Hegel, Georg, 16
Helms, L. Jay, 27–67, 158
Hirschleifer, Jack, 89
Hotelling, H., 72, 76
Hume, David, 17
Huntington, Samuel P., 10, 11
Hurst, James Willard, 159

Income distribution
　best distribution equity in, 48–51, 54–59
　government growth and, 84–85
　Malthusian theory and, 30
　Marxist theory on, 30–31
　rent seeking and, 90–93
　second-best problems and, 40–41
Income tax, 101

INDEX 173

Industrial Revolution, 30
Inflation, and tax revenues, 102
International Encyclopedia of the Social Sciences, 1

Johnson, Lyndon, 135
Joint Economic Committee, 7, 9

Kalecki, Michal, 109
Kautsky, K., 153
Kennedy, John F., 9
Keynes, John Maynard, 31
Keynesian economics and politics, 2–9
  autonomy of national policy and, 5–6
  focus on long-term structural forces in government in, 8
  government in, 3
  political and administrative requirements in model in, 5
  presumptions about political process in, 4–5
  pursuit of power in government in, 3–4
  recognition and response lags to recessions in, 7–8
  stagflation responses in, 8–9
  utility functions and compromises in, 6–7
Klein, Philip A., 63–67, 168, 170
Knight, Frank, 159
Koopmans, Tjalling, 32
Kuhn, T., 154

Laffer curve, 102
Laissez-faire, 29, 36, 48, 64
Lancaster, Kelvin, 51
Land, primacy of, 29, 30
Lenin, V. I., 152, 153
Levi, Margaret, 114–118, 169
Liberalism, 16–19
Lindahl, Eric, 72, 76, 83
Lindblom, Charles E., 11, 159
Lindsay, Cottom M., 89
Lipsey, Archibald, 51
Lowi, Theodore J., 11, 12

McCormick, Robert E., 87
Mackay, Robert J., 87
McKenzie, Richard D., 99
Madison, James, 11, 16–17, 18, 19, 162
Malthus, Thomas, 30
Market mechanism
  concept of utility in, 31
  neoclassical approach to, 31–32
  public choice and, 21
  stagflation and, 9

Marshall, Alfred, 2, 31, 160
Marx, Karl, 30
  on class, 126
  notion of democracy in, 15–16
  socialism and universal suffrage in Britain and, 15
Marxism, 1, 11, 13–19
  analyses of states in, 14–15
  approaches to political economy in, 13, 14
  bourgeois democracy in, 153
  classical economics and, 2, 3
  class struggles in, 128
  class theory in, 126
  common themes in, 13–14
  completion of social analysis in, 125–136
  contradictions in state in, 137–142
  demystification of liberal capitalist state in, 16–17
  forms of surplus labor in, 126–127
  functional-purposive fallacy in, 15
  fundamental class process in, 127
  implications of state theory of, 142–148
  liberalism and control of political power in, 16–19
  neoclassical public finance and, 30–31
  notion of democracy in, 15–16
  overdetermination in, 123
  ruling class in, 122
  social conflict in, 17–18
  social theory in, 127–128
  state and class in, 131–137
  themes of, 30–31
  theory of state in, 121–125
Middle class, in supply models, 94–95
Miliband, Ralph, 15, 17
Mill, John Stuart, 2, 31
Mitchell, William C., 69–118, 158, 169
Monopoly, in supply models, 87
Mueller, Dennis C., 87
Musgrave, Richard A., 83, 106

Neoclassical public finance, 27–67, 158
  classical economics and, 28–30
  criteria of public allocation in, 66
  first-best problems in, 40
  first-best taxation and expenditure policies in, 40–51
  general equilibrium theory in, 31–32
  historical setting for, 28–32
  Marxist theories and, 30–31
  Pareto optimality in, 158, 161
  prices in, 31–32
  relevance to policy problems of, 65–66

Neoclassical public finance *(Continued)*
  second-best problems in, 40
  second-best taxation and expenditure policies in, 51–59
  welfare economics in, 32–40
Niskanen, William A., Jr., 86, 87, 89, 98, 99
Nixon, Richard M., 8, 108
Normative microeconomics, 67
North, Douglas C., 117

O'Connor, James, 11, 12
Olson, Mancur, Jr., 71, 93, 114, 116
OPEC, 8
Oppenheimer, Joe A., 93
Ordeshook, Peter C., 87
Overdetermination, in Marxist theory, 123, 154, 167
  cultural processes and, 123–124
  social processes and, 124–125
  surplus labor in, 127
  voting and, 125
Owen, Bruce M., 89

Pareto optimality, 65
  central planning in welfare economics and, 33, 34, 35–36
  competitive equilibrium and, 38, 39, 40
  First Fundamental Theorem of Welfare Economics with, 38–39
  neoclassical economics with, 158, 161
  production with large fixed costs and, 45, 47
  second-best analysis with, 63, 64
Paris commune, 15
Parrington, V. L., 11
Peltzman, Sam, 87, 89
Penner, Rudolph G., 96
Physiocrats, 29
Pigou, Arthur Cecil, 21, 158, 160
Police functions, and state, 147
Political economy, 1–23
  approaches to, 1–2
  distribution in, 166
  Keynesian economics and politics in, 2–9
  legal-economic nexus in, 169
  Marxism in, 13–19
  political theory on, 9–12
  power and decisions in, 165
  productivity and exploitation discursive systems of, 160–162
  public choice and, 19–22
  toward a positive discursive system of, 162–170

Political processes
  capitalist societies and, 133
  state and, 130
Political science, professionalization of, 10
Political theory, 9–12
  Madison on, 16–17
  models used in, 10–11
  theories of the *Many* in, 10–11
  welfare state in, 11–12
Politicians, and public choice, 71
Pollution tax, 52
Poor, in supply models, 94–95
Posner, Richard A., 89
Power, and decisions, 165
Prices
  classical economics on, 29
  concept of utility in, 31
  neoclassical approach to, 31–32
Progressive historians, 11
Property rights, and public choice, 20–21
Property tax, and voter revolts, 97–98
Proposition 13, 105–106
Pryor, Frederick, 159
Public choice, 19–22
  characteristics of economic man in, 19–20
  classic economics and, 2
  competitive vote-maximizing parties and budgets in, 74–80
  constitutional spending limitations and, 97
  definition of, 20
  demand-based models in, 72–85
  distribution of benefits and costs by government and, 89–90
  elements of, 70–72
  entitlement in social programs and, 109
  fiscal behavior of democratic state and, 69–118
  institutional focus in economic analysis with, 21–22
  Pareto optimality in, 161
  political economy in terms of, 159
  politicians and, 71
  power distribution in society and, 115–116
  property rights and, 20–21
  property tax revolts in, 97–98
  redistribution and government growth in, 84–85
  research agenda in, 110
  revenue choices in, 82–84
  spending choices in, 80–82
  supply models in, 86, 110

transaction costs and, 116–117
unitary governments in, 73
Public finance
  features of, 27
  neoclassical approaches to, *see* Neoclassical public finance
Puviani, Amilcare, 100, 101, 102

Reagan, Ronald, 6, 7, 9, 108, 135
Recessions, recognition and response lags to, 7–8
Redistribution of income, *see* Income redistribution
Rent seeking, and income redistribution, 90–93
Republican Party, 130
Resnick, Stephen, 121–155, 158
Ricardo, David, 30
Riker, W., 95
Roberts, Paul Craig, 104
Roosevelt, Franklin D., 135
Rose-Ackerman, Susan, 87
Rousseau, Jean Jacques, 15
Ruling class, and state, 122

Samuels, Warren J., 157–170
Samuelson, Paul A., 3, 21, 32, 48, 76, 83, 164
Sartori, Giovanni, 18
Say's Law, 3
Schattschneider, E. E., 104
Schumpeter, Joseph, 15
Sidgwick, Henry, 160
Silver, Morris, 87
Sirkin, Gerald, 87
Smith, Adam, 29, 67
Social conflict, in Marxist theory, 17–18
Socialism
  Engels on state and, 14
  Marx on universal suffrage in Britain and, 15
  theory of state in, 143, 144
Social processes
  capitalist society and, 129–130
  overdetermination and, 124–125
Social-security programs, 101, 109
Social theory, in Marxism, 127–128
Solo, Robert, 170
Stagflation, 6, 8–9
State
  citizen pressures on, 141–142, 146
  class and, 131–137
  classic economics on, 3

class process and, 154–155
concept of, 128–131
contradictions in, 137–142
cultural processes and, 129–130
economic processes and, 129, 132–133
education and, 130, 147
foreign policy and, 136
fundamental class process in, 144–145
implications of Marxist theory on, 142–148
liberalism and control of political power in, 16–19
Marxist analysis of, 14–15, 121–155
model of policy making in, 117–118
police functions and, 147
political process and, 130
ruling class and, 122
as site in society, 130–131, 154
social conflicts within, 17–18
social processes and, 129–130
transaction costs and, 116–117
wage levels and, 140–141
see also Government
Stigler, George J., 84, 85, 87, 89, 91, 94
Supply models, 86–110
  bureaucracy in, 98–99
  constitutional spending limitations in, 96–97
  distribution of benefits and costs by government in, 89–90
  entitlements in social programs and, 109
  entrepreneurs, policy innovation, and supplies in, 93–98
  fending off taxpayer revolts in, 106–110
  history of, 86–88
  nature of public supply and excessive provisions in, 88–90
  obtaining revenue in, 99–103
  poor and middle class benefits in, 94–95
  private monopoly in, 87
  rent seeking and income redistribution in, 90–93
  slow growth, retrenchment, and taxpayer resistance in, 105–106
  social loopholes (tax expenditures) in, 103–105
Surplus labor
  forms of, 126–127
  overdetermination of, 127
Surplus value, 131
  capitalist state taxation of, 138–140
  state functionaries and, 138
  worker ownership of means of production and, 145–146

Taxation
  capitalist state and surplus value and, 138–140
  competition for votes and, 74–75
  constitutional spending limitations on, 96–97
  distribution equity in, 48–51, 54–59
  entitlements in social programs and, 109
  fending off revolts against, 106–110
  first-best problems and, 40–51
  inflation and revenues from, 102
  obtaining revenue in, 99–103
  production with large fixed costs in, 45–48
  recognition and response lags to recessions and, 7–8
  reforms in, 101
  second-best, and expenditure policies, 51–59
  social loopholes in, 103–105
  taxpayer revolts against, 97–98, 105–106
  visibility of information in, 100–101
  voter choice of, 82–84
Tax expenditures, 103–105
Technological externalities, 41–42
Thatcher, Margaret, 9
Third World countries, 121
Thompson, Earl A., 98–99
Tiebort, Charles M., 76
Tobin, James, 8, 9
Tollison, Robert D., 87
Transaction costs, 116–117
Treaties, 136
Truman, David B., 11, 12
Tullock, Gordon, 71, 78, 82, 84, 86, 89, 91, 94, 99, 114

Unemployment
  capitalist societies with, 132–133
  Keynesian remedies for, 4
Utilitarianism, 48
Utility, and demand, 31

Voting
  budgets and competition in, 74–80
  limited opportunities in, 76–77
  Marx on socialism in Britain and, 15
  median-voter theories on, 79–80
  nature of goods involved in public production and, 78–79
  overdetermination and, 124, 125
  power distribution in society and, 115–116
  property revolts by, 97–98, 105–106
  revenue choices in, 82–84
  size of budget and, 77–78

Wade, Larry L., 1–23, 157–158, 163, 168
Wage levels, in capitalist state, 140–141
Wagner, Richard E., 87, 88, 101, 104, 109
Wald, Abraham, 38
Wallis, W. Allen, 94
Weaver, Carolyn L., 87
Weber, Max, 153
Welfare economics, 72
  central planning in, 32–35, 64
  competitive equilibrium in, 35–38
  fundamental theorems of, 38–40
  neoclassical approach to, 32–40
  Pareto optimality in, 65
  relevancy to policy problems of, 65–66
Welfare state
  Marxist view of, 15
  political theory on, 11–12
Wicksell, Knut, 83
Wildavsky, Aaron, 69
Williamson, Oliver, 116
Wilson, James Q., 11, 12
Wittman, Donald, 87
Wolff, Richard, 121–155, 158

Young, Oran R., 93

Contributing Authors

Andrzej Brzeski is Professor of Economics at the University of California, Davis. He studied economics, law, and sociology in his native Poland, where he also worked in central-planning institutions and as a journal editor and writer. A student of comparative economics and especially of East European socialism he has contributed to the scholarly literature on those subjects and has lectured widely in Europe, Asia, and the United States.

L. Jay Helms is a member of the economics faculty, University of California, Davis. His current research involves the effects of state and local taxes on economic growth and the assessment of price stabilization policies on consumer welfare. His work has appeared, among other places, in the *Bell Journal of Economics* (1978) and the *Journal of Public Economics* (1981).

Philip A. Klein is Professor of Economics, The Pennsylvania State University; Research Associate, Center for International Business Cycle Research, Rutgers University; and Adjunct Scholar, American Enterprise Institute. In addition to his extensive research, consulting, and teaching experience abroad at the London School of Economics, the Organization for Economic Development and Cooperation, the United Nations, the University of Zagreb, and the European Institute of Business Administration in France, he has been a frequent contributor to the scholarly literature. Recent work includes *Growth Cycles in Postwar Sweden* (1981) and articles in *Applied Economics* (1981) and *Journal of Economic Issues* (1980).

Margaret Levi is Associate Professor of Political Science and Public Affairs at the University of Washington. She is currently working on a book, tentatively titled *The Predatory Theory of Rule*, which offers an historical account of revenue production and fiscal policy. She previously authored *Bureaucratic Insurgency: The Case of Police Unions* (1977).

William C. Mitchell has been Professor of Political Science at the University of Oregon since 1965. He has been visiting professor at Northwestern University, UCLA, the University of California, Berkeley, and Cornell University. He has been a Fellow of the Center for Advanced Study in the Behavioral Sciences and a member of the Social Science Research Council Committee on the Comparative Study of Public Policy. His several books and monographs include *The American Polity* (1962), *Sociological Analysis and Politics* (1967), *Political Analysis and Public Policy* (1971), *Why Vote?* (1971), *The Popularity of Social Security: A Paradox in Public Choice* (1977), and *The Anatomy of Public Failure: A Public Choice Perspective* (1978).

Stephen Resnick is Professor of Economics, University of Massachusetts and has also taught at Yale University, City College of New York, and the University of the Philippines. A prolific contributor to the economic literature, some of his most recent work appears in the *Journal of Economic History* (1982), the *Review of Radical Political Economics* (1979, 1982), and in L. Hollist and J. Rosenau, eds., *World System Structure* (1981). A book with Richard D. Wolff, *Epistemology and Class in Marxian Theory*, is forthcoming.

Warren J. Samuels is Professor of Economics at Michigan State University. He has written extensively in the history and methodology of economics, law and economics, and public-utility regulation. He was editor of the *Journal of Economic Issues*, 1971–1981 and is currently the editor of *Research in the History of Economic Thought and Methodology*. He is the author of *The Classical Theory of Economic Policy* (1966) and *Pareto on Policy* (1974), the coauthor of *Law and Economics* (1981), the editor of *The Economy as a System of Power* (1979) and the coeditor of *Taxing and Spending Policy* (1980).

L. L. Wade is Professor of Political Science at the University of California, Davis. He has been a National Science Foundation Fellow at the London School of Political Science and Economics, a Fulbright Lecturer at Waseda University (Tokyo) and a Fulbright Researcher at Seoul National University. He is the author or coauthor of *A Theory of Political Exchange* (1968), *A Logic of Public Policy* (1970), *The Elements of Public Policy* (1972), *Democracy in America* (1976), and *Economic Devel-*

opment of Korea (1977). He has coedited *Taxing and Spending Policy* (1980) and two forthcoming volumes, *Public Policy Across Nations, States and Cities* and *Comparative Resource Allocation*

Richard D. Wolff is Professor of Economics, University of Massachusetts. In addition to a major monograph, *The Economics of Colonialism: Britain and Kenya, 1870–1930* (1974), he has published extensively in the periodical literature, including the *American Economic Review* (1970), *Monthly Review* (1971, 1976, 1978), *Social Text* (1981, 1982), and the *Review of Radical Political Economics* (1982, 1983). He is currently writing a book-length study, *Epistemology and Class in Marxian Theory,* with Stephen Resnick.